P9-CSC-132

Outdoor Survival Guide

RANDY GERKE

Human Kinetics

BOCA RATON PUBLIC LIBRARY
BOCA RATON, FLORIDA

Library of Congress Cataloging-in-Publication Data

Gerke, Randy, 1954-
  Outdoor survival guide / Randy Gerke.
     p. cm.
  ISBN-13: 978-0-7360-7525-1 (soft cover)
  ISBN-10: 0-7360-7525-9 (soft cover)
  1. Wilderness survival. 2. Survival skills. I. Title.
  GV200.5.G47 2009
  613.6'9--dc22
                              2009021964

ISBN-10: 0-7360-7525-9 (print)   ISBN-10: 0-7360-8619-6 (Adobe PDF)
ISBN-13: 978-0-7360-7525-1 (print)   ISBN-13: 978-0-7360-8619-6 (Adobe PDF)

Copyright © 2010 by Human Kinetics, Inc.

All rights reserved. Except for use in a review, the reproduction or utilization of this work in any form or by any electronic, mechanical, or other means, now known or hereafter invented, including xerography, photocopying, and recording, and in any information storage and retrieval system, is forbidden without the written permission of the publisher.

This publication is written and published to provide accurate and authoritative information relevant to the subject matter presented. It is published and sold with the understanding that the author and publisher are not engaged in rendering legal, medical, or other professional services by reason of their authorship or publication of this work. If medical or other expert assistance is required, the services of a competent professional person should be sought.

The Web addresses cited in this text were current as of May 2009, unless otherwise noted.

Acquisitions Editor: Tom Heine; **Developmental Editor:** Heather Healy; **Assistant Editor:** Carla Zych; **Copyeditor:** Robert Replinger; **Permission Manager:** Martha Gullo; **Graphic Designers:** Nancy Rasmus and Keri Evans; **Graphic Artist:** Tara Welsch; **Cover Designer:** Keith Blomberg; **Photographer (cover):** ©Human Kinetics; **Photo Asset Manager:** Laura Fitch; **Visual Production Assistant:** Joyce Brumfield; **Photo Production Manager:** Jason Allen; **Art Manager:** Kelly Hendren; **Associate Art Manager:** Alan L. Wilborn; **Illustrators:** Kay Wiemer Gerke and Randy Gerke; **Printer:** United Graphics

Human Kinetics books are available at special discounts for bulk purchase. Special editions or book excerpts can also be created to specification. For details, contact the Special Sales Manager at Human Kinetics.

Printed in the United States of America   10 9 8 7 6 5 4 3 2 1

The paper in this book is certified under a sustainable forestry program.

Human Kinetics
Web site: www.HumanKinetics.com

United States: Human Kinetics
P.O. Box 5076
Champaign, IL 61825-5076
800-747-4457
e-mail: humank@hkusa.com

Canada: Human Kinetics
475 Devonshire Road Unit 100
Windsor, ON N8Y 2L5
800-465-7301 (in Canada only)
e-mail: info@hkcanada.com

Europe: Human Kinetics
107 Bradford Road
Stanningley
Leeds LS28 6AT, United Kingdom
+44 (0) 113 255 5665
e-mail: hk@hkeurope.com

Australia: Human Kinetics
57A Price Avenue
Lower Mitcham, South Australia 5062
08 8372 0999
e-mail: info@hkaustralia.com

New Zealand: Human Kinetics
Division of Sports Distributors NZ Ltd.
P.O. Box 300 226 Albany
North Shore City
Auckland
0064 9 448 1207
e-mail: info@humankinetics.co.nz

E4525

This book is dedicated to my father, Robert William Gerke, who instilled in me an appreciation of adventure and a love of nature when I was a very young boy.

CONTENTS >>

SURVIVAL SKILLS QUICK REFERENCE »

(continued)

Survival Skills Quick Reference *(continued)*

✚ INJURIES AND ILLNESS

(continued)

Survival Skills Quick Reference *(continued)*

PREFACE >>

EACH year thousands of people venture off the beaten path to find adventure or enjoy nature and all that it has to offer. Some travel as groups of friends, others travel as families, and still others choose to go it alone. Their reasons for seeking wild places are as varied as their background and experience. Some prefer to experience nature under their own power by hiking, climbing, biking, skiing, or paddling. Others enjoy using motorcycles, ATVs, snowmobiles, four-wheel-drive vehicles, or even the family car to take them to less-traveled areas. No matter the reason, the method of travel, or the activity, these people have one thing in common: They must be able to survive on their own when unforeseen events arise that prevent them from returning to the safety of their vehicles, camps, and homes.

All too often we hear reports of tragedies that occur when people are suddenly thrust into an emergency survival situation. Many die needlessly because of poor preparation and lack of knowledge. Those who arm themselves with basic survival knowledge and carry a few simple items with them have a far better chance of returning home, maybe not unscathed, but returning home nevertheless.

Outdoor Survival Guide is a reference for those who want to be prepared for an unexpected outdoor emergency. The book is a valuable resource for people who consider themselves novices as well as those with experience in the outdoors. This reference is designed so that you can carry it along on all your adventures, whether traveling on a remote highway in a car, climbing a snowy peak far in the backcountry, or exploring a deep canyon in the warm desert. This book, along with a cool head and some common sense, can save your life.

Covering every aspect of the topic of survival would require several volumes. *Outdoor Survival Guide* contains the most important practical aspects of outdoor survival in a concise, easy-to-follow format. The material presented includes both primitive and high-tech skills and information. One of the most valuable aspects of this guide is its ease of use. The book is organized so that you can quickly find the critical information for a particular survival emergency. The "Survival Skills Quick Reference" on page vi can help you quickly locate the skills presented in the book.

The chapters are organized in order of priority, beginning in chapter 1 with how to assess your situation and avoid panic. Chapters 2 through 8 teach specific skills such as building shelters, making fire, obtaining water and food, navigating, and signaling. A special photo guide to edible plants is provided on pages 83 through 98. Chapters 9 and 10 cover injuries and common illnesses, dangerous animals, and survival in extreme environments. Chapter 11 is a guide to building or customizing your own survival kit.

Reading about outdoor survival and romanticizing the idea of living without the aid of modern technology is one thing. Being required to live that way because of an emergency is quite another. During the more than 30 years I've spent as a wilderness guide and survival instructor, I have had the opportunity to experiment with many outdoor skills and techniques. I have field-tested the information and skills contained in this book, and all have proved to be effective, and in some cases, life saving. If you are among those who enjoy the feeling of adventure that only an outdoor experience can provide but look forward to a hot shower and a warm bed when the adventure ends, *Outdoor Survival Guide* was written for you.

ACKNOWLEDGMENTS >>

WRITING a book is certainly not a one-person job; it requires an entire team laboring many hours to bring it to completion. It has been my good fortune to work with especially qualified and helpful people during this project.

I owe a special debt to Tom Heine, the acquisitions editor at Human Kinetics who first approached me about writing this book. He continued to encourage and gently push me along during the writing and submission process. Special thanks to Heather Healy, the development editor for the project. Her cheerful disposition, insightful comments, and thorough examination of the manuscript improved the book and helped me to improve as a writer.

To my wife, partner, friend, and illustrator, Kay Wiemer Gerke, I owe the most. It is a difficult challenge to blend a personal and business relationship. During the 33 years we've spent together teaching wilderness skills and raising a family, we've gained enough interpersonal survival skills to fill more than a few volumes. I'm grateful for the never-ending supply of patience, support, and encouragement she's shown me during our years together. These gifts have been especially appreciated during the writing of this book. Her skill as an illustrator has greatly added to the quality of this project.

I'm also grateful to the many students I've worked with over the last three decades, who have allowed me to learn with them and from them.

Thanks to my friends and associates at the Ouray Mountain Rescue Team of Ouray, Colorado. It's been one of the great experiences of my life to be a part of this team and to serve with some of the most skilled and dedicated people to be found anywhere. Ouray is the quintessential learning laboratory for the study of survival. The experiences I've had there have expanded my knowledge and skills and have motivated me to share what I've learned with others.

The Art
of Survival

WE live in an extraordinary age. Technology has provided our society with all the comforts and conveniences that we need for a high quality of life. We are no longer personally responsible for maintaining our physical existence. We leave this duty, for the most part, to public service agencies, which provide electricity, water, and heating fuel and even dispose of our waste. We no longer have to provide shelter for ourselves; we hire people to build our homes. All that we have to do is work in a specialized field to earn the money to buy the services that meet our needs.

Most of us can only imagine what would happen if we were suddenly cast into a desperate struggle for life. In this situation, reality quickly changes from all that we had considered normal to a strange new world filled with fearful and threatening circumstances. When placed suddenly and unpredictably in such a situation, technology seems far away, and we become keenly aware of our physical limitations. But in a survival situation, our emotional and psychological limitations can be more critical than our physical shortcomings. Normal ethics and standards crumble around us, and we are generally unprepared for the challenges that we must face. In an elemental struggle between human and the environment, money, position, and education are mostly worthless. This realization only adds to the already staggering challenge of staying alive. The survival skills and equipment that you possess are important in a survival situation, but how you score on this most difficult test depends largely on your attitude.

Characteristics of Successful Survivors

Successful survivors are stubborn, determined, and even fanatical about staying alive. They are not passive about their situation but instead struggle to gain control of themselves and their new environment. They continually stay busy and productive by working to improve their circumstances. They struggle aggressively against their situation but not against themselves or others. They are good to themselves and have a sense of personal worth.

No formula can predict who will survive and who will not, but odds favor those with reasonable knowledge about the environment and survival techniques, emotional stability, good health, a sound ego, and a history of active participation in normal life (see table 1.1). People

Table 1.1 Characteristics of Survivors and Nonsurvivors

Characteristics of survivors	Characteristics of nonsurvivors
Knowledgeable about the environment and survival techniques	Apathetic
Emotionally stable	Passive
Physically healthy	Fearful
Confident	Injured
History of normal life participation	Easily discouraged
Strong will to live	Isolated
Willing to improvise	Quick to anger
Eager to work with others	Impulsive

who are apathetic, passive, or fearful are less likely to survive; an injury also lessens a person's chance for survival. But one characteristic towers above all others when considering survival qualities—the will to live. No matter what the circumstances, no matter what threatens their existence, and no matter how long the ordeal lasts, those who survive possess a fierce determination to stay alive. Apathy and negativity can lead to death during survival experiences.

Without a positive attitude a person stands little or no chance of survival, no matter what equipment, food, water, shelter, or other resources may be available. Maintaining optimism in the face of a survival challenge can be the most difficult part of the experience. Those who have endured a survival situation detail their daily struggle to sustain a positive attitude. They describe a few natural high points, when rescue seemed inevitable, mixed with long, desperate battles with situational depression, apathy, and the desire to give up. Of course, the longer a survival situation continues, the more pronounced this battle becomes. The following strategies can help you maintain a positive attitude in a survival situation:

- **Stay busy.** Begin putting your plan into action. Set a series of obtainable and meaningful goals directly related to your immediate survival. This approach is critical to a successful outcome. Being productive accomplishes two important purposes. First, you are completing tasks that are important for physical survival, such as building shelter, collecting water, and so forth. Second, you are channeling thoughts and feelings in a positive direction. Too much idle time can allow thoughts to drift to the dark side of a situation and lead to apathy and discouragement.

- **Be determined.** To get through, you must draw on a belief or emotion as a source of strength. It may be faith in a higher power or a relationship with family, friends, or other significant people in your life. Some draw their strength from faith in themselves and their abilities. For a few, the smoldering desire for revenge has kept the fire of life burning. Survivors fight through the demons of discouragement and win. You may suffer situational depression, which can have an intensely dark and powerful influence on your attitude and productivity. You may have desperate feelings of hopelessness and begin to blame yourself and others for the awful predicament in which you find yourself. When these feeling begin to arise, you must recognize them for what they are—feelings, not facts. You must replace negativity with positive motion. Get up, get busy, and stay busy by doing something that contributes to your survival. Improve your shelter, make a needed tool, find food, collect water, sing a song, help the people around you, and take long, slow, deep breaths. You have more reason to live than to give up. Fill your mind with positive thoughts until they crowd out the negative voices. You must believe you will survive.

Survival Responses

At the outset of a survival situation, people display a variety of behaviors. Their responses are based on factors such as experience with similar circumstances, survival training, ego and self-esteem, and other inherited genetic factors. Each person responds in a unique way to survival stresses. Panic may grip some, whereas others may drift into a bewildered state of quiet lethargy. On the other hand, some will actively fight to improve their circumstances and seek to help others. From the latter group leaders will emerge to help bring order and hope out of chaos and discouragement. Although individual reactions are unique, most people respond in one of several ways.

The Proactive

Some people remain calm while doing their best to improve their situation. They may have minor injuries but are otherwise able to participate physically and emotionally in their survival. They are proactive in their approach to solving the problems at hand. They quickly identify needs in themselves and others and use whatever resources are available to meet the demands of survival.

The Panicked

Generally, a small percentage of a group will panic and be uncooperative, draining away vital energy and resources that could be used for positive purposes. These people are a danger to themselves and others. Their fear and panic can easily spread if left unattended. If possible, they should be moved away from the rest of the group, and their panic should be controlled as quickly as possible. Refer to the section "Panic Control" later in this chapter for specific information about how to control panic in yourself and others.

The Bewildered

Probably the largest percentage of people will be in a state of psychological shock. They will not panic, but the enormity of the situation will confuse and almost incapacitate them. They are generally cooperative and responsive to simple direction. With reassurance and leadership, these people can become an asset to the group during a survival situation.

The Injured

Some in the group may be seriously injured and unable to assist in their survival. These people could exhibit any of the behaviors previously described. They may be helpful, panicked, or bewildered and will have the same needs of emotional support and leadership as the rest of the group. But because of their injuries, their survival depends largely on others.

The Leaders

Out of the initial confusion that results from an unexpected emergency, leaders will emerge from the group. Natural leaders begin to come forward, giving direction and structure to an otherwise chaotic situation. This leadership arises out of necessity rather than assignment. The leader or leaders in a survival situation must be truthful about the circumstances, but at the same time they should offer hope by pointing out positive aspects and the possibility of rescue and survival. Good leadership can bring order and purpose to a difficult situation. A leader must try to create and maintain positive emotions and activity, endeavoring to surmount negative emotions like fear and anger. A successful leader does all that is possible to instill hope within the group. Ultimately, however, a leader does not have control over whether others in a group live or die.

Panic Control

In situations of severe emotional or physical stress, especially in unfamiliar surroundings and circumstances, your mental and emotional responses trigger physiological reactions designed to help you deal with those stresses. These natural responses increase as your anxiety increases, and if left unchecked they can quickly cascade out of control.

Your thoughts will begin to race, and your brain will search frantically for anything that can take you back to a place of safety and security. Your body will release adrenalin to energize your brain and body in an attempt to protect you from harm and to help you solve the problem at hand. Your pulse rate will increase, you will begin to breathe rapidly, and your imagination will run wild. You will be desperate to escape, to bolt, to return quickly to something familiar. This feeling, panic, is one of the most powerful natural forces known to humans. Its awesome and horrifying influence can arise in anyone under the right conditions, regardless of the person's survival experience. If you allow panic to control your decisions and actions, it will take you on a frantic ride that can have deadly consequences. At the very least, succumbing to panic will prolong your survival experience.

A person who says, "I have no fear" is guided by foolish pride. Every person has fears about something. Nature has endowed us with fear to protect us from the natural dangers in the world. The goal is not to eliminate fear but to face it and understand it. Placing fear in the proper perspective can help you avoid or reduce the feelings that cause panic. Whether you find yourself in circumstances that are out of control because of your own decision making or through no fault of your own, the stresses to your mind and body will be similar. When you perceive yourself as not being in control of a situation, a combination of feelings can temporarily overload you and trigger the panic response.

Panic can overtake and control anyone. Does this mean that panic is inevitable? Absolutely not. Each person has the ability to control panic. The following steps can help you control panic in yourself:

1. Stop and sit down.
2. Breathe slowly and deeply. Inhale through your nose, completely filling your lungs. Purse your lips and exhale slowly and completely.
3. Stop negative thoughts and feelings, and replace them by taking positive action (see table 1.2). Remember that panic originates in the mind, and fearful thoughts will continue to promote panic. A helpful approach is to shout, "Stop! I'm going to be OK!" When the cycle is broken, panic will begin to subside in a few minutes.
4. Make a plan. Think about what you can do to survive, find your way, or increase your chances of being rescued. Redirect your thoughts away from what you or someone else did that led to the circumstance in which you find yourself. Focus instead on what can you can do immediately to improve the situation.

Channel whatever anger you may feel toward yourself or others into useful energy for survival.

5. Begin doing something constructive, such as gathering firewood, preparing a shelter, or signaling.

Table 1.2   Replacing Negative Thoughts With Positive Actions

Common negative thoughts	Positive replacements
Feeling overwhelmed and debilitated by the seriousness of the situation.	Begin working on one thing that you can do immediately to improve your condition.
Feeling angry and blaming others or yourself for getting into the predicament.	Assigning blame serves no useful purpose at this point. Transform anger into action by creating and following a plan for survival.
Becoming bored after the initial excitement of the situation ends and the waiting for rescue begins. Boredom leads to apathy, which drains away the will to live.	Stay busy working on useful tasks. Schedule assignments for yourself throughout the day and into the next so that you will always be thinking and working toward survival.
Beginning to feel hopeless and isolated as the survival situation continues.	Focus your thoughts on the reasons you have to stay alive, such as family, friends, your faith, your career, and your passions.
Having general feelings of despair and depression.	Get up and get moving. Do some form of mild exercise, like walking or singing a song. Take long, slow, deep breaths, exhaling slowly.

After you have gained control of yourself, you can help others overcome their panic by using the following steps:

1. Have the person who is feeling panicky sit down in a safe place.

2. Refocus the person's fear onto something positive. Let him or her know that the situation will turn out OK. Be firm but kind. You may have to raise your voice to get the person's attention, but you need to be reassuring.

3. Help the person control her or his breathing. Have the person look into your eyes and breathe with you, following the breathing pattern described in step 2 for controlling your own panic.

4. When the person has calmed a bit, enlist his or her help and give the person a meaningful job to accomplish. Assign a task such as collecting firewood or materials for a shelter, caring for others, or performing some other useful activity.

Assess Your Situation

Whether the survival situation that you find yourself in has occurred suddenly (an aircraft crash) or developed slowly (becoming lost), you face the challenge of creating order out of a chaotic circumstance. You must approach this task in an organized way, sorting out the things that can help you from the things that can kill you. The information gained from each step of the assessment process will help you develop an effective plan for your survival and eventual rescue.

1. Evaluate the Scene

Evaluating your immediate surroundings for dangers and hazards is a critical first step for survival. Initially, people suddenly involved in a fight for survival often overlook life-threatening risks that can lead to even more difficulties during an already harrowing experience. When given a choice, diving headlong into a pool from a high ledge is never a good idea if you do not first learn how deep the water is. You should take the same approach when dealing with unfamiliar surroundings.

When you first (suddenly or slowly) realize that you are involved in a survival situation, take a moment to survey the area for obvious and hidden dangers before exposing yourself to potential risks. Examples of such hazards include unstable wreckage from vehicles or aircraft; danger from falling rock, snow avalanches, or mudslides; flashfloods in gullies or narrow canyons during a rainstorm; imminent danger from leaking fuel, fire, explosion, smoke, or inhalation of dangerous gas; immediate threats from dangerous animals, including insects and reptiles; and danger from severe weather. If these or any other immediate hazards exist, quickly move yourself and others to a safer location. When you can bring the hazards under control or the area becomes safe, you can return to retrieve gear and collect useful materials and resources.

When entering or reentering an area with possible dangers, always move slowly, using all your senses to detect possible hazards. Stop occasionally and look overhead, to the sides, and behind. Listen for any unusual sounds that may warn of danger, such as the sound of approaching rushing water, the snap of a tree trunk or branch, the rumble of an avalanche, or the sharp slap of rocks falling. Be alert for the smells of smoke, animal scat, or dead animals. All these things can be a threat to your survival.

2. Evaluate Physical Condition

After you secure a safe location, the next step is to evaluate your physical condition and the condition of others, checking for significant injuries related to airway, breathing, and circulation. You must take care of yourself first before you begin helping others. This principle is based not on selfishness but on self-preservation. In an airline emergency, parents are instructed to put on their own oxygen masks before placing masks on their children. Both parent and child have a much better chance of survival if the adult pursues self-preservation first. A survival situation is similar. You cannot render aid to others until you first care for your basic needs.

Take a quick inventory of yourself. Check yourself for injuries by looking and feeling from head to toe. At this point, the focus is addressing life-threatening issues. Do not worry about cleaning wounds or splinting fractures or sprains at this time. You can deal with scratches, scrapes, and other shallow wounds later (see chapter 9 for more details about specific medical problems and their treatment). Treat your injuries as best you can with what you have. If you are alone, evaluating and correcting some problems may be difficult. If you have no pulse, your troubles are over or just beginning, depending on your perspective.

After you have assessed and addressed your condition, you can look to help others. Be sure to focus on treating life-threatening injuries first. The priority is to secure a good airway, stop severe bleeding, and make sure that blood is circulating (see chapter 9). Do not waste time on broken bones at this point. Although they are painful and some are spectacular in appearance, they are not usually life threatening in the short term. If you must hastily move yourself or others with fractures, you can use your hands to stabilize the fracture in its found position. After you relocate to a safe place and take care of all life-threatening injuries, the treatment of fractures and minor wounds and injuries can continue.

This process of prioritizing people for treatment according to the seriousness of the injury and the medical resources available is known as triage. You want to apply your limited resources where they will do the most good. This process can help guide you in choosing which injuries should receive priority. First, sort injuries as to whether they are life threatening or not life threatening. Treat life-threatening injuries first. Someone who has a deep laceration and is bleeding profusely has a life-threatening injury. A person who is not breathing and has no pulse certainly has a life-threatening injury or illness. On the other hand, someone who is walking but has pain in the ankle probably does not have a life-threatening injury.

Now imagine a scenario in which two people have life-threatening injuries: One is severely bleeding, and the other is not breathing and has no pulse. Which one should you treat first? If you are the only person available to render aid, this dilemma can be difficult. Obviously, you cannot help both at the same time. You must ask this question: Who has the best chance for survival? In this example, the person who is bleeding severely has the best chance. Done correctly, firm direct pressure can stop bleeding rather quickly. This single action can absolutely save a life. The other patient would likely require CPR and advanced medical care, and may not survive even with this treatment. Meanwhile, the bleeding person would likely die from blood loss while awaiting your help. In other circumstances, sufficient help may be available to treat all those with life-threatening injuries.

3. Inventory Your Resources

Now that you are in a safe place and have stabilized all urgent medical problems, you should evaluate the survival resources available in your situation. The items that you find available combined with a creative and positive attitude are the resources that will make it possible for you to survive. Identify all equipment, gear, clothing, food, liquid, and other items that could be useful for survival. Do not forget to check luggage and pockets. Inventory all physical and mental skills that you and the members of the group possess. The following types of resources can be helpful in a survival situation:

- **Human resources.** The collective personalities, knowledge, life skills, attitudes, and survival skills of you and members of the group will be by far the greatest resource during a survival situation.
- **Equipment resources.** These resources include camping or climbing gear, clothing, food, water, survival gear, firearms,

medical gear, rope, tools, medications, and so on. Search through luggage, pockets, storage compartments, and any other locations that may contain useful items.

- **Salvaged resources.** Salvageable items like fabric, metal, wire, glass, fuel, rubber, insulation, batteries, mirrors, grease, cord, and other items from aircraft and vehicles can be useful in a survival situation. Be creative and think like a caveman, not a businessman.

- **Natural resources.** Firewood, bark, rocks, wild game, water sources, natural shelters, shelter-making materials, edible plants, fire-making materials, and many other natural materials are useful in improving your chances of survival.

4. Make a Plan

Now that you know what you have to work with, begin developing a strategy for your survival that will ensure the most efficient use of your resources. The plan that you develop should take into account many factors and should encompass both short- and long-term needs. Consider such items as climate, the likely temperature range, and current weather; your condition and the condition of the group; immediate hazards (rockfall, snow avalanche, grizzly bear den nearby, and so on); proximity to civilization or help; and the likelihood that a search effort will be initiated.

Survival Is Not a Democracy

In a survival situation people may believe that the group should vote to determine what course of action to take. But unless all members of the group have experience and knowledge with rescue and survival and are familiar with the particular environment in which they find themselves, voting may lead to an incorrect approach to solving survival problems. Voting about what to do in a survival emergency, as in politics, often involves the pressure of group dynamics and the persuasiveness of personalities. Emotions also play a role in how a person votes. A better way to approach the many dilemmas that arise during a survival situation is to take a moment to study the possible choices and apply well-reasoned survival principles to find the right solution.

Begin the plan as a basic framework and add details as required. Perform this process quickly; the plan need not be elaborate. The main idea is to focus your limited resources in one direction so that you can begin to implement the plan promptly. You must be flexible and willing to adapt to the needs of a complex and ever-changing situation. Be stubborn in your resolve to survive but be flexible if a plan is not working. Reevaluate your objectives and progress often and make adjustments when necessary, but do not second-guess yourself. Make well-reasoned decisions with the best information and resources that you have. Be deliberate, have faith in yourself, and never, ever give up.

Execute Your Plan

Each survival situation requires the adjustment of priorities based on a variety of variables. Each circumstance will have critical needs. No listing of priorities should be set in stone. Always be thoughtful and flexible in your approach to solving survival problems. In the realm of survival, there is always more than one right way to accomplish a task.

The following list of priorities applies to all environments. For example, shelter is not just essential in cold conditions. In hot and sunny conditions, shelter from the sun is critical, and cool nights can require shelter for warmth. In hot and humid conditions, shelter from rain is desirable. Even in hot conditions, a fire is important for light and security. In some circumstances, the order of the priorities may change. For example, if you can hear or see an aircraft or people in the area, you should forgo the building of a shelter and begin signaling immediately. In cold environments, building a fire first may be prudent, but even without fire a proper shelter can be lifesaving.

1. Stay put. Do not travel away from the area of the incident site (where you first discover that you are lost, where your plane has crashed, where your vehicle has become stuck or stalled, where your bicycle fell apart), except when you can see or hear that help is nearby.

2. Survey the immediate area within view of the incident site for available resources.

3. Find or build shelter.

4. Build a fire. Fire is important as a source of heat, light, signaling, and security.

5. Begin signaling.

6. Locate a source of water or devise a method to produce it (see chapter 4).

7. Locate a source of food.

You should organize and accomplish these tasks as soon as possible. By doing this you are improving the situation, staying busy, and avoiding apathy and depression, which are by far the most deadly hazards.

Learning to improvise is one critical way to be thoughtful and flexible in any survival situation. The ability to improvise may also be the most useful skill for survival. Simply put, improvising is making or fabricating a substitute for something out of the materials that are immediately available. You can develop this skill with practice. The key to effective improvising is learning to see a situation from a different perspective. To survive, you must become a creative scavenger, always searching for the multiple ways in which you can use available natural and manmade materials.

If, for example, you have just been involved in a crash landing of a small aircraft, you may initially look at the wreckage as merely a crashed plane. When you begin to think of it as a pile of raw material, you have entered the world of improvisation. The wreckage can provide you with resources for shelter, fire, signaling, and tools; the materials to construct traps and snares for food; and even the means to collect and carry water. Here are a few examples of how you might use materials from an aircraft for survival:

- Fuel can be used to make a fire that will provide light, security, a source of signaling, and a heat source for warmth and cooking.

- Wire can be used as cordage to construct shelters, traps, and snares and to meet many other needs.

- Fabric and padding from seats and headliner work well as shelter, insulation, bandages, shoes, and clothing.

- Batteries can provide an electrical source to create a spark to ignite a fire, by connecting a piece of wire to each terminal and striking their ends together.

- Glass is useful as a reflector for signaling.

- Tires can serve as fuel, especially for a smoky daytime signaling fire. You can strip rubber from the tires and make it into fastening material, carrying straps, and snowshoe bindings.

- Metal from the skin of the plane makes good shelter material. Metal can also be used as sleds, snowshoes, fabricated pots and containers, and cutting tools.

- Magnesium engine parts can be scraped and shaved to provide a source of fire-starting materials (see the section "Metal Sparking Tools" in chapter 3). Placed in a fire, magnesium parts burn very hot and bright.

- Landing lights contain parabolic reflectors that can be useful in starting fires (see the section "Optics" in chapter 3). A reflector can also be used for signaling purposes.

- Aircraft control cables provide strong cordage for fastening needs and for construction of implements and tools.

Shelter

DURING normal living conditions you may give little thought to the idea of shelter. You work and live in relative comfort and for the most part take no active role in sheltering yourself from uncomfortable environmental conditions. Modern technologies allow people to thrive in locations that are extremely hot or cold. Even while traveling, people are sheltered from the elements. You can adjust your comfort by touching a button or turning a dial. As long as these technologies are available and functional, you move forward with your life, happy to be putting your effort toward loftier ideals.

But when circumstances change, either because of choice or accident, your priorities change immediately. Suddenly, you may be left standing on a windswept plain, on a steep snow-covered slope, or in the searing heat of a vast desert. Unfamiliar sounds may fill your ears as dark clouds gather and night approaches. In that moment, shelter becomes your most desperate need.

Being able to create shelter is a crucial survival skill. Shelter is not just an option for comfort; it is a vital element that may save your life. A properly constructed shelter accomplishes two essential goals. The first is providing protection from a particular set of environmental conditions such as wind, heat, cold, rain, or snow. The second is assisting the occupant in retaining heat or staying cool.

You can build a variety of shelters. Determining which type to build depends on the terrain, season of the year, and conditions under which you will build it. An emergency shelter constructed in the woodlands of North Carolina during the summer will be far different from a shelter built above timberline in Colorado during the winter. Shelters need not be elaborate to be functional, and they can be created from any available material, including logs, sticks, grass, leaves, conifer boughs, pine needles, rocks, dirt, sand, snow, and plants. Found materials might include plastic, articles of clothing, cardboard, and materials salvaged from aircraft, vehicles, and equipment.

Strategies for Building Effective Shelters

Before beginning to build a shelter, make a quick survey of the area, searching for any natural features that you can use as a shelter. Look for rock overhangs, rock outcroppings, caves, fallen trees and logs, and trees with overhanging boughs and branches that reach close to the ground. If you can find one of these, you can make a serviceable shelter with little modification. Weigh the expenditure of energy against the benefit received. If a natural shelter can provide good protection, then you should not squander your personal resources to build something from scratch.

Rock overhangs can provide good protection from wind, rain, and snow. They are an especially welcome site in an emergency. If plastic or other tarp material is available, you can quickly enclose the open side of an overhang to keep wind and moisture out. Sandstone overhangs, however, should be used with caution. Sandstone is soft and porous, so it is weaker and more unstable than other types of rock formations, and it tends to fracture in layers. Deaths and injuries have resulted from slabs of sandstone releasing from the roofs of overhangs while people used the area below for shelter. Before using a sandstone overhang, look on the ground for any broken slabs that originated from the overhang, which indicate instability. Because fire and heat affect the stability of rock, especially if the rock is moist, avoid building large, hot fires under any overhang.

Whether you incorporate natural features, such as trees and over-hangs, or build from the ground up, following these simple tips will help make your shelter safe and efficient:

- Avoid building shelters in areas that may contain hazards such as snow avalanches, rockslides or mudslides, floods and high water, noxious plants and insects, animal dens and nests, and timber that may fall because of high winds.
- Avoid building shelters in the bottom of canyons or near creeks and streams because cooler air sinks into these low areas.
- Locate shelters near resources such as firewood and water.
- Place the entrance of the shelter away from the prevailing wind.
- Keep entrances small and low to reduce heat loss.
- Build shelters just large enough for the number of people that they need to accommodate. In most cases, the only heat source inside the shelter is body heat. Think of a shelter as an insulated cocoon or natural sleeping bag. The smaller it is, the easier it will be to heat.

Ground Insulation

When using a shelter most body heat is lost by way of conduction to the ground. To avoid this heat loss, use insulating materials to protect the body from the ground. Use natural insulating material, such as leaves, pine needles, and conifer boughs. Because these materials compress and become less effective during use, gather a generous amount. Extra clothing can also serve this purpose. Place enough insulating material on the ground inside the shelter to provide several inches beneath you and plenty left over to cover you completely when you are inside. When you enter, burrow a tight space into the insulation and pull some of the extra material into the entrance opening to keep wind and weather out and to keep heat in.

What to Expect

How warm will a shelter be? The answer varies according to several factors, including the temperature and weather outside and the experience and condition of the occupant. You can assume that you will not be as warm or comfortable as you would be if you were in a sleeping bag, but if you follow the steps provided in this chapter, you will significantly reduce heat loss from your body, thus reducing the possibility of cold injury and illness. People have spent many comfortable and restful nights in the types of shelters explained here.

Lean-To

The lean-to is a versatile shelter that can be used in any season and in a variety of locations with great success. A lean-to derives its name from its appearance—a collection of materials leaned against a framework. Lean-tos can be built in various sizes and configurations, including closed or open, depending on the need. A properly constructed lean-to is a simple shelter to use in a wilderness environment. Try to locate a site that is well protected by natural features such as trees, rocks, or land formations. Enlist as much help from nature as it has to offer. Choose a flat area for the floor. Plan the opening of your shelter away from the prevailing wind if possible. Place a windbreak or fire reflector made of dirt, rocks, or logs parallel to and 2 to 3 feet (60 to 90 cm) from the shelter entrance for added protection and heat retention.

A closed lean-to is an efficient and easy shelter to construct (see figure 2.1) using the following steps.

1. **Create the shelter framework.** Locate a strong stick to use as the main supporting member for the roof structure. It should be a little longer than your height or that of the tallest occupant. One end of the roof support will rest on the ground, forming the rear of the shelter. The other end will become the entrance and should be elevated 2 to 3 feet above ground level. The elevated end can be secured to a tree, rock wall, or dirt brim. If natural features are not available, make a tripod using the elevated end of the long support and two sticks of adequate length to form the entrance. Keep the top of this opening as low as possible while still affording access into the shelter. A low entrance retains more body heat within the shelter and allows less to escape to the outside air.

2. **Construct the roof and sides.** Start by laying several strong sticks perpendicular to the main roof support and sloping down to touch the ground. Spread them out evenly over the entire width of the main support. If the shelter is for a single person, it need not be much wider than 3 feet; allow about another 3 feet for each additional occupant. If sufficient material is available, try to place the roof poles no more than 6 inches (15 cm) apart.

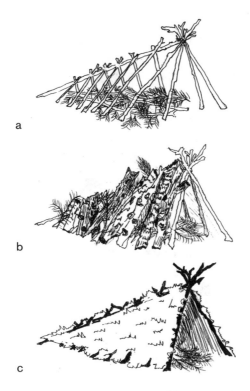

a

b

c

FIGURE 2.1 Construct a closed lean-to by *(a)* creating the shelter framework, *(b)* adding material to the frame, and *(c)* adding layering to insulate the shelter.

3. **Add layering.** When the framework is complete, begin gathering smaller sticks and laying them in the spaces between the framework. As the process continues, use bark, leaves, pine needles, or any other natural forest debris to create insulation. Completely cover the roof and sides with this material. The thicker the insulation is, the more effective your shelter will be. Conifer boughs, bark, and plant material work well for the layering material. If a sheet of plastic, rain poncho, or tarp is available, place it on top of the shelter and hold it in place with sticks to provide added protection from the elements.

4. **Finish the entrance.** After placing insulation on the ground, cover the bulk of the entrance, leaving only a small opening into the shelter.

An open lean-to can be constructed by placing the main roof support between two uprights (see figure 2.2). Space the uprights so that the area between them is large enough to accommodate the intended

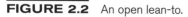

FIGURE 2.2 An open lean-to.

number of people lying sided by side. The main support forms the top of the entrance into the shelter. Keep the top of this opening as low as possible, just high enough to afford access into the shelter. To make the roof, place strong sticks, long enough to accommodate the height of the tallest occupant, perpendicular to the main roof support and sloping downward to the ground. Spread them evenly over the entire width of the main support. To close the sides of the shelter, lean smaller sticks from the ground up to the framework at a steep angle. Add layering and insulation as described in step 4 of the instructions on page 19 for the closed lean-to. Sleep with your feet at the closed end of the shelter.

Hasty Shelter

In severe conditions such as wind-driven snow and rain, finding or building shelter quickly is vital for survival. Protection from wind is especially important because of its deadly ability to rob the body of precious heat. These situations require fast action, which may not allow time to build a traditional shelter.

In forested areas, burrowing under a partially fallen log or crawling under natural foliage is far quicker than spending time collecting and constructing a conventional shelter. In open areas look for natural mounds and depressions in the ground that you can use as cover. If natural barriers are not available, stacking rocks or pushing dirt into a mound will make an effective barrier against the wind. A simple roof added to a wind barrier makes an effective hasty shelter. Use a sheet of plastic, emergency blanket, tarp, or poncho secured by rocks, sticks, or dirt to accomplish this.

Wikiup

Certain nomadic tribes of Native Americans used a shelter called a wikiup (also spelled wickiup). Historically, two types were used. One was a domed-shaped shelter consisting of a framework of sticks, usually willow or oak. The second and more practical version for survival purposes is built on a main framework of poles set in the formation of a tripod or tipi shape. Follow these steps to construct a wikiup:

1. **Set the tripod.** Gather three poles that are long enough for the size of shelter that you are creating. For a small one- or two-person wikiup, the tripod poles need to be about 5 feet (1.5 m) long. A good way to determine the length of the main poles is to draw a circle on the ground large enough to accommodate the required group size. Gather two poles that you estimate to be of sufficient length and place one end of each pole on the circle 180 degrees from one another. Lean them at a steep angle toward the center of the circle where they should meet and cross. If the poles are long enough, find a third pole of similar length and create a tripod by tying them together with cordage where they cross. If cord is not available try to find one pole with a fork at the proper length. Place a second pole into the fork, locking it into place. The last pole should also have a fork at the correct location to complete the tripod.

2. **Complete the framework.** When the tripod is complete, begin leaning poles of the same length into the tripod to form the main framework (figure 2.3). Leave an area open for the entrance.

3. **Finish the exterior.** Lay additional poles and sticks against this main framework and add insulating materials until the outside of the shelter is completely covered except for a small entrance opening. You can build a small and efficient wikiup for a single person or a larger one for several people. If you leave a vent hole open in the top of the shelter, you can make a

FIGURE 2.3 Framework for a wikiup shelter.

21

small fire inside. If plastic or a tarp is available, apply it to the main framework and lay on additional materials to secure it. You can fashion a durable and weather-resistant shelter in this manner.

Poncho Shelter

A high-quality waterproof poncho is one of the most useful and versatile items to carry with you as a survival aid. Rain ponchos are typically made of coated nylon or plastic, and most have grommets installed at the corners and along the edges. Ponchos are available at outdoor stores and camping stores and range in price from about $15 to $50. A low-tech poncho shelter (see figure 2.4) is quick to set up and amazingly effective in a variety of conditions. Locate the shelter on flat ground near a small sapling or a tree with low, flexible branches. The low branches of a tree or the tip of a bent sapling will provide upward tension on the center of the shelter to keep it in place.

1. **Line up one corner to the tree.** Begin by placing one corner of the poncho within a few inches (about 10 cm) of a small sapling or within 2 feet (about 60 cm) of a larger tree. This corner will connect to the tree with cordage and become the entrance.

2. **Stake the other corners.** Stake down the other three corners of the poncho with small sticks or use rocks to weigh them down.

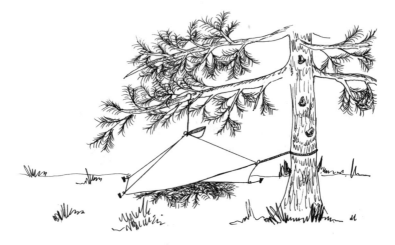

FIGURE 2.4 A poncho shelter.

3. **Create the roof.** To pull the roof of the shelter up and taught, tie the hood of the poncho to a flexible overhead branch or bent sapling.

4. **Set up the entrance.** Tie a loop of cordage through the grommet near the entrance and around the tree or small sapling. You can slide this loop up and down the trunk of the sapling to open and close the entrance. During inclement weather, slide the cord tied to the entrance corner down to the bottom of the tree, completely closing the entrance to create a weather-tight shelter. Used in place of cordage at this location, an elastic shock cord with hooks installed makes the shelter easier to set up and use.

Snow Cave

Snow can pose an enormous challenge to human survival. But snow can be a useful survival tool as well. The greatest benefit of snow is its effectiveness as an insulator when used to fabricate shelters. Many types of snow shelters are used throughout the world, but one of the most common and easiest to construct for emergency use is the snow cave shown in figure 2.5. Almost any improvised tool can be used, even the hands if nothing else is available. But for a planned and comfortable cave, a shovel is best. Small collapsible avalanche shovels work well for building snow shelters. Usually made from metal or polycarbonate plastic, these shovels range in price from $35 to $85. You can find them at ski shops, climbing and mountaineering stores, and snowmobile dealers.

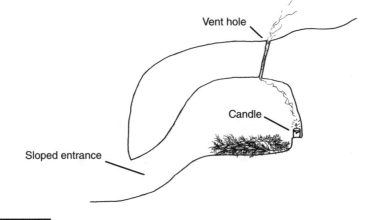

Vent hole

Candle

Sloped entrance

FIGURE 2.5   A cross section of a snow cave.

When choosing a site for a cave, avoid areas exposed to natural hazards such as avalanches. You would probably not choose to build a snow cave on a steep slope where avalanches form because of the difficulty of doing so, but even on gentler terrain you should stay well away from the base of steep slopes where avalanche debris accumulates during a slide. Snow depth is an important consideration when choosing a location for a snow cave. A depth of 4 to 5 feet (120 to 150 cm) is helpful. Look for a drift or swale (depression between slopes) near ridges or trees. Try to arrange the entrance to the cave so that it is on the leeward side (the side away from the wind) of a slope. Be sure to begin building your cave early while plenty of light remains. Construction becomes difficult in the dark.

Many areas of the world do not receive enough snowfall for the snow depth to reach 4 to 5 feet (120 to 150 cm). You can overcome this problem by forming a large pile of snow. To form the snow pile, shovel or move snow onto a site that will provide a flat and stable base. Continue adding snow to form a rounded pile at least 4 feet deep. The pile should be large enough in length and width so that the eventual shelter will accommodate the number of people who will occupy it. Start with more snow than you think you will need.

Leave the newly formed pile undisturbed for at least an hour before attempting any digging. This interval allows the snow crystals to bind together, which will give the snow cave strength and stability. The binding time will vary depending on the type of snow, the moisture content, and the air temperature. In some conditions, especially during spring, the snow crystals may require double the time to form this bond, and occasionally a bond will not form at all. In these situations you should consider other types of shelters. When the snow depth is limited or difficult snow conditions exist, smaller snow shelters will be easier to build. If the group is large, the most effective approach is to build several smaller caves. When you have found an appropriate site or finished forming a pile of snow, you can use the following steps to construct a snow cave:

1. **Prepare to dig.** In cold conditions, moisture is a deadly enemy. Remember, dry is warm. While building snow shelters you can become extremely wet. Before the actual digging begins make sure that you are wearing the proper clothing, including layers and a breathable, waterproof shell on the outside. If proper clothing is not available, use special care to stay as dry as possible. A large scoop shovel is helpful for heavy digging, although smaller

avalanche shovels also work well. In an emergency a shovel may not be available, so use whatever you can improvise, including your gloved hands.

2. **Dig a pit.** Begin by digging a pit downward into the snow. The purpose of the pit is to get you deep enough into the snow so that you can then dig a cave in the snow to the side of the pit and allow adequate thickness (minimum 12 inches, or 30 cm) on the top and sides. Make the pit wide enough to work in. As you dig, place the snow that you remove onto the roof area of the cave. If the snow is 4 or 5 feet (120 to 150 cm) deep, dig down until the pit is deep enough that the surface of the pile comes to about to the top of your chest. If the snow is deeper, make the pit as deep as you are tall.

3. **Prepare the entrance.** The next step is to make the entrance. Do this by shaving the snow flat and vertical on the front face of where you will create the general entrance area of the cave. At a point at about knee level, make the entrance by using the front edge of the shovel to make cuts in the snow in the shape of the entrance, which should be slightly wider than your body.

4. **Tunnel in.** Now begin tunneling in by digging at a slight upward angle from the entrance. Ideally, the cave end of the tunnel should be at least 12 inches (30 cm) above the entrance to help prevent warm air from escaping the shelter, but this may not be possible because of the lack of snow depth. Do your best to make the sleeping portion of the cave higher than the entrance. At the upward end of the tunnel hollow out a space as large as your body. Moving the snow becomes a major task at this point. Use the shovel in front of your body to dig in. As you move forward use your feet to move the snow out of the entrance. Now you are ready to begin shaping the cave.

5. **Shape the cave.** The ceiling and the walls of the shelter should be dome shaped and smooth, and the space should be large enough to sit up in. Try to eliminate sharp edges or ridges on the walls and ceiling of the cave. The temperature in a snow cave commonly rises above the freezing mark, which creates snowmelt. If the ceiling and walls of the cave are domed and smooth, the water droplets will run down to the edges. On the other hand, water droplets will gather at ridges and edges and fall to the floor from those locations. If drips do occur smooth those spots with a tool or your hand.

6. **Create a ventilation hole.** Another necessary feature is a ventilation hole to release the carbon dioxide produced by your breathing and the carbon monoxide produced by using a candle in the cave. Never build a fire in a snow cave because fire produces so much heat that it melts the snow and uses most of the available air, creating a carbon monoxide hazard. With a stick or other object, make a hole about 2 inches (5 cm) in diameter in the top of the cave. Check the vent hole at regular intervals to be sure that it does not become clogged. A convenient way to do this is to insert a small stick or other object into the hole. The stick should be only half the diameter of the vent hole. Leave the stick in place and occasionally push it up and down.

7. **Add platforms and shelves.** An elevated sleeping platform is a feature that allows you to be nearer the warmer air in the upper part of the cave. Create platforms and shelves for gear and equipment by placing and compacting snow in the desired locations. You can also make a shelf for a candle. One lighted candle can increase the air temperature in a small cave by as much as 20 degrees Fahrenheit (9 degrees Celsius). You can block the entrance to the cave with a snow block or other piece of gear to reduce air movement and increase the temperature inside.

On occasion during the construction of a snow cave, especially in poor snow conditions, a collapse can occur. A good practice is to build caves in teams of two. During construction, one person should always remain outside. In case of a collapse the person outside can then rescue the person digging. Rarely does a snow cave collapse after construction,

Emergency Snow Cave

When time is short and you are in trouble, find a drift or ridge of snow and dig the cave straight into the bank. You can skip the tunnel. Make sure that the roof is 12 inches (30 cm) thick and that you have not built the cave below a cornice or avalanche hazard. Dig the cave only as large as the space your body needs when sitting with your knees drawn up to your chest. Line the cave with conifer boughs or other dry material. If you have a little more time, you can start with a short tunnel, but at the end of the tunnel hollow out the same space as previously noted. You can straighten your legs in this type of shelter by sitting in the cave and stretching your legs into the tunnel.

especially after the temperature drops at night. Cold temperatures tend to increase the overall strength of the shelter. The ceiling of a snow cave can sink as much as 2 inches (5 cm) per day because of normal settling of the snowpack. During a heavy storm the settling can increase dramatically. Always keep your shovel or digging device next to you in a snow cave in case a collapse does occur.

Snow Trench

A snow trench, which is simpler and less time consuming to build than a snow cave, is extremely effective when constructed properly (see figure 2.6). Snow trenches work well where the snow is not deep or when time is a consideration. Besides requiring much less time to build than a snow cave, a snow trench greatly reduces the possibility of getting wet, an important consideration for a person without proper clothing.

1. **Dig a trench.** Construct this shelter by creating a trench about 3 feet (90 cm) deep. The trench should be just long enough to accommodate the tallest person in the group. The size of the group lying side by side determines the width. As with other shelters, keep the entrance to the shelter small. Steps cut into the snow at the entrance of the shelter work well. In an emergency the trench can be used with no further modification. As is, the trench will break the wind and provide a small degree of insulation.

2. **Add a roof.** To increase the effectiveness of the snow trench, start by laying larger sticks across the width of the opening to create the main supporting members. If the trench is wide, additional vertical sticks from floor to roof may be needed for support. Then add smaller sticks until the roof is well covered. If a sheet of plastic or a tarp is available, place it over the roof.

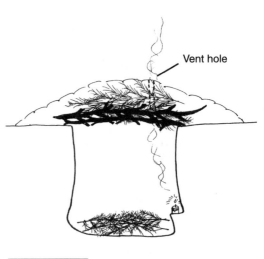

Vent hole

FIGURE 2.6 A cross section of a snow trench.

3. **Add snow insulation.** The next step is to place a layer of snow 12 inches (30 cm) deep on top of the roof of sticks. The snow will add a great deal of insulation to the snow trench.

4. **Add heat.** As in snow caves, you can light a candle in a snow trench to add heat. Be sure to provide a vent hole in the roof (as described on page 26) for fresh air.

Tree Pit

As you walk through the woods when snow is on the ground, you may have noticed that around the downhill sides of trees the snow is farther from the trunk. This effect is caused by the plastic properties of snow. Gravity pulls at the snowpack and begins to stretch it away from trees. In addition, trees absorb heat from the sun and earth. This heat is transferred from the tree trunk into the snow, causing the snow to melt away from around the trunk. These effects create the beginnings of a natural winter shelter known as a tree pit (see figure 2.7). To finish what nature started, follow these steps:

1. **Find an appropriate tree.** Look for a large tree with a good hole around the trunk. A tree with low branches that reach toward the ground is ideal because the branches provide overhead cover.

2. **Enlarge the hole.** You want to make the hole just large enough to accommodate the number in the group. Building steps down into the pit eases entry.

3. **Add a roof and insulation.** If necessary, construct a roof by laying roof supports across the width of the pit and adding material using the technique used for the snow trench. To complete the shelter, line the floor with conifer boughs or any other dry material for insulation. If you decide to use a candle for heat, make sure that you create a vent hole in the roof to supply fresh air.

FIGURE 2.7 A cross section of a tree pit.

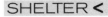

Shade Shelter

Most shelters are designed to protect people from cold conditions. In hot conditions, however, you will need to create a shelter that provides protection from the heat. The most important aspect of this kind of shelter is shade. Seek shade wherever you can find it. Do not wait until you feel hot. Find or prepare your shelter during the cool of the morning or evening. If available, natural overhangs and caves can provide needed shade. If you are in a disabled car or truck, get out of the vehicle and seek shade underneath. Because vehicles contain so much metal, they conduct and reflect the heat. You will be much cooler underneath the vehicle than in it.

You can also use the following steps to deal with heat and create artificial shade:

1. **Search for cooler ground.** Digging into the ground will uncover cooler soil. Even a depth of a few inches will expose cooler dirt. Digging near dry washes or riverbeds may expose cool moist soil. You can dig with your hands, a stick, or an improvised shovel.

2. **Create a lightweight framework and covering.** Construct a framework from sturdy sticks over the area of soil that you have chosen. The structure could be fashioned similar to an open sided lean-to. In this situation the entrance can be high and the sides should be left uncovered. The only purpose of this shelter is to create shade and encourage heat loss by providing plenty of airflow. Lay bark, plant material, a rain poncho, an emergency blanket, or opaque plastic or fabric over the framework to create shade. Then lie down on the soil and wait out the heat of the day. Do the bulk of the work on a shade shelter during the cool of the morning or evening. If a tarp, a poncho, or other fabric is available, any of these items can be used as the roof for the shade shelter. If enough material is available, create a double-layered roof by placing two pieces of material one above the other with about 5 or 6 inches of air between the layers. The double-shade layer further decreases the temperature inside the shelter.

Shelter in Your Vehicle

People often overlook the shelter value of vehicles and aircraft. During cold weather the risk of being stranded or stalled in a vehicle is far greater than it is at other times of the year. Many people die each year in their vehicles because they are either unprepared or uneducated about what to do. The two most common causes of death in these situations are hypothermia and carbon monoxide (CO) poisoning.

Spending the night inside a vehicle with no protection other than the clothes on your back can be cold, but the addition of a few items can create an adequate if not comfortable shelter. By enclosing yourself in a vehicle, you are already sheltering yourself from wind and wet weather. The most effective method of modifying a vehicle for shelter is to reduce the area being heated. You can enclose a space in the front or back seat using emergency blankets, tarps, or plastic along with duct tape or cold-weather electrical tape and then heat the area with a candle. Covering glass is especially important in reducing heat loss. The following precautions can help you avoid carbon monoxide poisoning when staying in your stalled or stuck vehicle during cold conditions:

- **Use a CO detector**. Always keep a CO detector in your vehicle. A simple and inexpensive type is a card that contains a colored spot that darkens in the presence of dangerous levels of carbon monoxide. This type of detector costs less than $10 and can be ordered from aircraft pilot supply shops. Various styles of electronic detectors are also available. Place the detector in a location at about eye level and monitor it frequently.

- **Open a window slightly**. A small opening allows fresh air to enter and helps reduce moisture buildup caused by condensation.

- **Run the engine at intervals**. Warm the cab of the vehicle until comfortable and then turn off the engine. Wait until you become uncomfortably cool before starting the engine again. This method conserves fuel and reduces the possibility of carbon monoxide poisoning.

- **Check for tailpipe obstructions**. Frequently check to be sure that snow or other debris is not obstructing the tailpipe. This practice is especially important during windy conditions when snow is on the ground.

Fire

TO the primitive cultures, the discovery of fire was a vital milestone of survival. Fire was used for heat, light, cooking, and the manufacture of tools. It offered safety and security and became the centerpiece for social gatherings and tribal meetings. To early societies, fire came to symbolize life itself, and each person learned to become a proficient fire maker at a young age.

With the ever-increasing emphasis and dependence on technology, our culture has lost the sharp-edged technique of fire making because we are not required to use it as a matter of course in day-to-day living. Modern equipment and clothing have considerably enhanced our ability to survive in difficult environments, but sometimes everything else fails and a simple low-tech fire saves the day and saves a life. Fire-making skills still reign supreme as a priority for those who venture into challenging environments.

Components of Fire

Three ingredients are essential for creating a successful fire: oxygen, heat, and fuel. The right combination of the three will produce and maintain a fire. People often overlook the importance of oxygen when building a fire. Although you cannot create oxygen (it is contained in the surrounding air), you can make sure that the fire has enough of it. One way to ensure that a fire has sufficient oxygen is to avoid adding too much fuel in the early stages of a fire, which can quickly smother it. Blowing air directly into the base of the fire is also a method of getting oxygen to a fire. This technique is especially useful when attempting to burn damp fuel.

The heat, or ignition source, can come by means of primitive or modern methods. The ignition source might be a hot spark created by flint and steel, a smoldering ember created by the friction of a bow drill, or the heat from a match. To produce a successful fire, you will also need to find and prepare the right kinds of dry fuels. Even if you are carrying modern fire-starting tools, do not be fooled into believing that you can skip the vital steps of fuel gathering and preparation. The extra time spent at that task will pay big dividends later when a desperate struggle to survive becomes merely an uncomfortable night next to a fire. To build a fire, you need tinder, kindling, and firewood.

Tinder

Tinder is the most important fuel in the fire-making process. It is the first material that the ignition source comes into contact with, and it should be fine, dry, and supple enough that a tiny spark can ignite it. Without good, dry tinder, the rest of your efforts will be difficult and frustrating. Dry barks, grasses, plant fibers, weed tops, and even animal nests and lint from clothing make good tinder. Down from thistle, cattail, and milkweed as well as the inner bark of cottonwood, aspen, cedar, sagebrush, cliffrose, and juniper work well. You should prepare barks and plant material by breaking down the fibers until they become feathery and light. Twisting and rubbing the material against itself, between the hands, or mashing it between two rocks does this effectively. Gather an amount the size of a bird's nest.

Always be thinking ahead, gathering plenty of material before you need it. Whenever you see something that would work well for a fire starter, collect and save it. You may not have the same opportunity when conditions change. Placing tinder in your clothing close to your body can dry damp materials, but avoid putting tinder next to your skin because it will absorb moisture from perspiration.

Kindling

Kindling is slightly larger than tinder, requires more heat to ignite, and is not consumed as quickly. Any material that is dead and dry will work as kindling. Sticks, twigs, and dry conifer needles can be used. Gather them in various sizes from the diameter of a guitar string to the size of your little finger.

In wet areas, look for materials that have been protected from the weather. A good place to look is under logs and at the base and trunks of conifers where the boughs have protected dead wood on the tree. During wet weather, collecting enough small, dry kindling is sometimes difficult. In cases like these you can make a fuzz stick from a thicker branch. Using a knife, begin by stripping the damp outer part of the stick until you reach dry wood. Then make a series of shallow angled cuts on the shaft of the stick along its length without cutting completely through the material. This process creates thin slices, which you leave attached to the shaft. You should have several fuzz sticks ready to go before attempting to start the fire.

Firewood

When you have collected enough tinder and kindling, begin gathering various sizes of dry wood for fuel. You will need several armloads to keep a fire going through the night. The driest and most usable wood will be standing dead wood. When possible, avoid rotten or pithy material or wood lying on the ground because these will contain more moisture. A good way to carry fuel wood is to create a bundle and tie it with cordage or wrap it with a belt or strap. Long logs that are large in diameter need not be broken; you can feed them slowly into the fire as they are consumed.

In an area of sparse woodland, search for sagebrush and other natural woody growth. This fuel is usually smaller in diameter than tree growth and will not burn as long, so you will need to collect more of it. Dried cattle and animal dung can also be gathered in quantities and burned. Manure fuel produces a lot of heat but not as much light as wood fuel does.

How to Build a Fire

The difficulty of building a fire can range from easy to nearly impossible, depending on the materials available, the weather, and the skill of the fire maker. In extreme cases you may have only one chance at a fire, and your survival may depend on it. To give yourself every advantage, follow these six basic steps to starting a fire:

1. **Prepare a site for the fire.** In dry conditions, clear dead brush and wood away from the site and be aware of any low-hanging branches that may catch fire. Dig a small depression to contain the fire. Choose a site that is protected from the prevailing wind and weather. You may need to improvise a windbreak from available materials. If you are building a fire in snowy conditions, choose a location away from overhanging branches that could dump snow and extinguish your fire. If you have to build a fire near a tree, shake any snow from the branches before you start. If you need to build a fire in a snow-covered area, dig down to the ground if possible. If the snow is too deep to dig out, then compact the snow and make a platform of solid logs to build the fire on.

2. **Collect plenty of fuel.** Place the fuel items within easy reach of the fire-starting area. In a survival situation, building a fire is a matter of life and death. Lighting a fire quickly is a priority, but caution is in order here. Take enough time to collect the best dry fuels that you can find. A little extra time spent during this step can save hours of frustration later and may affect the ultimate outcome of your experience.

3. **Prepare a tinder bundle.** When you have prepared the tinder for use, form it into a bundle. The completed bundle should look like a birds nest with a depression in the center. Combining different materials together can help hold the bundle in the proper shape. Place the finest and lightest material in the depression of the nest.

4. **Prepare the kindling.** After you light the tinder bundle (step 5), you will need to be able to place the flaming bundle under the kindling. A way to facilitate this is to form some kindling into a small upright triangle or tipi shape. Add more kindling to the framework until you have a loose bunch of kindling with a hollowed out place in the middle into which you can place the flaming tinder.

5. **Introduce the spark or heat source.** You want to place the spark into the depression in the tinder bundle. After the spark is in the depression, begin blowing gently into the nest onto the spark or ember to add oxygen to the burning fuel and spread the fire into the tinder. As the material begins to light, start folding the nest around the glowing tinder. As the heat intensifies you can blow with greater pressure. Use long, slow breaths, occasionally turning your head away to draw fresh air into your lungs. As the heat increases hold the bundle with the ends of your fingers. The tinder bundle will soon burst into flame. When materials are damp, this process will take longer. But do not give up; if you persevere the tinder will eventually catch flame.

6. **Place the flaming bundle into the prepared kindling.** You then place the flaming bundle inside the kindling tipi. After the kindling begins to burn you can be begin to add more kindling. Take care not to smother the fire by adding too much kindling at once. Add a few small pieces at a time until the fire is producing enough heat to add more fuel.

When materials are damp the fire needs much more oxygen to produce enough heat to maintain itself. Blow directly into the hottest portion of the fire using long, slow breaths. Keep at it, and eventually the fire will produce enough heat on its own to overcome the moisture in the fuel. When the fire is burning on its own, you can place damp wood near it to dry.

Ignition Sources

Many methods exist for starting fires, from striking a match to using a bow drill set. All these techniques have one thing in common: They produce a hot spark, ember, or other ignition source. These various ignition sources provide the heat needed to produce fire. The more fire-starting methods you have available, the greater the likelihood of success.

Primitive Methods of Fire Starting

Several primitive fire-starting methods are extremely effective. Some require more skill and practice than others. These methods require patience and perseverance, but anyone can learn them with practice and experimentation. Most of these techniques are based on the principle of fire by friction. The available materials will drive the decision as to which method you choose in a particular situation.

Flint and Steel

The flint and steel method of fire starting requires the use of steel in some form. The principle of this method is based on the interaction of two different materials by friction. Steel is struck against the sharp edge of a hard stone, and sparks form as the rock peels away tiny pieces of heated steel. The sparks are directed to the tinder bundle that has been prepared to accept them when they fall. The spark is then blown into flame. The disadvantage of this method is that steel is difficult to find in the wild.

As indicated by the name, you need two items to start this type of fire: flint and a piece of steel. With some searching, you can find an appropriate piece of flint. Flint rocks, such as quartz, agate, chert, and jasper, which are high in silica content, are needed for striking fires. These stones have a smooth, glassy appearance. Stones that are easy to grasp in one hand are the ideal size. Smaller stones, which you can hold with your fingers, will also work, but they may be more difficult to use because you will need to hold the stone in a stationary position when creating a spark. You can strike a flint rock against another stone or other hard object to create sharp edges, which will enhance your ability to make good sparks with the stone.

High-carbon steel works best because it is soft and produces large sparks easily. Stainless steel is too hard and brittle to be effective. Pocketknife blades and steel files are two of the most common sources for the steel. Pocketknives made of high-carbon steel are typically less expensive than those made of stainless steel. Stainless steel blades usually have a stamp or engraving indicating that they are made of stainless steel. Steel files, available at hardware and building supply stores, work best when broken into pieces 4 to 5 inches (10 to 12 cm) in length.

For a flint and steel fire to be successful, you must use very fine, dry tinder. Sparks created in this manner are short lived and need to fall onto material that will capture and retain the small amount of heat generated. It is helpful to use charred powder, charred cloth, extra-fine steel wool, or some other spark-enhancing medium, which you place into the depression of the tinder bundle. These materials act as a vehicle to hold and spread the heat from the small steel spark. You can obtain charred powder by scraping the burned wood from an old campfire or forest fire, but charred cloth is a better spark-enhancing medium.

Making Charred Cloth

You can make good charred cloth by burning 100 percent cotton fabric until it is black and then starving the oxygen from it. You can make charred cloth in two ways. One method is to hold a stick in one hand and drape cotton fabric over it. Move the fabric over a fire or burning candle to ignite the cloth. Allow the fabric to burn until completely blackened and then smother it from oxygen by pressing it tightly to the ground with a flat object of sufficient size such as the bottom of a can or cooking pot or a flat rock.

The other method is to cut several pieces of cotton cloth so they fit inside a small tin like the ones that mints come packaged in. Stack the cut pieces of cloth loosely into the tin. Then punch a single hole about 1/8 inch (.3 cm) in diameter in the center of the lid. Secure the lid in place and put the container in a fire. Keep the tin out of the hottest section of the fire. Placing it on hot embers works even better. As the cloth begins to char, smoke will rise from the hole in the lid. When the smoke stops coming from the hole, remove the container from the fire. The cloth should then be sufficiently charred. Wait for the tin to cool before removing the lid. If you remove the lid while the cloth is too hot, the addition of oxygen will burn the cloth too much, rendering it useless. If you do the procedure correctly, the finished charred cloth should be completely blackened but not burned to ash. If the cloth is still brown, it needs more time in the fire.

To strike a spark with flint and steel, follow these steps:

1. Kneel on the ground, place a tinder bundle in front of you, and crouch over the bundle. If you are using charred cloth, place a piece into the depression of the tinder bundle before you begin.

2. Hold the steel in one hand between your thumb and index finger. If you are using a pocketknife, hold the closed knife in the same fashion with the back of the knife blade facing the rock (see figure 3.1).

3. Grasp the flint in the opposite hand with the sharpest edge toward the steel.

4. To generate sparks, strike the steel against the sharp edge of the rock with a quick downward motion. Use deliberate, powerful strokes, directing the sparks toward the tinder bundle. Besides

having the charred cloth in the tinder bundle, try holding a small piece under your thumb against the flint near the striking edge. Many times sparks will deflect upward away from the steel as it strikes the flint, and the cloth may catch them. Incorporating this technique can greatly increase your chances of catching a viable spark.

5. When you see a spark fall into the tinder, immediately give a light puff of air onto the tinder bundle. Alternatively, if you catch a good spark on the charred cloth under your thumb, quickly transfer it to the tinder bundle and blow it into flame. If the spark has begun to ignite the tinder, a small wisp of smoke will be present, and you should see a tiny glow in the bundle. Continue to blow the tinder into flame. If the tinder does not catch, continue striking sparks. In bright and sunny conditions, place the tinder bundle

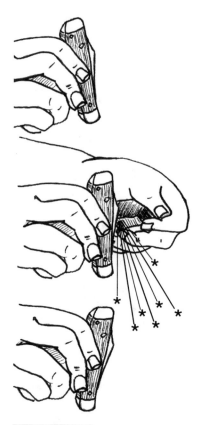

FIGURE 3.1 Proper technique for striking a spark with flint and steel.

in the shade or position yourself so that you cast a shadow over the tinder. That way you can see where the sparks are falling and whether the tinder is beginning to burn.

Bow Drill

With the bow drill method, you place a spindle made of wood on a fireboard with a notch cut into it and hold the spindle in an upright position with a hand socket. You turn the spindle back and forth very rapidly by using a bow and string. Friction and heat build until the spindle in contact with the fireboard begins to char. Hot charred powder is produced by the spinning action of the spindle against the fireboard and deposited into the notch. When enough hot material accumulates in the notch, it becomes an ember. You then place the ember into the tinder bundle, where you can blow it into flame.

You need the following components to use the bow drill method (see figure 3.2):

- **Spindle.** The spindle should be about 3/4 inch (2 cm) thick and at least 8 inches (20 cm) long, and the shaft should be smooth and symmetrical. The easiest way to make a spindle is to use a straight stick with the proper diameter. The upper end, which fits into the hand socket, should be shaped into a rounded point. The lower end, which mates with the fireboard, must be blunt and rounded. You can also make a spindle by splitting a smaller piece of wood from a log and shaping it with a knife or scraping it with a stone. Woods that make good spindles include cottonwood, sagebrush, yucca, willow, sycamore, cedar, poplar, tamarack, and aspen. These woods are considered medium in hardness. You will obtain poor results by using woods that are too soft, too hard, or rotten. Also, avoid using resinous or pitchy materials such as pine, spruce, and fir. As with any material for fire making, using extremely dry dead wood is the key to success.

- **Hand socket.** The hand socket can be made from a stone or piece of wood. A stone with a depression near the center that fits your hand works well. You can fabricate wood with a knife or abrade it with a stone to create a depression near the center to accept the sharpened end of the spindle, and you can shape it to fit into your hand.

- **Bow.** You can use live or dead woods of various types to make the bow. The easiest way to begin is to find a stick 2 to 3 feet (60

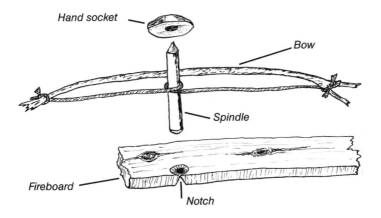

FIGURE 3.2 Bow drill components.

to 90 cm) long with a diameter of about 3/4 inch (2 cm). Any cordage can be used as a bowstring. To string the bow, attach the cord to one end of the stick. Do this by cutting a notch in the end of the stick or by choosing a stick with a small fork at one end. Tie the cord onto the opposite end of the stick, leaving it a little slack. This end of the cord needs to remain adjustable. The tension needed on the string depends on the diameter of the spindle and the stiffness of the bow. Pay special attention if you use shoelaces, leather, or other flat cordage because the spindle can catch and drag with these materials. To prevent these problems, secure the cord to one end of the bow and begin twisting until it becomes rolled and round and no visible flat areas remain. If possible, avoid using twine with loose, hairy fibers because the loose fibers tend to wrap around the spindle, causing dragging and binding.

- **Fireboard.** The optimal fireboard will be about 1/2 inch (1.25 cm) thick and at least 2 inches (5 cm) wide. A minimum length of about 12 inches (30 cm) works best. The fireboard should be straight and flat enough so it will be stable under your foot. The spindle and fireboard can be made from the same or different woods, but they should be similar in hardness. To prepare the fireboard, you need to create a socket in the fireboard to accept the bottom end of the spindle. The socket should be located 2 to 3 inches (5 to 7.5 cm) from one edge of the fireboard (or you can measure in and place the socket at a distance of about two-thirds the diameter of the spindle). Use a knife or sharp stone to make a small pit or depression in the fireboard. Then use the spindle, bow, and hand socket to drill the socket into the fireboard just deep enough to seat the spindle (see the steps on page 41). After you have made the socket, cut a narrow V-shaped notch through the entire thickness of the fireboard that reaches from the outside edge to the center of the socket that you have just created. The notch should also be slightly flared toward the underside of the board. Careful preparation of the notch is critical to success because this is where the hot wood fibers created from the friction between the spindle and fireboard are deposited and where the ember forms.

Now that the bow drill set is complete, you are ready to make fire. Contrary to what you may have seen in the movies, a novice cannot quickly make a bow drill fire. You have created the tools; now you must prepare yourself mentally to keep trying until you accomplish the goal of making fire. You will likely need several attempts before you create an ember, but you must not become discouraged. Your technique will improve as you persevere. By following these steps and by using the troubleshooting tips in table 3.1, you will be successful:

1. Prepare a flat, dry spot on which to place the fireboard.

2. Place a thin, flat piece of wood or bark beneath the notch. You will use this wood or bark to catch the ember and transfer it to the tinder bundle.

3. Lubricate the top end of the spindle to decrease the friction between it and the hand socket. Rubbing it against your nose or through your hair can do this.

4. Twist the spindle onto the bowstring so that the string is wrapped once around the spindle. If you have the proper tension, the spindle will feel as though it is trying to roll out of the string, and it will if you do not keep a hand on it.

5. If you are right-handed, kneel with your right knee on the ground while placing your left foot on the longer portion of the fireboard but near the notch (see figure 3.3 on page 43). Grasp the end of the bow with your right hand and arrange it so that the string is toward you with the bow on the outside. Then lean over so that your chest is resting on your left knee. Place the blunt end of the spindle into the socket on the fireboard. With your left hand, grasp the hand socket and place it on top of the spindle.

6. Brace your left arm securely against your upright leg. While putting pressure on the spindle, slowly begin pushing the bow back and forth, using long slow stokes. Take care to keep the bow parallel to the ground. Go easy at first until you are secure with the technique and then increase the speed of the bow and the pressure on the spindle.

7. As the spindle and fireboard begin to char, smoke will begin to rise from the fireboard. The smoke will become thicker as you continue. Keep going until enough charred material has been deposited into the notch to create an ember. When you think you have reached this point, continue for several strokes more and stop.

8. Very gently blow on the notch. This will reveal a small glowing ember. Carefully transfer the ember to the tinder bundle and blow it into flame.

Table 3.1 Bow Drill Troubleshooting Tips

Common problems	Potential causes	Solutions
Spindle stoppage or slippage	• Loose bowstring • Bow that is too limber • Too much downward pressure on the spindle	• Tighten the bowstring • Use a stiffer bow • Try using a little less pressure on the spindle
A smoking hand socket	• Insufficient lubrication • Top end of the spindle too blunt	• Add more lubrication • Reshape the upper end of the spindle into more of a point
Good technique but not much smoke	• Not enough downward pressure on the spindle • Glazing (from use) on the spindle and fireboard that prevents good contact between the two surfaces • Glazing caused by woods that are too hard or contain resins	• Push harder on the hand socket to create more downward pressure on the spindle • Remove the black glaze from the spindle and fireboard • Make sure that the materials used for the fireboard and spindle are of medium hardness and contain little or no pitch or resin
Lots of smoke and charred powder but no ember	• Poorly formed notch	• Make sure that the notch extends close to the center of the depression in the fireboard • Check the width of the notch (a notch that is too narrow prevents collection of the charred powder; a notch that is too wide prevents collection of the powder in a tight bunch that will become an ember)

FIGURE 3.3   Proper technique for starting a fire with a bow drill.

Modern Methods of Fire Starting

Modern, high-tech fire starting methods are convenient, laborsaving, and a great advantage to those who know how to put them to use, but they do not eliminate the need for fundamental fire-making skills. These materials and methods merely provide an easier means of producing the initial heat source for making a fire. To be fully prepared, you should carry a least three reliable methods of fire starting.

Matches

Matches are the most common and reliable method used in fire making. They are inexpensive and easily obtained and have no moving parts that can malfunction. Matches are lightweight, easy to carry, and require little training or expertise to use. The most dangerous enemy to matches is moisture because over time moisture can be absorbed through the matchstick, rendering them ineffective.

The most effective way of keeping matches reliably dry is to store them in a waterproof container or match safe. The container should include an O-ring seal and a threaded lid. Always store a match striker inside the container with the matches. (Sandpaper or emery cloth does not work as a striker). Regular box or book matches require two chemical components to ignite. One of the components is contained in the match head, and the other is in the striking surface on the box or matchbook. Remove the striking surface and enclose it with the matches in the match safe. You can mount the striking surface to a piece of thin wood or plastic for rigidity and durability. Strike-anywhere matches contain both chemical components on the match head and do not require a special striking surface, but they are hard to find in stores because they are now considered a hazardous material.

Another option that you may want to consider is waterproof and windproof matches. You can buy waterproof matches from outdoor and camping stores for less than $3 a box. You can also make them by dipping regular wooden strike-on-the-box or strike-anywhere matches in heated candle wax or paraffin and completely coating and sealing the entire match in wax. Dipping matches in fingernail polish and allowing them to dry is another excellent method of waterproofing matches. You can also buy matches that are windproof and waterproof. These matches burn hot and quickly and are made with a waterproof, windproof material that ignites in almost every condition. They can usually be found at the same stores that sell waterproof matches, but they cost a bit more.

As with regular matches, waterproof and windproof matches should be stored in a waterproof match safe. All matches degrade over time, and moisture will eventually find a way to render even waterproof matches useless. It is difficult to say how long a particular container of matches will stay fresh. You should frequently check your matches to make sure that they still light. Replace them as needed. Do not wait until your life depends on them to discover that they have become useless.

Metal Sparking Tools

Manufacturers make a variety of metal sparking devices that have many different names. These tools, available at outdoor and camping stores, range in price from $5 to $25. Most have no moving parts, are easily carried and stored, and are not affected by moisture. This type of tool is reliable and worth using as a primary ignition source.

Most spark-making tools are made from ferrocerium, a manmade alloy composed of rare earth elements. A knife blade or sharp piece of steel scraped along the alloy rod creates sparks. The procedure is similar to that used with flint and steel, except that in this case the sparks come from the alloy rod, not the steel. These tools produce a shower of extremely hot sparks, which provide the needed ignition source for fire. One variation of this product includes a magnesium block with a ferrocerium rod attached. You use a knife to scrape a small pile of shavings from the relatively soft and burnable magnesium. You then ignite the shavings with sparks created by the ferrocerium rod.

Fire-Starting Aids

The following fire-starting aids cannot produce heat or sparks on their own, but they can hold a spark or flame after one has been produced, thus aiding in the fire-making process:

- **Petroleum-based products.** Products designed with petroleum as the key component can be useful. These include paste, soft cubes, small bricks, and solid sticks. When ignited, these items burn for up to a couple of minutes, providing time to ignite tinder and kindling for a fire. They are available from outdoor and camping stores and range in price from $5 to $10. You can make your own fire-starting aids by completely saturating cotton balls with petroleum jelly and storing them in a small sealed container. When you are ready to make a fire, remove a ball from the container and light it with a spark or flame. The petroleum ball lights easily and burns for a minute or two.

- **Candles.** Candles are a reliable, low-tech aid for starting fires, especially with damp material. Used candle stubs work well, as do small inexpensive tub candles available at outdoor stores or craft supply stores. You can light the candle and hold it under the tinder for an extended time to give the material enough time to dry and ignite, or you can drip wax onto the wood itself and burn it, giving an extra boost to materials that are difficult to ignite.

- **Steel wool.** Steel wool is an extremely helpful aid in fire making, and it can be purchased in small quantities from hardware and building supply stores for less than $5. Steel wool is made in various thicknesses from coarse to very fine. The thickness of the material is identified by the number of 0s printed on the package. For example, 000 is coarser than 00000. Steel wool in a thickness range of 000 to 00000 is best for fire starting, although the finest material is preferred. Steel wool can be ignited with a spark or electrical current. It is a good medium to hold a spark or ember, and it will not absorb moisture. If it does become wet, a quick shake renders it ready for service again.

Lighters

Several types of lighters are on the market. These range from inexpensive disposable lighters to expensive windproof firelighters. Most lighters have adjustable flames, and many are refillable. A few of the high-end gadgets will light and stay burning in high wind. Even an empty, inexpensive lighter that uses a flint-type igniter can be used to strike a spark and make fire because the flint in modern lighters is actually ferrocerium.

Although convenient, lighters suffer from reliability issues. All lighters rely on several tiny moving parts and mechanisms, which are subject to failure. Temperature, moisture, and altitude may affect them. They contain liquid fuel that may leak and leave you out in the cold and dark. The fuel that they contain may become unstable in high temperatures. In several documented cases, lighters have malfunctioned and caused injury to the user. Lighters range in price from $2 to about $100 and can be found in grocery and convenience stores, as well as outdoor and camping stores.

Emergency Flares

Handheld or road flares provide an excellent means of creating fire. When activated, they emit a high intensity heat source for several minutes. They burn hot and long enough to be extremely useful in starting a fire with damp fuels. The disadvantages of flares are their size and weight. Aerial flares can be used as fire starters, but their use is discouraged because the signal meteor, which is propelled from the flare tube, has a burn time of only a few seconds, can be hard to control, and may cause injury. Emergency road flares are usually stocked at auto parts stores.

Electrical Current

You can create an intense heat source for a fire by using the electrical current from batteries to heat and ignite the tiny filaments of steel wool. Two 1.5-volt flashlight batteries can be used as a source of electrical current. The minimum voltage required for success with standard size batteries seems to be 3 volts. Two AAA batteries will produce just enough current, but larger batteries are better. Batteries from cell phones, PDAs, laptop computers, GPS units, music players, two-way radios, test equipment, or any electronic gear can be used to create fire using this method.

To begin, take a small bunch of very fine steel wool (00000 works best) and thin it by pulling it apart and removing some of the filaments. Form the thinned filaments into a loose narrow strand long enough to reach the length of the two batteries. Then hold the batteries in line in the palm of one hand near the fingers so that the positive terminal of one battery is touching the negative terminal of the other. Fold your fingers around the batteries, holding them tightly in position. Place one end of the steel wool strand on the terminal near your thumb. With your thumb holding the strand in place, use your other hand to touch the other end of the strand to the opposite terminal on the other end of the batteries. The current flowing through the fine steel filaments will cause it to ignite. As soon as it ignites, quickly place it into the tinder bundle and begin blowing it into flame. With larger batteries such as 9- or 12-volt batteries, the ignition is immediate and dramatic. Take care not to burn yourself.

Electrical Sparks

You can use a vehicle battery to create sparks by shorting a metallic object across the opposite poles at the same time. The most effective and safe method is to use jumper cables. By extending the cables away from the vehicle you reduce the risk of explosion and injury. Hook the leads of one end of the jumper cables to the positive and negative contacts of the battery, as if you were going to give another vehicle a jump start. Take care not to touch the leads of the loose end of the jumper cables together until you are ready to create sparks. By striking the leads of the loose end of the cables together, you will create sparks that can ignite tinder or other flammable materials.

Using electrical sparks to ignite a gasoline-soaked rag seems like an easy proposition, but the process is much more difficult than you might imagine. The vapors from gasoline are what make it easy to ignite. When you apply gasoline to an absorbent piece of fabric and place it out in the open, the vapors from the fuel are carried away into the open air. A fuel-soaked rag will ignite easily when exposed to an open flame, but it is much more difficult to ignite with only sparks. Attempting to enclose or capture the vapors from the fuel and ignite them could cause an explosion. Avoid performing this type of science experiment during a survival situation. A far better choice is to use the sparks to ignite the types of fuels discussed earlier in the chapter.

Optics

The sun generates a tremendous amount of heat and energy that you can focus with a magnifying glass, camera lens, or parabolic mirror into a pinpoint of heat to create fire. The main drawback to using the sun as a heat source is that the sun's rays are often not accessible, and you need bright midday sun for fire-starting purposes.

Magnifying glasses work best for this method. Other types of lenses can be tried individually and in combination with one another. To create a fire with a magnifying glass, hold the lens so that it directly faces the sun. Position your tinder bundle on the ground in line with the lens and the sun. Begin moving the lens toward the tinder, keeping the lens facing directly into the sun. You will begin to see a bright circle of light being focused from the sun into the tinder. Continue moving the lens toward the tinder until the circle of light is about as large as a pinhead. Hold the pinpoint of light steady on the same spot. Eventually smoke will begin to rise from the tinder. If the material does not begin to flame you may need to blow it into flame.

The reflector of some flashlights can be removed and used as a parabolic mirror to focus the sun's energy and create fire. To use this method, place the tinder in the bottom or small end of the reflector and point the reflector at the sun. The mirror will collect the sun's rays and focus them on the tinder, eventually creating an ember.

You can also use a headlight from a vehicle or landing light from an aircraft as a parabolic mirror. Remove the light and carefully break or remove the lens from the light. Take care not to break the reflective dish. Place tinder on the beam filament and point the headlight toward the sun until it focuses onto the filament. The tinder will begin to smoke almost immediately. Then move the smoldering piece of tinder into the tinder bundle and blow it into flame.

Water

HUMANS are resilient and adaptable creatures who live and thrive in all climates and in nearly every corner of the world. Documented accounts exist of people surviving weeks without food while enduring epic conditions. Although humans may be able to live without food for many days or even weeks, the same does not hold true for water. For humans, water is life. Next to oxygen, water is the most precious commodity needed for sustaining life. With no water to drink, unprepared people exerting themselves in a hot environment can die from dehydration in a matter of hours.

The human body is an amazingly complex system that is made up of approximately 75 percent water. This water must be continually replenished to keep the major organs functioning at an optimum level. Water is lost from the body in three major ways: perspiration, urination, and respiration. You cannot control respiration and urination, but you can control perspiration by properly using a layering system in cold weather and by regulating activity level and staying in the shade during hot conditions.

In comfortable, nonstressful conditions, the body requires a minimum of two liters of water per day. Those living in a survival situation are rarely comfortable and usually burn more calories and water because of an added workload. In hot environments the body can lose as much as two liters of perspiration an hour. The idea that dehydration is less likely to occur in a cold environment is a common misconception. In fact, living in cold conditions requires a substantial intake of fluid. Dehydration under these conditions can contribute greatly to hypothermia and cold injuries. When temperatures are cold the thirst mechanism can become suppressed, so you must consume water out of habit.

Dehydration Basics

Because the human body consists mostly of water, it makes sense that maintaining a constant level of tissue saturation is a high priority. In simple terms, water is required to transport life-giving oxygen and nutrients to the vital organs and brain, while at the same time removing life-threatening toxins from those same organs. Water is also critical for proper thermoregulation of the body. Human organs function at maximum efficiency in a narrow temperature range. Tiny fluctuations in core temperature immediately begin to have negative effects. Water is the critical element needed for normal operation of this temperature regulation mechanism.

Although the body can temporarily compensate for changes in internal and external conditions, lack of water and dehydration quickly take their toll on all major systems of the human body. How quickly and to what extent dehydration occurs depends on several factors, including temperature, general fitness, activity level, and fluid intake. The effects of varying levels of dehydration are shown in table 4.1.

Sweat is mostly water but also contains sodium, chloride, and small amounts of potassium and other elements. During periods of heavy activity, significant amounts of these electrolytes are lost and must be replaced. The correct balance of electrolytes is necessary to regulate hydration and is important for nerve and muscle function. Generally, the intake of meals and snacks replaces electrolytes. During an emergency when limited water and food are available, it is vital to limit the loss of water and electrolytes by reducing perspiration.

Avoiding dehydration requires a basic understanding of why and how the body needs and uses fluids. But you also need to stay vigilant and disciplined, taking every opportunity to replenish your body

Table 4.1 Effects of Dehydration

1–5% water loss	6–10% water loss	11–12% water loss	More than 12% water loss
Thirst	Dizziness	Delirium	Death
Loss of appetite	Headache	Severe lack of coordination	
Flushed skin	Labored breathing	Swollen tongue	
Increased core temperature in normal and hot environments	Numbness in extremities	Inability to swallow	
Decreased core temperature in cold environments	Decreased blood volume	Deafness	
Increased pulse and respiration	Absence of salivation	Dim vision	
Nausea	Cyanotic (blue) appearance of skin	Shriveled appearance of skin	
Concentrated urine	Slurred speech	General numbness	
Little or no urine output	Lack of coordination		

with the right kinds of fluids. The following actions can help you stay hydrated:

- Be prepared. Always carry more water than your anticipated need.
- Drink before you become thirsty. Be aware that dehydration begins before the thirst mechanism kicks in.
- When you have an opportunity to drink, consume more than you need to satisfy your thirst.
- Force yourself to drink fluids at regular intervals during cold weather.
- Drink plenty of fluids at regular intervals, especially if you are at high altitude. Higher altitudes accelerate dehydration and

dampen the thirst mechanism, so you must drink regularly even if you do not feel thirsty.

- Do not drink alcohol, which not only depresses the nervous system but also requires fluids to break it down, hastening dehydration.

- Avoid caffeinated drinks and fluids with high sugar content. These substances require considerable body fluids to process.

- Do not drink urine, blood, or seawater. The concentrations of salts and other elements contained in them will only worsen the effects of dehydration. These liquids can, however, be added to a solar still (see the section "Solar Still" in this chapter).

- Breathe through your nose to reduce evaporation from respiration.

- Do not eat if limited water is available. The digestion process requires considerable fluid. Eating without drinking sufficient fluids only accelerates dehydration. Water-rich foods are an exception.

- Wear a hat in sunny and hot conditions. A wide-brim hat that provides protection to the neck and ears is best. If a hat is unavailable, fashion one out of other clothing, plant materials, or salvaged items.

- Wear sunglasses, if you have them, to protect your eyes from the sun. If you do not have any sunglasses, you can create them from fabric, cardboard, wood, bark, or anything that you can find. Make small horizontal slits in the material and place the item over your eyes. In this case function takes precedence over fashion.

- Wear light-colored, loose-fitting clothing. Long pants and long sleeves are best because they prevent direct sun exposure of the skin.

Dehydration Check

Urine output and color is a more accurate gauge of dehydration than thirst. When you are fully hydrated, your urine will be nearly colorless. More concentrated and darker colored urine indicates more advanced dehydration. If you are not producing urine at all, you are significantly dehydrated. Trying to hold urine in the bladder does nothing to prevent dehydration and contributes to other medical problems.

Priorities in a Waterless Environment

When water resources are limited, you should clearly define your priorities. You must use a combination of strategies that includes conserving, locating, and manufacturing water.

Conserve Water

In an environment with a limited supply of water, you should immediately begin conserving the moisture within your body by reducing your perspiration output. You should ration sweat, not water. Reducing your workload and activity level is the best way to do this. In hot weather find or make shade during the hottest part of the day. Slow down! Perform activities such as travel and searching for water and food only in the cooler evening and morning hours. If you are in cold conditions, adjust your layering to reduce perspiration and thus decrease the rate of dehydration. Limiting perspiration is also important in preventing hypothermia. In cold environments, perspiration and the resulting effects of evaporation can lead to hypothermia.

If you find yourself with a limited water supply, you should know that rationing water does little to slow dehydration. In fact, people have been found dead from dehydration with a partially filled canteen. Therefore, you should store water in your stomach, not in your canteen. Small amounts of water may give temporary refreshment, but they do not return the body to the saturation point. You will become less dehydrated if you drink the water that you have and reduce your sweat output by resting in the shade and reserving physical activity for a cooler time of day.

Find Water

Look for sources of water nearby. Three major indicators can aid you in locating water: plant life, animal life, and geological features of the landscape. By studying your surroundings you will gain important clues about the likely locations of water. Before attempting a search for water, ask yourself how much water (sweat) you will lose from the work performed trying to obtain more water. In the end, will you be water ahead or will you have added to your water deficit? You must be honest with yourself and methodical when evaluating whether or not to pursue a particular course of action where water is concerned.

If you cannot calculate a net gain in fluid, then you should set aside the idea and search for other solutions. Your life depends on it.

Plant Indicators

Botanical indicators of water include cattail, bulrush, cottonwood, willow, tamarack, Russian olive, grasses, and reeds. Locations that support these plants contain water either on or close to the surface. The lush green of these plants will stand out from the surrounding landscape. In open areas, climbing to an elevated observation point where you can visually survey the area will save time and energy in the search for water.

When you locate an area containing plants that indicate the presence of water, do not be discouraged if surface water is not present. In these cases, you may need to dig to get to the water. Digging for water in likely areas can produce enough water to sustain life. Note that in arid environments where water is scarce, small springs and seeps often disappear underground during the heat of the day but reappear during the night and early morning hours.

To obtain water from under the surface, dig a small seep hole in damp soil to collect the water. If possible, dig the hole in a shady area to reduce water loss through evaporation. The shade will also provide a cooler place for you to work and wait. Dig until you reach moist material and then make the hole large enough so that you can use a container (or other improvised implement) to dip the water out. Be patient and wait for water to collect in the bottom of the hole. Depending on conditions, you may have to wait for several hours. When water collects in the hole, remove it with a container or implement. If nothing else is available, use a piece of cloth as a sponge. Then squeeze the water into a container or directly into your mouth. If the first hole is successful, dig a few more in the same area.

Animal Indicators

Observing the movement of animals may help lead you to water. Game trails usually converge toward a water source. Birds commonly gather at a water source in the morning and evening hours. Ants and bees never venture far from water. Pay attention to their movement and direction of travel.

Watch and listen for game. If animals are moving in a determined manner and are not fleeing predators, they may be heading for water. Using all your senses to collect information about your surroundings will be a powerful aid in locating water.

Geological Indicators

Geological features can help you find water. Look for signs of water near the base of cliffs or the foot of outcroppings. Low spots in valleys may also contain water. Sharp bends in dry streambeds are a good place to search for pools and seeps. Tanks and potholes (depressions in rock or solid ground) tend to fill with water during rains or periods of runoff from melting snow. The size of potholes can vary from as small as a teaspoon (15 ml) to several feet (a meter or more) across and several feet deep. The larger tanks can hold water for several weeks after spring runoff or a storm.

Collect and Manufacture Water

We are surrounded by water, even in the arid landscape of the desert. Soil, plants, and air contain small amounts of water. Although you cannot simply create water, you can collect it and patiently coax it out of the materials around you.

Dew

Dew is a good source of water that is often overlooked, but with some effort you can collect sustainable quantities of water. Early in the mornings when dew is heavy on plants and grasses, you can drag a cloth or piece of clothing over the ground to collect it. After you have saturated the cloth, wring it out into a container.

Water From Vegetation

Only a few plants contain enough moisture to be used to alleviate dehydration. Although all plants contain some degree of moisture, most do not contain enough to justify the effort required to extract the usable water from them. In arid regions, the prickly pear cactus (see page 82) and barrel cactus can supply some water. Contrary to what the old Western movies would have you believe, cacti do not contain an everlasting supply of clear, cool water, but they do contain some moisture that you can use. To obtain water from the prickly pear cactus, remove the outer spines and hard outer skin. You can then squeeze or chew the inner pulp to extract a milky fluid. To obtain the moisture, you can also eat the inner meat, which has some food value. With some effort, you can cut away the top of a barrel cactus to expose the inner pulp. You then mash the pulp with a stick, from which you can squeeze a milky substance. The pulp is not suitable as food, but you can use the bitter-tasting liquid.

The stalks of the common thistle plant (see page 101), which is found throughout most of North America, can be chewed to obtain moisture. The young stalks are sometimes compared with celery. They contain more moisture during spring when the plants are young.

You can obtain water from some trees in the form of a clear sap. Maple, white pine, birch, walnut, hickory, and aspen can be used during spring for this purpose. Tap the tree by drilling a hole into the trunk with a knife or other sharp object. Ideally, the hole should be about 3 inches (7.5 cm) deep. Insert a hollow stem or reed into the hole and collect the liquid in a container. This process requires several hours but does produce usable liquid.

Snow and Ice

Eating snow or ice is not recommended. The energy and fluid required for the body to melt the snow and use the water outweighs the benefits. In addition, eating snow in a weakened condition in cold weather can contribute significantly to hypothermia and in severe cases could mean not surviving. You can make drinkable water from snow and ice by melting it various ways.

The quickest method for melting snow or ice is to place it in a container and heat it over a fire or stove. Ice will yield more water than snow using the same amount of fuel. If a heat source is not readily available, you can use solar heat. Containers or plastic bags work well for warming ice and snow in the sun. You can speed the process by breaking ice into small pieces before placing it in the container and by hanging the container from a branch of a tree in the sunlight. Another method is to place the container near the body between layers of clothing to cause melting.

Ice-Cold Water

When gathering water from lakes and streams during winter, take care not to get too close to the bank. Snow on the edge can give way. Avoid areas where snow has created a deep embankment next to the water. Look for game trails leading to the water. The packed-down snow in those areas will provide easier access. If you cannot safely access the water, fasten a container onto a long stick to retrieve water. If you do fall in, immediately roll in the snow. Snow will act as a sponge to absorb a large amount of moisture from clothing.

If a container or bag is not available, you can melt snow and ice using a snow basin. Begin by making a depression in the snow and filling it partially with small sticks and brush. Line the basin with plastic, bark, or other waterproof material and spread a thin layer of snow in the depression. As the snow begins to melt, add more. Drink the water or collect it in a container. You should always be making and storing water.

When collecting snow for melting, avoid any pinkish snow. This color is characteristic of toxic algae that cannot be removed by conventional filtering or purification methods. Find another source for clean snow.

Solar Still

A solar still (shown in figure 4.1) uses the rays of the sun to distill water from the ground, plants, and anything that contains moisture. The real advantage of a solar still is that impure substances, which are useless in an ordinary situation, can be used to produce usable water. These items include blood, urine, salt water, and plant material. Keep in mind that building a solar still is labor intensive and that you will lose water through sweat while constructing it. You must calculate the net benefit of constructing a solar still. If your estimates do not show a positive result in terms of fluid gain, look for another solution. If you decide to construct a solar still, perform this and similar activities in the early morning or evening hours when it is cooler.

1. A solar still (see figure 4.1) is made by creating a small pit in the ground. The pit should be 3 to 5 feet (90 to 150 cm) in diameter and about 2 feet (60 cm) deep.

FIGURE 4.1 A cross section of a solar still.

2. When the pit is complete, line it with plants and other materials that contain moisture. Make sure that the plant materials are not poisonous (see pages 105 to 108).

3. Place a small container in the center of the pit. This will act as a catchment for the moisture. If tubing is available, run it from the bottom of the container up and out of the pit.

4. Position clear plastic over the pit and pull it down to a sharp point in the middle so that the tip of the point is directly over the container. Use a rock in the center of the point to maintain the shape in the plastic. Secure and seal the edges of the plastic with rocks and soil. An airtight seal will improve the efficiency of the still. (Note that dark plastic or a reflective material such as an emergency blanket will cause the still to work much slower. The rays of the sun must penetrate the cover for it to work as intended.)

5. Wait for the sun to create the solar effect, which causes the water to distill out of the plants and soil. This distilling effect takes several hours, depending on the intensity of the sun, and the amount of water created from one still is relatively small. When the still begins to work, you will see water droplets forming and running down toward the center of the plastic and dropping off the tip into the container.

6. When enough water has collected in the container, you can drink it by sucking on the end of the tubing. If tubing is not available, lift an edge of the plastic, remove the container, and drink directly from it. Replace the container and plastic quickly so that you do not interrupt the distillation process. Realistically, you would need to construct several stills to provide the minimal water requirements for just one person.

Modified Solar Still

A simple above-ground variation of the solar still is to place a clear plastic bag over the end of a leafy tree branch, plant, or leafy bush that is located in direct sunlight. Tie the end of the bag closed with a cord or other material, and the same distillation process will take place. Water will begin to collect on the inside of the plastic and collect at the lowest spot. When enough has collected, open the bag and remove the water. Another variation is to place moisture-bearing materials in a clear plastic bag and seal it. Place the bag in the sun until the moisture has been extracted from the materials.

Water Contamination

The days are gone when a person could be assured of drinking pure, untainted water in wild places. Waterborne pathogens carried by humans and animals have been detected in some of the most remote regions of North America and the world. They travel and thrive in the warm intestines of their hosts and enter the environment by way of feces. Many of these organisms survive long enough to make their way into streams, lakes, and rivers where they can be ingested and take up residence again in a warm and fertile digestive tract. If enough of these tiny creatures find their way inside you, they can multiply rapidly and throw an abrupt and uncomfortable monkey wrench into an otherwise smoothly operating digestive system.

Water purity should be a concern to those who spend time away from civilization. Drinking any untreated water carries with it the risk of ingesting waterborne pathogens. In North America, protozoan cyst, bacteria, and viruses are the three major types of bugs that cause illness. Manmade toxins and chemicals are another potential threat.

Protozoan Cyst

Two protozoan cysts are blamed for most of the problems associated with people drinking untreated water in the wilds. These are Giardia lamblia (commonly called Giardia), which range in size from 5 to 15 microns, and Cryptosporidium (commonly referred to as Crypto), which range in size from 2 to 5 microns. These parasites consist of a single cell protected by a hard shell, which make them resistant to the outside environment. When a human or other mammal ingests the cysts in sufficient concentration, the parasites attach themselves to the wall of the small intestine and begin to reproduce at a rapid rate. Some people may become ill, whereas others may carry the parasites but never suffer the symptoms of the illness. Either way, the tiny animals are excreted in feces and the cycle continues.

The symptoms of infection from Giardia and Crypto are similar. Both can cause severe gastrointestinal problems including diarrhea, stomach and intestinal cramps, severe gas, and nausea. The average time from ingesting the cysts before symptoms are felt is about seven days, although this interval can vary widely. The onset can be quite sudden and debilitating. Large quantities of fluids and electrolytes can be lost in a short time, contributing to dehydration. If untreated, symptoms can continue for several weeks, often diminishing for a time and then reappearing as the concentration of protozoa increase. If you suspect that you have become ill because of contaminated water, drink plenty of purified water to replace the fluids that you have lost. Try to eat as well to replace the electrolytes that you have lost. When you return to civilization, seek medical treatment, even if your symptoms have diminished.

Although Giardia cannot survive freezing, it can live for several weeks in cold water. Crypto, on the other hand, can live for long periods in a frozen condition. With both types of cysts, the warmer the temperature is, the shorter the life span is. Protozoan cysts can be removed or killed with boiling, filtering, or chemical treatment.

Bacteria

Most of these organisms are smaller than protozoan cysts and range in size from .2 to 10 microns. North American varieties include E. coli, salmonella, and Campylobacter jejuni. The one most commonly found in wilderness environments is Campylobacter. The most common symptom of infection from this bacterium is diarrhea, which usually begins within two to five days but can occur within a few hours. Symptoms of campylobacteriosis usually disappear within five days. Boiling, filtering, or chemical treatment can remove or kill bacteria.

Viruses

The tiniest of the pathogenic offenders, viruses range in size from .004 to .01 micron. Although viruses are the least common threat to wilderness water in North America, they should be taken into consideration, especially when choosing a purification method. Hepatitis A, Norwalk virus, polio, and rotavirus are some of the common viruses that pose a potential threat. As with the other pathogens, the most significant and dangerous symptom of these viruses is diarrhea, which

Do Not Deny Yourself Water

Water is vital for survival. Without it, dehydration occurs, and eventually death. During emergency survival conditions you may not have the resources available to filter or purify water. In this situation if you have a choice of water sources, select the one that appears to be most pure and drink it. Do not hesitate to drink. You must drink to live.

can quickly cause or hasten dehydration. Viruses can be killed with boiling or chemical treatment. Filtering is ineffective against viruses.

Toxins and Chemical Pollutants

This category includes chemicals that have migrated into the water supply from mining, industrial, and agricultural activities. Such toxins include pesticides, detergents, selenium from irrigation wastewater, petroleum products carried by storm water, and many others far too numerous to mention here.

Ingestion of these toxins can cause a variety of problems. They can affect every major system and organ of the body and cause long-term deficits. Unfortunately, these materials are some of the most difficult to eliminate from drinking water and require special industrial treatment. Boiling and filtering can only partially neutralize toxins. These types of toxins are not common in remote wilderness environments, but if you suspect toxins in a particular water source, try to find another source. If you are unable to find another source and you must drink, collect moving water that appears the cleanest. Allow the water to stand in a container until the solids settle to the bottom. Use the water from the top of the container and filter it if you have the capability. Then boil the water. If you follow these steps, you will have done all that you can to purify the water.

Water Treatment

Take all reasonable precautions to treat water before drinking it. All water is suspect. Even clear water splashing from a high mountain snowpack may contain troublesome organisms. Take preventative measures against these small but powerful creatures.

Filtration

Water filters come in a variety of sizes and configurations. The effectiveness of a particular filter against a specific pathogen depends on the absolute pore size of the unit. This information should be included with the filter. To be effective against Giardia and Cryptosporidium, an absolute pore size of 1 micron or less is required, whereas an absolute pore size of .2 micron or less is required to capture bacteria. Filters are not effective against viruses because they are extremely small and will pass through a filter.

Choosing a Purification Device

Most purification devices eliminate the threat posed by protozoan cysts, bacteria, and viruses by combining microporous filtering with chemical exposure. Some technologies for purification pass water through a special filter that has an electrostatic charge to capture organisms. Choose a device based on size, weight, ease of use, and effectiveness against a wide range of pathogens.

If you need a filter only for yourself, choose one that is small and lightweight and will produce purified water at a sufficient rate for your individual needs. If the filter is for group use, it needs to be larger and able to produce purified water at a faster rate. You may want to consider buying a unit that comes with a prefilter that helps to capture large particles and reduces the need for frequent cleaning and replacement of the main filter. Be sure to consider the estimated lifespan of filters and the cost of replacements, which can help you determine the actual cost of various units. Filters can be purchased from outdoor and camping stores at prices from $25 to about $900.

Chemical Treatment

Exposing water to chemical halogens, such as iodine or chlorine bleach, is an effective treatment for disinfection of bacteria, viruses, and Giardia cysts. Cryptosporidium is resistant to these chemicals and must be neutralized by boiling or filtration. Water purification tablets can also be an effective method. Available at outdoor and camping stores, several types are on the market. Potable Aqua, the most common brand, costs about $6 for a bottle of 50 tablets. Most water purification tablets are iodine based. Be sure to read the manufacturer's information before deciding to use them. The product label should list the types of pathogens that the tablets are effective against. Follow the manufacturer's recommendations for use of these products.

Be aware that iodine can present health risks to people with iodine allergies, those with thyroid conditions, and pregnant women. Iodine should be used only for a few weeks. For extended purification needs, consider other methods. The effectiveness of chemical treatment depends on the temperature and clarity of the water, the concentration of the halogen, and the contact time as shown in table 4.2.

Table 4.2 Chemical Disinfection of Water

| Water characteristics | INSTRUCTIONS BASED ON CHEMICAL TYPE | | | |
| | Iodine (2%) | | Chlorine bleach* | |
	Drops per liter	Exposure time before drinking	Drops per liter	Exposure time before drinking
Clear water 77 °F (25 °C) and above	5	30	2	30
Clear water below 77 °F (25 °C)	5	60	2	60
Cloudy water	10	30	4	30

*Use only ordinary household liquid bleach with no additives.

Adapted from U.S. Environmental Protection Agency, 2006, Emergency disinfection of drinking water. [Online]. Available: http://www.epa.gov/safewater/faq/emerg.html [April 29, 2009].

Boiling

Heating water to a high enough temperature for a long enough time is a sure and simple method to kill all three of the dangerous waterborne pathogens. All you need to do is bring water to a rolling boil to kill all offending organisms. The U.S. Environmental Protection Agency recommends boiling water for one minute. Because water boils at a lower temperature at high altitudes, you should extend the boiling time to three minutes if you are located at an elevation above 5,000 feet (1,500 m). After the water has cooled, you can aerate it by pouring it back and forth between two containers a few times, which will improve the taste. Boiling provides only partial purification of water contaminated with chemical toxins, so that type of water may not be safe for drinking even after it has been boiled. In those circumstances you should search for an alternative water source.

Food From Plants

FOR short-term survival, food is not the highest priority. The human body can go for a few days without food with little or no adverse effects, and many survival situations are resolved within the first three days. In these cases, food is an option but not a necessity. Extremely cold or hot conditions, preexisting medical problems such as diabetes, or a survival situation that extends into several days increases the need for sustenance.

Wild Edible Plants

Edible plants are an important source of food during a survival situation. Even during winter or in arid climates, plant resources are available that can significantly improve your condition. Being able to identify plants suitable for food is the key to unlocking the benefits of this resource.

Many so-called taste test procedures have been published to describe how to differentiate between edible and poisonous plants. But this method of identification is extremely dangerous and may result in serious illness or death. You should taste or eat a plant only if you can positively identify it. A few people die each year because they begin grazing on unfamiliar wild fare. If you cannot identify it, do not eat it! Now that you have heard this warning, understand that many wild edible plants are easy to recognize. If you are confident that your identification is correct, do not hesitate to use them.

Gathering Wild Plants

To proficiently recognize and use wild edible plants, you must first observe the plant life in a particular habitat. Whether you live in a city, a rural area, or near the wilderness, wild plant life thrives nearby. Begin by learning to identify the most common plants in your area. Learn what parts are usable and how to prepare them. This process requires a bit of experimentation, but it is an important part of learning. Unless you are in an actual survival situation, take steps to minimize your effect on the environment. Collect only what you require to fulfill your immediate needs and avoid plants that occur infrequently. Collect edible or useful parts from several plants instead of destroying a single plant. The potentially edible parts of a plant include the tender shoots, stems, and leaves; berries; nuts; seeds; and roots. By following a few tips you can easily and safely harvest them.

- **Avoid treated or polluted habitat.** All living organisms absorb elements from their immediate environment. Plants that have been chemically treated or that grow near polluted water sources or wastewater areas will contain those chemical toxins to some degree. If you suspect that pollutants or toxins are present in the soil or water, avoid those areas altogether.

- **Gather new growth.** New tender growth on a plant is the most desirable to gather. During spring and early summer look for new shoots, leaves, and stem growth. In climates that are more arid this type of growth may appear soon after a rainstorm anytime during summer.

- **Pick berries and nuts.** Look for edible berries and nuts from midsummer to fall. The fruit and nuts can remain on many plants throughout the winter as well.

- **Dig roots.** Roots are easier to harvest with a digging stick. Begin with a piece of any type of green wood 1 to 1 1/2 inches (2.5 to 3.75 cm) in diameter and about 3 feet (90 cm) long. Strip the bark and flatten one end by removing material with a knife or by rubbing it on a rough stone. The tip should be rounded and somewhat sharp like a digging shovel. To increase the durability and strength of the digging stick, fire harden the tip by baking it without burning it. This procedure drives out the moisture and cures the sap in the wood. One method for fire hardening is to hold the tip end of the stick above the hot coals of a fire but not so near the flames that the wood fibers char and weaken the stick. Another method is to place the stick in the dirt just beneath the fire. In either case, you should turn the stick slowly so that all parts of the tip receive enough heat. Go slowly and use four or five applications of heat, allowing the tip to cool slightly between applications. The tip of a fire-hardened stick should be light brown in color, not black. (Fire hardening can be useful in creating a hard and enduring tip for any tool or implement.) To use the digging stick, thrust it into the ground alongside the plant and gently lever the plant out of the soil. Sometimes, lightly pulling on the plant at the same time can speed the process.

- **Gather seeds.** You can gather small amounts of seeds by hand and place them in a container or cloth. For gathering large quantities of small seeds, remove the stems containing the seedpods and pound them on a hard, flat surface. Then blow or winnow the chaff away from the seeds. After you have separated the seeds, grind them between two rocks to make meal or flour (see page 68).

Preparing Wild Plants

If you do not have a fire or are on the move, eating plants raw is a quick and simple way to use wild food. But in some cases, cooking will enhance the flavor of a plant or render it available for another use. For example, roasting a particular root allows it to be ground into flour or meal. Boiling can tenderize tough plants parts or create nutritious teas and soups. The method used depends on your preferences, skills, and available resources.

- **Roasting.** Next to eating plants raw, roasting is the simplest and most nutritious method of preparing wild foods. A fire is all that is needed. Roots, seeds, and nuts roasted over or next to a fire can render foods more flavorful and prepare them to be ground into flour or meal.

- **Boiling.** All plant parts can be boiled. Boiling is often the best method for older leaves, stems, and roots. Some foods, like acorns from many varieties of oaks, have a strong or disagreeable taste. In these cases, boiling with a change or two of water can moderate the flavor and render these foods more palatable. Keep boiling times to a minimum because the process lessens the food value. You can make tea from the leaves of plants by bringing water to a boil, removing it from the fire, and then allowing the leaves to soak or steep in the hot water. Tea made from the leaves of some wild plants provides nutritional as well as medicinal value.

- **Drying and smoking.** Drying is an excellent way to preserve many kinds of wild foods. Small nuts, seeds, and roots can be dried whole and set aside for later use. You should crush larger items before drying. Begin by placing the food on a flat surface with good exposure to the sun or hang it from tree branches or a makeshift rack. You can also arrange food items so that the smoke from a fire filters through them. Smoke will hasten the preservation process.

- **Making flour or meal.** Many plant parts such as seed, nuts, and roots can produce a type of flour or meal. Dry the plants thoroughly first. You should boil and shred roots before drying. Many ancient civilizations used two stones (known as a metate and mano) to make flour, and you can use this method in a survival situation. The metate is a large flat stone with a natural shallow depression in the center. Place the grain or seeds in the depression. The mano is a smaller stone that you hold in both hands to pulverize and grind the seeds against the metate. Creating meal or flour offers variety and preserves the plant so that it can be more easily stored. You can mix flour and meal with other foods or make it into a type of thin cake and bake it. Plant flour can also be made into soups and gruel.

Guide to Edible Plant Varieties

This section describes some of the most common wild edible plants in North America, although many of them are found in other areas of the world. The listing is not comprehensive, but it includes plants that grow in many regions. Photos of each of the plants described in this section are included on pages 83 through 98. Note that these photos show the best representative sample of a particular plant specimen. Unlike the scientific classification of plants, common plant names are not universal. A particular plant species may be known by several different common names. The following guide lists the common name first, then the scientific names for the genus and, if appropriate, the species. In cases where many closely related species exist, only the genus is given. For example, the currant (page 76) is classified in the (Ribes) genus. There are about 150 different species in this genus. All are closely related in appearance, with variations in the color of the berries and flowers based on the location and habitat. Therefore the genus is provided along with a broad description of the possible variations. Many factors affect individual plant appearance and size, including the soil composition in a particular location, moisture, general climate, elevation, sunlight exposure, and many others. For this reason, the color and size of plants of the same species may vary considerably.

The plants represented in the photos are fully mature specimens. In early spring when the plants are young they may appear quite different. A useful exercise is to go out early in spring to search for new growth and then return to the plants frequently to observe their development to maturity until you can identify them. When attempting to identify plants, pay particular attention to the shapes of stems and leaves, which are the most reliable characteristics, especially when the flowers of the plants are not in full bloom. As you begin your study of wild edible plants, you no doubt will find some that are already familiar to you, such as the cattail, strawberry, dandelion, asparagus, and others. Begin your learning with the plants that you already know and branch out from there, adding more to your knowledge each time you identify a new plant.

Amaranth *(Amaranthus retroflexus)*

Description   These annual plants grow 1 to 5 feet (30 to 150 cm) tall. The stem is erect and sometimes branched. The plant has a red taproot. Amaranth has alternate egg-shaped or lance-shaped leaves. (Alternate leaves grow singly from each node, and leaves alternate direction along the stem.) The plant bears small greenish flowers in dense clusters at the top. Seeds are black, shiny, and plentiful, and when ripe are found amidst the flower clusters.

Habitat   Amaranth grows along roadsides, in disturbed areas, or as weeds in crops. The plant usually grows below 9,000 feet (2,700 m) throughout North America.

Food   All parts are edible. The young leaves can be eaten raw. Older leaves can be boiled. The tiny seeds are best harvested in late summer or fall by shaking the mature or dried plant. Seeds can then be eaten raw or ground into flour or meal. Used as a cereal, the flour is very nutritious.

Other Uses   Long stems from the plant can be used as a spindle for bow drill fire making.

Arrowhead *(Sagittaria)*

Description   Arrowhead is a perennial plant characterized by arrow-shaped leaves, which are deep green and grow about 4 to 16 inches (10 to 40 cm) in length. The leaves grow from a single stem. The small white flowers are present midsummer to fall. The fruit grows in a cluster containing numerous seeds. During fall, tubers form on the ends of the long rootstocks, which are often located some distance away from the main plant.

Habitat   Arrowhead grows in marshy areas and shallow water near streams and lakes in North America.

Food   Roots and tubers can be eaten raw or cooked. Eaten raw they are quite bitter, but when roasted, they have a flavor and consistency similar to that of a potato. They can also be baked or dried, pounded into powder, and used as flour.

Asparagus *(Asparagus officinalis)*

Description   During spring the young shoots of asparagus look like a small bunch of green fingers protruding from the ground, much like cultivated asparagus. The mature plant grows tall and branching, producing small greenish flowers and red berries.

Habitat   Asparagus grows in moist soil near roads and in open fields throughout North America.

Food   The young shoots can be eaten cooked or raw.

Biscuit Root *(Cymopterus)*

Description   Biscuit root is a member of the carrot family, which includes several species. All the edible species are similar in appearance and difficult to distinguish from one another. All grow in dry soils and have elongated taproots with fernlike leaves near the base. The plant produces small flowers in compound clusters, which may be white, yellow, or reddish. Exercise care when identifying this plant. Several related species are poisonous, including poison hemlock (see page 108), which can be deadly. The poisonous members of the family grow in moist or damp soil, are much larger, and have leaves growing from the upper part of the stem.

Habitat   Biscuit root grows in dry soil on hillsides or open plains in the western United States.

Food   The leaves of the young plant can be used as a salad. They can be eaten raw or cooked. Roasted roots can be ground into flour or meal.

Blackberries *(Rubus)*

Description   Blackberries have prickly or thorny stems that grow upward and then bend toward the ground. The plants are 1 to 6 feet (30 to 180 cm) high. The leaves are alternating and compound, meaning that more than one leaflet, usually several, are attached to the same leaf stalk. The fruit may be red, black, or salmon colored.

Habitat   Blackberry grows in open areas and thickets along lakes and streams in North America.

Food   Berries and young shoots can be eaten raw. The fruit can be dried and used with other foods or stored.

Other Uses   The dried leaves can be used to make tea.

Blueberries *(Vaccinium)*

Description   These shrubs grow from 1 to 10 feet (30 to 300 cm) tall. The alternating leaves are finely toothed. Teardrop-shaped flowers are white to rose colored and about 1/4 inch (.6 cm) long. The smooth berries may be dark blue, red, or black.

Habitat   The plant grows in damp areas, forests, woodlands, and on mountain slopes in North America.

Food   Their fruit can be eaten raw, cooked, or dried.

Bracken Fern *(Pteridium aquilinum)*

Description   This large fern grows rapidly to a height of 1 to 6 feet (30 to 180 cm). The mature plant branches out, bearing light green fronds. Bracken usually grows in patches

Habitat   Bracken fern grows in North America in open woods or open slopes in dry or moist soil.

Food   Young unfolding fiddleheads (frond) can be eaten raw or cooked. The starchy rootstock can be dried and roasted. Flour can be made by pounding the inner part of the rootstock into powder. Older plants have a stronger bitter taste.

Other Uses   Soap can be made from the rhizome, the thick elongated node from which roots and sprouts grow. Dried, pulverized rootstock makes good tinder.

Burdock *(Arctium lappa)*

Description   Burdock is a large biennial plant that has a fleshy taproot. Coarse, many-branched stems have wavy-edged, egg-shaped leaves and flower heads in burrlike clusters. Burdock grows 1 to 6 feet (30 to 180 cm) tall and produces rose-colored or pink flowers.

Habitat   Burdock grows in open waste areas (unused and uncultivated areas such as ditch banks, roadsides, and vacant fields) and disturbed soil, usually below 8,000 feet (2,400 m) in North America.

Food   Tender young shoots and leaves can be cooked or eaten raw. The roots of the first-year plants can be peeled and used as food. Because older leaves and roots may have a bitter taste, boil them and change the water several times.

Cattail *(Typha latifolia)*

Description   Cattails grow in clusters from thick underground root-stalks and can reach a height of up to 8 feet (240 cm). They have green, blade-shaped leaves that grow up to an inch (2.5 cm) wide and tall stalks that have tubular-shaped seed heads. The flowers are at the top of the plant stalks. The male flowers are located above the female and contain the pollen that eventually turns golden. The female, seed-bearing portion of the stalk ultimately transforms into the fluffy down-filled seedpod. Late in the season the seed head is brown and empty.

Habitat   Cattails are found throughout most of the world in shallow water along the edges of lakes, ponds, and streams.

Food   Young shoots can be pulled from the rootstocks and eaten raw or cooked. Shoots are numerous in spring but also grow during summer. Remove the outer leaves from the shoots to expose the tender meat. The young seed heads can be harvested before the pollen appears and prepared by removing the outer covering and boiling them. When the yellow pollen appears, it can be stripped, collected in a container, and used as a flour.

   The starchy rootstocks are an excellent food source. Look for buds that contain new shoots, which are located at the base of the plant a few inches (about 10 cm) below the soil. Peel the outer portion to reveal the white inner core, which can be eaten raw or cooked. To make the root hearts into flour, dry and pound or mash them. Then soak and shred the root hearts in a container of water until the root fibers are completely washed. Let the flour settle on the bottom of the container, pour off the water, and begin working the dough.

Other Uses   Dried cattail leaves can be used for weaving and insulation material. The downy seeds make good insulation and excellent tinder. The dried plant stalks are useful in fire making and tool construction.

Chickweed *(Stellaria media)*

Description   Chickweed is an annual plant that grows 4 to 16 inches (10 to 40 cm) tall. The finely stemmed, many-branched plant has leaves about 1 inch (2.5 cm) long. The small white flowers have two rounded sections at the top and are about 1/4 inch (.6 cm) long.

Habitat   Chickweed grows in North America in waste places, in disturbed soils, and in fields and shaded areas.

Food   The young leaves and stems can be eaten raw. Older and tougher plants can be boiled.

Chicory *(Cichorium intybus)*

Description   Chicory is a perennial plant that grows 1 to 3 feet (30 to 90 cm) tall from a deep, fleshy taproot. The plant has leaves at the base of the stem and some leaves on the stem that are 2 to 6 inches (5 to 15 cm) long and resemble a dandelion. The flowers are similar to those of the dandelion but are blue and stay open only on sunny days.

Habitat   Chicory grows in North America in waste areas, along roadsides, and in open fields. It usually grows at lower elevations.

Food   The young leaves and shoots can be eaten raw or cooked. The roots should be cooked with a change of water to reduce the strong taste. For use as a coffee substitute, roast the roots until dark brown and then pulverize them.

Clover *(Trifolium)*

Description   Clover is a low-growing plant that reaches 2 to 20 inches (5 to 50 cm) in length. The finely toothed leaflets, which are heart shaped or ovate (like a pointed oval) nearly always occur three together. The elongated flowers spike upward and group in small clusters at the top of the plant. Flowers are white, pink, or yellow and grow up to 1 inch (2.5 cm) long.

Habitat   Clover grows in North America in disturbed and dry soils and in sunny to partly shaded areas. Open fields and partially wooded areas are common habitats.

Food   The leaves can be eaten raw or cooked. The seeds can be dried and ground as flour. The flowers can be eaten raw or used to make tea.

Cottonwood *(Populus)*

Description   The cottonwood is a deciduous tree that grows up to 100 feet (30 m) tall. Mature cottonwoods have deeply rough, gray bark. Flowers grow in long hanging catkins (slim, cylindrical flower clusters). The leaves are finely toothed, shaped like hearts, and have long stems.

Habitat   Cottonwoods grows near rivers, creeks, and streams in North America.

Food   Catkins can be eaten raw or cooked. The inner bark can be stripped and eaten fresh or dried.

Cowlily _(Nuphar lutea)_

Description   Cowlily is a floating leaved plant that is anchored to the sediment soil in ponds and lakes by thick rootstocks. The leaf blades, from 8 to 16 inches (20 to 40 cm) long, are connected by long stalks to the thick roots. The bright yellow, ball-shaped flowers are made up of several broad yellow leaves with petals inside. In the center is the pod, which contains many large seeds.

Habitat   Cowlily grows in ponds, lakes, and slow-moving streams in North America.

Food   The roots can be collected and eaten raw or cooked. When dried, the root can be ground into flour. The seeds can be roasted or dried and ground into a powder.

Cow Parsnip _(Heracleum)_

Description   This tall, spreading biennial plant grows 3 to 7 feet (90 to 210 cm) tall. Leaves are large, sometimes over 1 foot (30 cm) long, and have large segments. The stems are slightly ridged and hairy. The white flowers grow in flattened compound umbels (umbrella-shaped clusters). Cow parsnip has a strong, pungent smell.

Habitat   Cow parsnip grows in North America in partial shade in moist ground, in woodlands, and along ditches and roadsides.

Food   Young shoots can be eaten raw or cooked. The root can be cooked and eaten. The peeled stem can be eaten raw or cooked. Because of the strong taste of this plant, cook the peeled stem in two changes of water.

Warning   Cow Parsnip can be confused with Water Hemlock or Poison Hemlock, which are both poisonous. To distinguish between the species, pay close attention to the stems and to the smell of a crushed portion of the plant. Cow Parsnip stems are slightly ridged and hairy and are _not_ spotted, while the stems of Water Hemlock and Poison Hemlock are smooth and have purple or brown spots. Crushed Cow Parsnip will have a strong licorice odor, whereas Water Hemlock or Poison Hemlock will have a distinct bitter mousy odor. If you are not able to absolutely identify the plant, then do not consume any portion of it.

Currant *(Ribes)*

Description   A sprawling shrub with spreading braches, the currant grows 3 to 6 feet (90 to 180 cm) tall. Twigs may or may not have spines. Leaves are up to 3 inches (7.5 cm) wide. The white, yellow, or pinkish flowers are 1/4 to 1/2 inch (.6 to 1.25 cm) long. The red, black, or orange fruit is 1/4 to 1/2 inch (.6 to 1.25 cm) in diameter, globed shaped, and either smooth or bristly.

Habitat   In North America this plant grows in damp wooded areas, canyons, and fields.

Food   Fruit can be eaten raw, cooked, or dried and mixed with other foods. The flowers can be eaten raw.

Dandelion *(Taraxacum officinale)*

Description   Dandelion plants are perennial and grow from a taproot. Leaves have a jagged edge, grow close to the ground, and are usually 2 to 12 inches (5 to 30 cm) long. When fully open the bright yellow flower heads are up to 2 inches (5 cm) across and have small seedlike fruits in the center. The hollow flower stalks are leafless and excrete a milky sap when cut.

Habitat   Dandelions are a North American plant that grows in open, sunny locations such as fields, meadows, and disturbed ground at elevations up to 10,000 feet (3,000 m).

Food   Young leaves can be eaten raw or cooked. Boil older leaves with a couple of changes of water to eliminate the bitter taste. The roots can be roasted and ground into a coffee substitute, and dried leaves can be used to make tea. The live flowers can be eaten raw. Dandelions are high in vitamin C.

Daylily *(Hemerocallis)*

Description   Daylilies are perennial plants that grow in patches with thick tuberous roots. The stems are 1 to 5 feet (30 to 150 cm) tall and bear flowers 3 to 5 inches (7.5 to 12.5 cm) long. The flowers have unspotted, tawny orange blossoms that are open for only one day. The plant has green, swordlike basal (forming the base of the plant) leaves.

Habitat   Daylilies grow predominantly in the eastern United States in waste ground and along ditches and roadsides.

Food   Young green leaves and shoots as well as tubers are edible raw or cooked. Flowers can be eaten raw or cooked.

Elderberry *(Sambucus)*

Description   Elderberry is a large shrub with a brown stem that bears opposite, compound leaves. (Opposite leaves are paired at each node and grow in opposite directions.) The plant grows up to 15 feet (4.5 m) tall, and white flowers are borne in large flat-topped clusters from 2 to 8 inches (5 to 20 cm) across. The fruit are small berries about 1/4 inch (.6 cm) in diameter that are purple, red, or black when ripe.

Habitat   Elderberry grows in North America in damp soil along creeks and streams and in canyons at the base of cliffs.

Food   The purple or black berries can be eaten raw, cooked, or dried. Avoid the red berries, which have a stronger, bitter taste. The flowers are edible and can be used to make tea. Do not eat the leaves, stems, and roots, which are poisonous.

Evening Primrose *(Oenothera)*

Description   The evening primrose is a biennial plant that grows 1 to 4 feet (30 to 120 cm) tall. Clusters of basal leaves form the first year and flower the second year. The unbranched, rough stem stands erect. The leaves are 2 to 6 inches (5 to 15 cm) long and lance shaped. The yellow flowers are about 2 inches (5 cm) wide, consisting of four heart-shaped petals. The fruit is a long, narrow pod about 1 inch (2.5 cm) long. The flower opens at night and usually closes by midday.

Habitat   This plant grows in North America in sandy soil, along roadsides, and in open areas.

Food   Young shoots and leaves can be eaten cooked or raw. The roots of the first-year plant can be boiled with one or two changes of water. The seeds can be eaten or ground into meal.

Fireweed *(Epilobium angustifolium)*

Description   This smooth-stemmed perennial plant grows 2 to 8 feet (60 to 240 cm) tall. Stems are erect and typically unbranched. Fireweed has large, showy, pink flowers and lance-shaped leaves, which are 2 to 6 inches (5 to 15 cm) in length. The flowers have four petals that are about 1 inch (2.5 cm) long. Seedpods are 2 to 4 inches (5 to 10 cm) long.

Habitat   Fireweed grows in North America in sunny open areas, in open woods, on hillsides, and on stream banks. It is especially abundant in burned-over areas.

Food   Young shoots and leaves are edible raw or cooked. Stems of older plants can be split open, and the tender pith can be eaten raw.

Jerusalem Artichoke *(Helianthus tuberosus)*

Description   Growing up to 10 feet (2.5 m) tall, the Jerusalem artichoke is a perennial plant with rough, hairy, slender stems. The large yellow flowers are 2 to 3 inches (5 to 7.5 cm) wide and have 10 to 20 bright rays. The leaves are up to 8 inches (20 cm) long and ovate to lance shaped. The numerous edible roots produce tubers, which are just below the ground. They are knobby and can be several inches thick. They are usually white or yellow but may be red or purple as well.

Habitat   This North American plant grows in disturbed ground, open areas, and fields.

Food   During fall, winter, and spring the tubers can be eaten raw, boiled, or baked like potatoes.

Juniper *(Juniperus)*

Description   Junipers, sometimes called cedars, are a shrublike tree with very small scalelike leaves that grow densely on the branches. The leaves are about a 1/4 inch (.6 cm) long. The small berrylike fruits are greenish blue and have a white waxy coating.

Habitat   Several varieties grow throughout North America in dry open areas, especially in the foothills and deserts of the West.

Food Juniper berries are edible but have a strong, resinous taste. Boiling or roasting improves the flavor. The thin wax coating on the berries can be removed by boiling and then skimmed from the water to make an aromatic wax. The inner bark layer is a useful emergency food.

Other Uses The outer shaggy bark of some varieties of the tree is one of the best tinder materials available for fire making. The bark can also be used as insulating material for shelters and to fabricate emergency sandals and blankets.

Lambs Quarters *(Chenopodium album)*

Description Lambs quarters is an annual bluish green plant with small flaky white scales. The many-branched stems are grooved and grow from 1 to 5 feet (30 to 150 cm) tall. Leaves are up to 5 inches (12.5 cm) long and vary from ovate to lance shaped. The small flowers lack petals and are usually in greenish clusters. The black seeds are tiny and numerous.

Habitat The plant grows on fields, waste ground, and disturbed soil in North America

Food The seeds can be gathered and boiled or ground into flour. The young leaves and shoots can be boiled or eaten raw.

Mallow *(Malva neglecta)*

Description This annual plant grows from 6 to 24 inches (15 to 60 cm) tall. The prostrate stems are spreading and have several branches with rounded leaves containing several scalloped lobes. The small five-petaled flowers are white, pink, or pale blue. The disklike fruit has a flattened top and bottom, and appears in flat, rounded clusters.

Habitat Mallow grows in North America in disturbed ground and cultivated soil, usually at lower elevations.

Food The leaves and young shoots can be eaten raw or cooked. The young cheeselike fruit can be eaten raw. The tiny seeds can be collected and ground into meal. A tea can be made from the dried leaves.

Milkweed *(Asclepias)*

Description   Milkweed grows in patches from thick rootstocks. The gray green stems, which are straight, sturdy, and grow to a height of 2 to 5 feet (60 to 150 cm), have a milky sap inside. The thick leaves are opposite and oblong in shape. The flowers grow up to 1/4 inch (.6 cm) long, appear in clusters, and are dull white to rose colored. The seedpod is teardrop shaped and has knobby prominences on the surface.

Habitat   This plant grows in fields, along roadsides, and in disturbed ground in North America

Food   This plant should not be eaten raw. The young shoots are best harvested when they are 4 to 8 inches (10 to 20 cm) long. Boil them for 15 to 20 minutes with at least two changes of water to remove the milky sap and bitter taste.

Other Uses   The silk from the seedpod can be used as insulation and padding. The fiber from dry stalks makes excellent material for cordage and is a good source of tinder.

Miner's Lettuce *(Claytonia perfoliata)*

Description   Miner's lettuce is a short-lived succulent herb with spreading stems about 3 to 10 inches (7.5 to 25 cm) tall. The basal leaves have long stalks and are ovate in shape. The two upper leaves are opposite, and their bases are joined together. The white or pinkish flowers are five petaled and about 1/4 inch (.6 cm) long.

Habitat   The plant grows in shady moist ground and on slopes in North America.

Food   All parts of the plant are edible raw or cooked.

Mountain Sorrel *(Oxyria digyna)*

Description   A perennial plant growing low from thick taproots, mountain sorrel is only 2 to 12 inches (5 to 30 cm) tall. The fleshy, kidney-shaped leaves form on the lower part of the stem. The small greenish or reddish flowers grow grouped in an upright cluster.

Habitat   Mountain sorrel grows in wet places, usually above timberline, in North America.

Food   The leaves can be eaten raw or cooked.

Mullein *(Verbascum thapsus)*

Description Mullein is a biennial plant that has a rigid stem and grows from 1 to 6 feet (30 to 180 cm) tall. Small yellow flowers are densely clustered on the upright stem that grows from a large rosette of leaves. The gray green, hairy leaves are 4 to 12 inches (10 to 30 cm) long.

Habitat The plant grows in loose, dry, disturbed soil in North America.

Food The dried leaves of the plant can be used to make tea.

Other Uses The dry stalks can be used as spindles for a bow drill for fire making. The flowering stems can be dipped in pitch from pine and spruce trees and used as torches.

Nettle *(Urtica)*

Description These leafy, erect plants grow from 2 to 6 feet (60 to 180 cm) high. They have small, green, inconspicuous flowers. Fine, hairlike, stinging bristles cover the stems, leafstalks, and undersides of leaves. The fruit consists of tiny seeds.

Habitat Nettles grow in North America in moist areas along streams, ditches, and canyons.

Food Young shoots and leaves are edible. Boiling the plant destroys the stinging quality of the bristles. Tea can be made from the leaves.

Other Uses Dried stems make good tinder and fibers for cordage.

Oaks *(Quercus)*

Description Oaks range in size from small shrubs to trees. The toothed leaves grow in alternating directions from the stem. Oaks produce acorn fruits.

Habitat Oaks are found in many habitats throughout North America.

Food The acorns are edible but bitter because they contain tannic acid. White oak acorns usually have the best flavor. To remove the bitter taste, the gathered acorns should be shelled, soaked, and boiled with several changes of water. They can then be dried or baked, ground into flour, and used alone or mixed with other foods.

Other Uses The water left over from boiling the acorns contains a high concentration of tannic acid that can be used in tanning hides.

Oregon Grape *(Berberis repens)*

Description   The Oregon grape is a creeping evergreen shrub. The stems grow to 1 foot (30 cm) long. The deep green leaves, which grow about 2 to 4 inches (5 to 10 cm) in length, have spiny, marginal teeth. These leaves resemble holly leaves and turn to a reddish color during fall. The small yellow flowers of the plant grow in close clusters. The fruits are round berries about 1/2 inch (1.25 cm) across or smaller and blue to dark blue. They resemble a blueberry.

Habitat   The plant grows on partially shaded slopes in dry to moist soils in the western United States.

Food   The berry fruit can be eaten raw, cooked, or dried.

Plantain *(Plantago)*

Description   This low-growing plant originates from a cluster of roots. The broad leaves are 2 to 12 inches (5 to 30 cm) long and ovate to lanceolate in shape. The greenish white flowers grow in concentrated, leafless spikes. (This plant is not related to the banana-like fruit-bearing plant grown in the tropics.)

Habitat   Plantain grows along roads, in fields, and in disturbed ground in North America.

Food   The young tender leaves are edible raw. Older leaves should be cooked.

Prickly Pear Cactus *(Opuntia)*

Description   A succulent plant with gray green pear-shaped pads, prickly pear cactus grows up to 2 feet (60 cm) tall. Two kinds of spines cover the pads. The most obvious are the large needlelike spines with barbs on the tips. Less obvious are the tiny hairlike spines, which are also barbed. The many-petaled flowers are 2 to 3 inches (5 to 7.5 cm) long and can be a variety of colors including yellow, pink, rose, or reddish. The reddish fruit borne below the flowers is 1 to 2 inches (2.5 to 5 cm) in length.

Habitat   The plant grows in deserts and dry sandy soils in North America.

Food   The pads can be peeled or scorched to remove the spines. The pulp can then be eaten raw or cooked. The inner pulp of the fruit is also a good food source. The seeds can be collected and eaten or ground into flour.

© JC Schou/Biopix

Photo courtesy of Mary Winter

Amaranth
(Amaranthus retroflexus)   Page 70

Arrowhead
(Sagittaria cuneata)   Page 70

© Henriette Kress

Asparagus *(Asparagus officinalis)*   Page 71

> PLANTS

Photo courtesy of Mary Winter

Biscuit Root (*Cymopterus*) Page 71

© Henriette Kress

Blackberries (*Rubus parviflorus*) Page 71

© Janet Horton

Blueberries (*Vaccinium uliginosum*) Page 72

© Randy Gerke

Bracken Fern
(Pteridium aquilinum)   Page 72

© JC Schou/Biopix

Chickweed
(Stellaria media)   Page 73

© JC Schou/Biopix

Burdock *(Arctium lappa)*   Page 72

85

© JC Schou/Biopix

Cattail
(Typha latifolia) Page 73

© R.A. Howard @ USDA-NRCS Plants Database

Chicory
(Cichorium intybus) Page 74

© Henriette Kress

Cottonwood *(Populus nigra)* Page 74

Clover
(Trifolium pratense)   Page 74

Cow Parsnip
(Heracleum lanatum)   Page 75

Cowlily *(Nuphar lutea)*   Page 75

87

© Hennette Kress

Currant *(Ribes uva crispa)* Page 76

© Janet Horton

Dandelion
(Taraxacum officinale) Page 76

Photo by G.A. Cooper, courtesy of Smithsonian Institution

Daylily
(Hemerocallis citrina) Page 76

Elderberry *(Sambucus nigra)* Page 77

Evening Primrose
(Oenothera biennis) Page 77

Fireweed
(Epilobium angustifolium) Page 78

Jerusalem Artichoke
(Helianthus tuberosus)   Page 79

Juniper
(Juniperus californica)   Page 78

Lambs Quarters *(Chenopodium album)*   Page 79

© Henriette Kress

Photo: J. E.(Jed) and Bonnie McClellan © California Academy of Sciences/Inset: © JC Schou/Biopix

© Henriette Kress

Mallow
(Malva neglecta)   Page 79

Milkweed
(Asclepias syriaca)   Page 80

© Randy Gerke

Mountain Sorrel
(Oxyria digyna)   Page 80

© Janet Horton

Mullein
(Verbascum thapsus)   Page 81

© 2005 Louis M. Landry

Nettle
(Urtica dioica) Page 81

© Henriette Kress

Oregon Grape
(Berberis repens) Page 82

© JC Schou/Biopix

Plantain *(Plantago major)* Page 82

© Scott Warren/Aurora Photos

Prickly Pear Cactus *(Opuntia)*   Page 82

© JC Schou/Biopix

Purslane *(Portulaca oleracea)*   Page 99

© 2002 Larry Blakely

Serviceberry *(Amelanchier utahensis)*   Page 100

Cassondra Skinner @ USDA-NRCS PLANTS Database

Ricegrass
(Oryzopsis) Page 99

© Henriette Kress

Salsify
(Tragopogon porrifolius) Page 99

© JC Schou/Biopix

Sheep Sorrel *(Rumex acetosella)* Page 100

Shepherd's Purse
(Capsella bursa-pastoris) Page 100

Thistle
(Cirsium vulgare) Page 101

Strawberries *(Fragaria vesca)* Page 101

© Henriette Kress
© Randy Gerke
© Henriette Kress

Watercress
(Nasturtium officinale)   Page 102

Wild Onion
(Allium cernuum)   Page 103

Tule Bulrush *(Scirpus acutus)*   Page 102

© Henriette Kress

Wild Rose *(Rosa canina)*

© Randy Gerke

USDA-NRCS PLANTS Database

Yarrow
(Achillea millefolium)

Yucca
(Yucca glauca)

Purslane *(Portulaca oleracea)*

Description   Purslane is an annual plant with fleshy leaves and stems. The stems, which may have a reddish tinge, spread low to the ground and grow from 4 to 12 inches (10 to 30 cm) long. The thick, oval-shaped leaves are about 1/2 inch (1.25 cm) long and grow grouped at the tips of the stems. The yellow flowers have petals about 1/4 inch (.6 cm) long and contain tiny black seeds.

Habitat   Purslane grows in open waste ground and disturbed soil in North America.

Food   Young shoots, leaves, and stems can be eaten raw or cooked. The seeds can be collected and ground into flour.

Ricegrass *(Oryzopsis)*

Description   Ricegrass, also known as Indian ricegrass (*Achnatherum hymenoides*), is a perennial bunchgrass with a delicate lacework of seed-pods. The stems grow erect up to 2 feet (60 cm) tall. The seed-bearing portion of the plant is about 1/4 inch (.6 cm) long.

Habitat   Ricegrass grows in the western United States in open slopes, valleys, and plains in dry, rocky, and sandy soil.

Food   The seeds can be collected and eaten raw, cooked, or ground into flour.

Salsify *(Tragopogon porrifolius)*

Description   Salsify is a perennial plant that grows from a thick taproot to a height of 1 to 4 feet (30 to 120 cm). The hollow, smooth stems contain a milky juice. The grasslike leaves are light green and contain a milky substance. The flowers, similar in appearance to those of the dandelion, are 1 to 2 inches (2.5 to 5 cm) long and yellow or purple. The fruit is seedlike and covered with projections of fuzzy hairs.

Habitat   Salsify grows in waste places, open fields, and disturbed soil in North America.

Food   The roots, leaves, and young shoots can be eaten raw, boiled, or roasted.

Serviceberry *(Amelanchier)*

Description Serviceberry is a shrub or small tree that grows from 5 to 20 feet (1.5 to 6 m) tall. Alternate leaves are 2 to 4 inches (5 to 10 cm) long and oval shaped with toothed margins. White flowers grow in long clusters, and the petals are about 3/8 inch (1 cm) long. When mature, the fruit looks like small purple or black apples.

Habitat Serviceberry grows in North America on stream banks, on hill slopes, in thickets, and in moist ground.

Food The berries can be eaten raw, cooked, or dried. Leaves can be used to make tea.

Sheep Sorrel *(Rumex acetosella)*

Description This perennial plant grows 6 to 18 inches (15 to 45 cm) tall from spreading rootstalks. Alternate leaves are 1 to 5 inches (2.5 to 12.5 cm) long and have arrowlike bases. Small greenish yellow or reddish brown flowers grow in clusters.

Habitat Sheep sorrel grows in North America in waste places, disturbed ground, fields, and roadsides.

Food The leaves are edible raw or cooked, and they can be used to make tea.

Shepherd's Purse *(Capsella)*

Description This annual plant has slender, erect stems growing from 6 to 16 inches (15 to 40 cm) tall. Leaves usually grow in clusters at the base of the plant and have an appearance similar to dandelion leaves. Stem leaves are sparsely placed. Tiny white flowers grow in clusters. Seeds develop in a triangular, flattened pod notched at the top of the stems.

Habitat Shepherd's purse is found in North America in disturbed ground and fields.

Food The young leaves can be eaten raw or cooked. The seeds can be eaten raw or dried.

Strawberries *(Fragaria)*

Description   Strawberries are a low-growing perennial plant about 3 to 5 inches (7.5 to 12.5 cm) tall. The leaves always have three well-defined leaflets about 1 to 2 inches (2.5 to 5 cm) long. The small white flowers have five petals. The fleshy fruit is red when ripe and has an appearance similar to the cultivated strawberry except that the wild variety is smaller.

Habitat   Strawberries grow in open woods and fields in North America, usually in partial shade and moist soil.

Food   The fruit is edible fresh, cooked, or dried. The leaves can be used to make tea.

Thistle *(Cirsium)*

Description   Thistle is a biennial plant that grows from a thick taproot with a straight stem that is branched or unbranched. The plant can reach a height of 1 to 6 feet (30 to 180 cm). The stems may or may not have spines. Leaves are alternate, lance shaped with several spiny lobes, and 4 to 10 inches (10 to 25 cm) in length. Flowers grow in a radial disk, are about 1 inch (2.5 cm) wide, and appear at the end of the stalks. They may be white, pink, or reddish. Egg-shaped seedpods lie underneath the flowers and contain a mass of hairy seed tufts.

Habitat   This North American plant grows in open light in disturbed and loose ground and in somewhat moist to dry soils.

Food   Young stalks can be peeled and eaten raw or cooked. The older stalks should be boiled before eating. Roots are edible raw or cooked. Tea can be made from the leaves.

Tule Bulrush *(Scirpus acutus)*

Description A dark green perennial plant, tule bulrush grows from scaly rootstocks with thick stems, reaching 4 to 12 feet (1.2 to 3.6 m) tall. Flowers are small and grow in small compact spikes arranged in dense brown clusters 1/4 to 1/2 inch (.6 to 1.25 cm) long.

Habitat Tule bulrush grows in shallow water, marshy areas, and wet ground in North America.

Food The rootstalks can be peeled and eaten raw or cooked. They can also be dried and pounded into flour. The base of the stems can be peeled and eaten. When the flowers are in bloom, the pollen can be collected and mixed with flour to make a variety of foods. After the flowers have bloomed, the seeds can be collected and ground into meal or flour. During fall, new shoots begin forming, and these can be harvested through the winter months. The young shoots are crisp and can be cooked or eaten raw.

Other Uses The dried stalks can be used for weaving.

Watercress *(Nasturtium officinale)*

Description Watercress is a low-growing, leafy, green perennial plant that grows partially submerged in water and forms a thick mat. The stems are fleshy and smooth. Three to nine oval-shaped leaflets grow directly from one another, and a single leaflet grows at the end of each stem. Flowers are white with four petals 1/8 to 1/4 inch (.3 to .6 cm) long.

Habitat Watercress is found in slow-flowing streams, springs, and mud in North America.

Food These plants should be gathered only from clean water sources. Plants growing from wastewater or other polluted sources will contain the impurities found in the water. The leaves and stems can be eaten raw.

Wild Onion *(Allium)*

Description Wild onion is a perennial plant that grows erect from an underground bulb to a height of 6 to 24 inches (15 to 60 cm). The leaves are slender and tubular to flat in shape. Flowers grow in clusters at the end of the stems. Each flower is about 1/8 to 1/4 inch (.3 to .6 cm) long and white or pink. When crushed, the flower and plant have a characteristic onion smell.

Habitat Wild onion grows in North America in open, sunny areas and in rocky or sandy soils up to 10,000 feet (3,000 m).

Food The bulbs and young leaves can be eaten raw or cooked. Be sure that the plant has an onion smell before using it as food. Death camas (see page 106) is sometimes confused with wild onion.

Wild Rose *(Rosa)*

Description Wild rose is a sprawling shrub with prickle-bearing stems that grow as tall as 12 feet (3.5 m). The alternate leaves have an odd number of fine-toothed leaflets. The flowers may be red, pink, or yellow. The fruit (called rose hip) remains after the flowers have died and is spherical, shiny, and red or orange.

Habitat Wild rose grows in moist ground in fields, open woods, and thickets in North America.

Food Flowers and buds can be eaten raw or cooked. The hips are edible raw or cooked and remain a viable source of food through early winter. The leaves and hips can be used to make tea.

Yarrow *(Achillea)*

Description Yarrow is a perennial herb that grows erect with grayish green stems that are usually unbranched. The plant grows 1 to 3 feet (30 to 90 cm) tall. The flowers are lacy and fragrant, growing in round, daisylike flower heads that are usually white. The leaves are grayish green, fernlike, and aromatic.

Habitat Yarrow grows in fields, meadows, and open areas in North America.

Food Leaves can be steeped to make an aromatic tea.

Yucca *(Yucca glauca)*

Description   Yucca is a perennial plant with a woody straight stalk that grows to a height of 2 to 6 feet (60 to 180 cm) from a crowded base of stiff, sword-shaped leaves. The leaves are up to 3 feet (90 cm) long and have sharp-pointed tips. The flowers, which appear in large clusters at the top of the stem, are white or cream colored, bell shaped, and 1 1/2 to 2 inches (3.75 to 5 cm) long. The fruit is an elongated capsule 1 to 2 inches (2.5 to 5 cm) long that contains large black seeds and grows from the stalk near the top.

Habitat   Yucca grows on dry slopes in rocky and sandy soil in the western United States.

Food   Fruit can be eaten raw or cooked. The inner part of the young stems can be cooked and eaten. The seeds can be ground or boiled. Flower petals can be eaten raw.

Other Uses   Roots can be crushed in water to make soap. Leaves can be used for weaving, and they can make an excellent emergency needle and thread. The pointed tip of a leaf can be used as a needle, and the broad part of the leaf can be stripped away, leaving a thin strand of material for thread. Large stalks from the plant can be used as spindles for making fire.

Poisonous Plant Varieties

Technically, most wild plants are edible. But some are not very palatable, and a few are poisonous to some degree. As with the edible varieties, poisonous plants are too numerous to allow a comprehensive list to appear here. The three poisonous varieties described in this section are common throughout North America. They are potent and can be deadly if ingested in sufficient quantity. As mentioned earlier in this chapter, there is no substitute for being able to make a positive identification of a plant. Be positive; if you are unsure about the identity of a particular plant, leave it alone.

Death Camas *(Zigadenus)*

Description   Death camas (*Zygadenus elegans* pictured here) is a perennial plant that grows from bulbs, which are 1/2 to 1 1/2 inches (1.25 to 3.75 cm) in diameter and produce a single, erect stem 6 to 24 inches (15 to 60 cm) in length. The narrow grasslike leaves are 4 to 12 inches (10 to 30 cm) long and crowded near the base of the stem. Flowers are greenish white to yellowish white, dish shaped, and clustered at the top of the stem.

Habitat   The plant grows in plains, open meadows, and open areas in forests up to timberline.

Threat Level   Death camas grows in the same habitat as wild onion and is similar in appearance. Every part of a wild onion plant has a distinctive onion smell, but death camas does not. The definitive test is to tear or crush a piece of the plant and smell it. If does not smell like an onion, leave it alone. The plant parts and bulbs contain alkaloids, which are poisonous to humans and many animals. Death camas is considered extremely poisonous.

Cassondra Skinner @ USDA-NRCS PLANTS Database

Water Hemlock *(Cicuta)*

Description   Water hemlock (*Cicuta douglasii* pictured here) is a perennial plant that grows from a thick tuberous rootstock. The stem has many branches and is smooth and hollow, except at the nodes. Purple spots are usually visible on the stem. Leaves are compound and alternating. Leaflets are 1 to 4 inches (2.5 to 10 cm) long and have toothed edges. Leaf veins run through the notches between the teeth. The small white flowers grow in multiple clusters at the top of the stems. When cut or crushed, the plant emits a rank, bitter odor.

Habitat   Water hemlock occurs in swampy areas, near creeks and streams, and in other damp locations in North America.

Threat Level   All plant parts and roots are extremely poisonous and deadly.

POISONOUS

© 2008 Margo Bors

Poison Hemlock *(Conium maculatum)*

Description   This biennial plant grows 2 to 10 feet (60 to 300 cm) tall from strong taproots. The stem is green, smooth, and usually spotted with brown or reddish brown spots. Leaves grow to over 1 foot (30 cm) in length and are finely divided and lacy, triangular overall, and fernlike. The leaves are made up of several coarse-toothed leaflets with veins that run through the tips of the teeth. The small flowers are usually white and grow in clusters at the top of the stems, 3 to 6 inches (7.5 to 15 cm) across. When crushed, the plant emits a rank, unpleasant odor.

Poison hemlock can be distinguished from water hemlock by the less finely divided leaves of the water hemlock. The leaf veins of poison hemlock run through the tips of the teeth, unlike those of the water hemlock, which run through the notches between the teeth. The root of poison hemlock is fleshy and unbranched, in contrast to the tuberous roots of water hemlock.

Habitat   Poison hemlock grows in moist ground and waste places at low to moderate elevations in North America.

Threat Level   All plant parts and roots are extremely poisonous and deadly.

© Henriette Kress

Food From Animals

AS discussed in chapter 5, harvesting edible plants can meet some nutritional needs and stave off starvation during a survival experience. To fill the need for food more completely, you should consider the animal resources in the area. Animals are a good source of protein and fat, and they provide other useful materials as well, such as hide, bone, and tendons, that you can use to make clothing and tools. You can catch a variety of animals with simple traps and snares. Fish can be harvested from lakes and streams.

Before you decide what to hunt or catch, take some time to discover and observe the animals that you are sharing the habitat with. When you have an idea of what kinds of wildlife are available, make a decision about which will be easiest to capture, trap, or kill. Your resources are limited, so a conservative approach is in order. The factors to consider are the type and abundance of wildlife; available tools; other resources such as wood, rocks, and cordage materials; your condition; and your skill level. Evaluating these factors will help you decide which animals to harvest and what method to use.

Building Traps and Snares

The technique of using traps and snares for obtaining small game can produce good results. Several types of traps and snares are easy to make and require few resources. All materials used in making traps and snares should appear as natural as possible. If the sticks that you choose to make your trap have bark on them, leave it on. After making notches and other cuts in the sticks, darken them with dirt or ashes from a fire. Rubbing the parts in dirt, ashes, or plants will also help hide the human scent on the trap.

Deadfall Traps

A trap that is particularly helpful is the deadfall trap, which uses the weight of a falling object, such as a rock or log, to capture and kill an animal. The concept is simple, and construction requires few materials. Deadfall traps are most effective for animals that range in size from a rodent to a fox. Small deadfall traps are appropriate for small game such as mice, chipmunks, ground squirrels, tree squirrels, and rabbits. As a rule, the object used as the deadfall should weigh about twice as much as the animal that you intend to catch, and the deadfall should be large enough to entrap at least the animal's head and shoulders.

Figure Four

The figure four derives its name from the shape of the finished trap. The completed trap is composed of three sticks that form the shape of an upright number 4 (see figure 6.1). Begin building the trap using

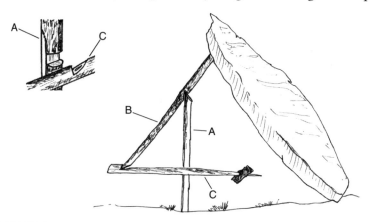

FIGURE 6.1   A figure four trap.

straight sticks that are about .75 inch (2 cm) thick. Stick A, which will be the upright, should be 6 to 7 inches (15 to 18 cm) in length. Stick B, the diagonal lever that the deadfall object leans against, should be slightly shorter than the upright. Stick C, the bait stick, should be 8 to 10 inches long. You will position it parallel to the ground and perpendicular to the upright.

Follow these steps to construct the trap:

1. On stick A, leave one end blunt and carve a squared chisel point on the opposite end.

2. On stick B, cut a shallow notch a few inches (3.75 cm) from one end and carve a squared chisel point on the other end. The face of the chisel point and the notch must be on the same side of the stick.

3. On stick C, create a shallow notch within 1 inch (2.5 cm) of one end and sharpen the other end. You will apply the bait to the point of this stick.

4. Now that the basic components are ready, you need to make some final cuts to the upright and the bait stick. Lay the pieces on the ground to create the 4 shape.

5. On the upright (A) and the bait stick (C), mark the location where the two sticks cross. At the mark on the upright, cut a squared slot into the stick. At the crossing point on the bait stick, cut a notch. This notch mates the squared area that you just prepared in the upright. When the figure four is set up, the notch in the bait stick locks against the squared section of the upright to form the trigger for the trap. As the animal pulls on the bait, the bait stick is dislodged from the upright and releases the deadfall. If the notch does not hold the upright correctly, the trap may not function correctly. If the notch is too shallow, the trap may be difficult to set or it may release prematurely before an animal arrives. If the notch is too deep, the release may be delayed or may not occur at all and the animal will escape with the bait.

6. Apply the bait to the bait stick. Use foods that will entice your intended target. Use fresh plant material such as buds, young shoots, succulent roots, animal fat or grease, or fresh animal entrails. Take care not to handle the bait, but instead skewer it onto the point of the bait stick. If you cannot skewer the bait, secure it to the bait stick with fine cord, taking care not to touch it.

7. To set the trap, kneel down and lift the deadfall, leaning it against your body. Place the upright stick perpendicular to the ground and slightly in front of the deadfall. Then place the lever stick that forms the descending top of the 4 in place and gently lower the deadfall onto the upper end of the stick while holding the lower end in position. At this point the entire weight of the deadfall will be on the lever stick. To set the trap, place the baited trigger stick in place.

Ultimately, the size of the animal that you want to catch determines the size of the sticks and the weight of the deadfall. Try setting and checking seven or eight traps each day. You will probably have better success using smaller traps. You can make more of them with less effort, and they are easier to set. The animals that you harvest will be smaller, but you will likely have greater success than you will by setting a few large traps and hoping for a larger animal. The ground where you place the deadfall must be solid for the trap to function properly. Soft ground allows the upright stick to sink and move, causing the trap to release. A soft base may allow an animal to escape or suffer unnecessarily. You may need to hollow out the soil where you will set the trap and place a flat rock, log, or thick piece of bark level with the ground. Limit the disturbance to the set area and conceal and camouflage it when you are done.

Paiute Deadfall

The Paiute deadfall uses cordage as part of the trigger mechanism. The upright and diagonal lever sticks are fashioned as in the figure four, but instead of carving a chisel point on the lower end of the diagonal, you tie a piece of cordage around the end of it (see figure 6.2). You tie the other end of the cordage to a short twig. To set the trap, wrap the twig around the upright and keep it in place with a long thin bait stick placed between the loaded end of the twig and the deadfall. The Paiute deadfall has the advantage of releasing more quickly than a figure four deadfall and is well suited for small animals such as rodents.

Follow these steps to construct a Paiute deadfall:

1. On stick A, leave one end blunt and carve a square chisel point on the opposite end.

2. On stick B, cut a shallow notch about 1 1/2 inches (3.75 cm) from one end. Leave the other end as is.

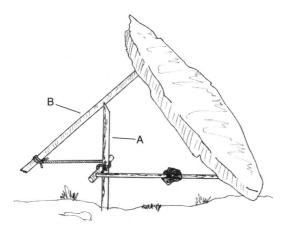

FIGURE 6.2 A Paiute deadfall trap.

3. At the lower end of stick B (opposite the end of the notch), tie a length of thin cordage within 1 inch (2.5 cm) of the end. To estimate the correct length for the cordage, lay sticks A and B on the ground to form the upright (stick A) and the descending top (stick B) of the 4 shape. The thin cord tied to the lower end of the lever stick should extend over to the upright stick and 1 inch (2.5 cm) or so beyond.

4. Tie a twig about 2 inches (5 cm) in length to the other end of the cordage.

5. To set the trap, use the technique discussed for the figure four but after placing the deadfall on the lever stick, pull the end of the cordage with the twig attached toward the deadfall and wrap it once around the upright stick.

6. Place a thin bait stick between the deadfall and the twig to hold the trigger in place.

Snares

Snares can be used to catch small game, but they also work well with larger animals, such as fox, coyote, and deer. You make snares with cordage formed into a self-tightening loop. Unbaited snares are set on animal runs and game trails. Make the loop from material strong enough to hold the weight of the captured animal. The loop should be just large enough for the intended animal to place its head through but not so large that the animal can pass its front legs through. As the animal travels through the loop, the cordage tightens around the neck, causing the trigger mechanism to release. The animal is lifted from the ground, tightening the loop even further. Snares designed for larger game require only that a foot be caught in the snare loop, which is anchored to an immovable object, such as a tree.

Spring Pole

The spring pole snare uses the tension of a sapling to capture an animal. This type of snare is quickly and easily constructed because it requires only a length of cordage and a trigger made from two hooked sticks (see figure 6.3). Secure one end of the cordage to the tip of a sapling and tie a short hooked trigger stick to the other end. Form a self-tightening loop or noose with cordage and tie it to the trigger stick. Drive a stationary hooked trigger stick into the ground near the sapling on a game trail with the hook facing downward. Then bend the tip of the sapling toward the ground so that you can interlock the hooked triggers. Complete the setup by positioning the snare loop on a game trail. When an animal becomes ensnared in the loop, the trigger hooks are displaced, releasing the sapling upward and causing the snare loop to tighten.

FIGURE 6.3   A spring pole snare.

Follow these steps to construct a spring pole snare:

1. Locate a flexible sapling within 2 or 3 feet (60 to 90 cm) of an active game trail or run.

2. Create two trigger sticks. One trigger, the floating trigger, should be about 3 inches (7.5 cm) long. You will tie this trigger to the spring pole. The other trigger, the stationary trigger, should be about 6 inches (15 cm) long. You will drive this trigger into the ground. The easiest way to make these triggers is to use sticks about 1/2 to 3/4 inch (1.25 to 2 cm) in diameter with a small fork near one end. You will use the forks as hooks to hold the triggers in place.

3. Drive the stationary trigger stick into the ground with the hook facing downward next to the game trail on the same side of the trail as the sapling.

4. Create the self-tightening snare loop and tie it to the floating trigger.

5. Tie the floating trigger with the hook facing up to the loose end of the cordage coming from the sapling.

6. Set the snare by bending the sapling toward the stationary trigger and placing the hooks against one another so that the tension from the spring pole holds them in place.

7. Then arrange the snare loop on the trail.

Lift Pole

If an appropriate sapling is not available near a game trail, you can create a lift pole, illustrated in figure 6.4. To do this, find a sapling with forked branches about 3 feet (90 cm) from a game trail. If a tree is not available, you can drive a forked stick vertically into the ground. Drive the stick in until the fork is about 3 feet (90 cm) above the ground. The bottom of the forked branches or stick is the fulcrum in the system. Then place a pole in the fork with one end extending over the game trail.

FIGURE 6.4 A lift pole snare.

This pole serves as the lever in the system. Tie weights made from rocks or pieces of wood to the other end of the pole to create enough lift to set the triggers and allow the snare to function. After you construct the lift pole, follow the steps described for the spring pole snare for making the triggers and setting the snare.

Placing Traps or Snares Properly

With patience and some experimentation anyone can build a usable trap or snare, but catching animals in the trap or snare is another matter. Procuring game for survival requires significant time and effort. Placing traps and snares in a suitable location is the key to success. Setting traps in random locations without regard to the indicators of game trails or other signs will produce disappointing results. You must search out places where animals travel and live and where they gather food and water. Set traps and snares on lesser-used game trails, at the entrance to burrows and dens, and near water holes where animal signs are present. Barriers made of upright sticks staked in the ground can direct animals into an area of a trap or snare. When you find these locations, you should set several traps and check them each day. The more traps you set, the better the chance you have of catching something.

All animals, no matter how large or small, are preyed on by other creatures in their native habitat. Suspicious by nature, they constantly watch, listen, feel, and smell for anything that might be dangerous to their survival. They have an especially keen sense of smell and hearing and can detect subtle vibrations and movements. Understanding these characteristics is important as you enter their world as a predator.

Unless you are an avid hunter, you are probably not in the habit of being stealthy, but this practice is essential if you want to be successful at catching game. You must make your presence less noticeable. Walk slowly and softly. Avoid making loud noises or sudden movements. Walk to the side of game trails or obvious animal tracks. Avoid touching objects with your hands and do not urinate or defecate in the area.

Frequently stop and observe. Most people are unaccustomed to standing still and being silent for even a few seconds, but you will gain more from a moment of observation than from an hour of thrashing through the woods. Be still and watch for motion in all directions. Listen for sounds such as movement through brush or trees, scratching, or pecking. Look on the ground for animal and bird tracks. Watch for broken or trampled brush, plants, and leaves. Look for scratch or chew marks on trees or brush. Use your sense of smell. Do you notice any particular smells? Do the odors change in intensity? Do you see animal scat on the ground? If so, is it warm, or does it appear to have been there for several days? All the signs that you observe tell a story about the types of wildlife present in the area—where they live, what they eat, and what their habits are. The more you know about them, the better your chances are of capturing them.

Cleaning and Skinning Animals

Most animals, whether large or small, are skinned and cleaned in the same way. The first stage in this procedure is to remove the blood from the animal and then the skin. The final step is to remove the internal organs. If you are dealing with a large animal far from camp, leave the hide on the animal. The hide will make it easier to drag the animal back to camp, where you can complete the skinning and butchering process.

Bleeding

Draining the blood thoroughly from the animal is important. If you fail to do this, the meat will spoil quickly. Gravity eases the process. Position the animal on the ground with the head downhill.

Blood contains valuable salts and nutrients, which you can add to soups and stews. If you plan to save the blood, cut only the jugular veins in the neck, located on either side of the windpipe, and avoid cutting the windpipe because an opening could release the contents of the stomach and contaminate the blood. Allow the blood to drain into a container. If preserving the blood is not a consideration, cut the entire throat including the windpipe to bleed the animal.

Skinning

Removing the skin is easier when the animal is still warm. This consideration is especially important with larger animals. Before beginning, know that most animals have scent glands. On animals such as deer, they are located on the hind legs, behind the knee. On smaller animals they are usually found on either side of the anus. Remove these glands early in the process. Fresh meat will become tainted if it is exposed to these glands. Urine from the bladder will also spoil the meat.

To skin an animal, begin by making a circular cut around the hind legs above the knee. Make similar cuts on the front legs. Cut the skin on the inside of each hind leg to an area near the genitals. Then make a circular cut around the genitals, taking care not to puncture the organs because they contain fluids that can taint the meat. From the genital area, continue cutting toward the middle of the belly to the neck. Finish the process by cutting up the inside of the front legs to the top of the chest.

The skin is then ready to be removed. Using your fingers, begin peeling the skin from the flesh at the rear legs. On larger animals using a fist can help. Skin each side of the animal, working outward from the belly to the spine. If possible, avoid using a knife, which can puncture the hide. When you reach the neck area, cut the remaining tissue attaching the head and remove it.

Gutting

Begin by cutting carefully into the abdominal cavity just in front of the anus, continuing through the chest cavity and up to the neck. Take your time and be careful not to cut into any organs while doing this. Reach high up on the windpipe and cut or pull this loose from the carcass. The remainder of the entrails will then be easy to remove. Continue removing them and pulling them down toward the tail of the animal. Separate the edible organs such as the lungs, heart, kidneys, and liver from the other entrails so that you can use them later.

Depending on conditions, the carcass may be ready for use or you can hang it to cool. In hot weather, raw meet can spoil quickly, so you should process it right away. Begin cooking and eating the meat immediately. One of the best ways to preserve meat is to dry or smoke it into jerky. Do this by cutting the meat into thin strips and hanging it so that air can get to all sides of the strips. You can build a primitive drying rack, shown in figure 6.5, with sticks in the shape of a tripod and then tie several horizontal rows of cordage or sticks between the tripod supports from which you can hang the meat. You can accelerate the drying process by moving the rack near a fire to receive the benefit of heat and smoke.

FIGURE 6.5 A drying rack used to preserve meat.

Catching Fish

Fish and related animals are an important food source to consider during a survival situation. You can catch fish in traps, with hook and line, with bare hands, or with a spear. As with all food gathering, the method that you use will depend on your location, the available resources, and your level of skill.

Fish are most active when feeding during the early morning and evening hours and just before a storm. These are the best times to try to catch them. During midday fish seek deeper, darker places, such as deep shaded pools or near undercut banks and outcroppings. Fish are highly sensitive to movement and sound on or beyond the surface of the water. You should approach fishing just as you would when hunting any other wild creature. Move slowly and quietly, keep a low profile, and take time to observe their behavior.

When you catch a fish, cut the throat and hang it with the head down so that the fish bleeds out. Remove the guts by making an incision from the anus to the throat and pulling out all the entrails. You can use the entrails as bait on a fishing line or for baiting land-based traps. Fish skin is nutritious, so you should leave it on. Scaling is not necessary in a survival situation. Small fish need not be cleaned and can be eaten as is.

Traps

Simple one-way fish traps are an effective means of capturing fish. You can make these traps from materials such as willows or saplings that grow beside lakes and streams. The trap is cone shaped and about 3 feet (90 cm) long. Begin by forming three rings from the saplings in graduated sizes (see figure 6.6). The first ring, which forms the mouth of the trap, needs to be about 12 inches (30 cm) in diameter. Make another ring 3 or 4 inches (7.5 to 10 cm) smaller than the first. The

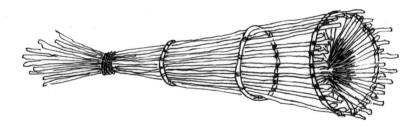

FIGURE 6.6   A one-way fish trap.

final ring should be about 6 inches (15 cm) in diameter. Then collect a bundle of straight, thin sticks about 3 feet (90 cm) in length. These sticks will become the main structure for the trap. An easy way to tie the parts together is to strip the bark from willows or saplings and use the flexible bark as cordage. To form the main structure for the trap, gather five or six of the straight sticks into a bundle. Line up the ends of the sticks on one end so that they are even with one another. Then tie this end of the bundle together to form the closed end of the cone.

To form the open end of the cone, take the largest ring and tie the loose ends of the bundled sticks to the ring at evenly spaced intervals. Then insert the medium-sized ring into the cone several inches (cm) beyond the first ring and tie the straight sticks to this ring as you did with the largest ring. Insert the smallest ring into the cone and place it farther down toward the closed end of the cone. Tie it to the sticks as before. Then tie straight sticks to the structure until the spaces between the sticks are no more than 1 inch (2.5 cm) wide at the open end of the cone.

You can give the trap a one-way entrance by constructing a much shorter cone and attaching it to the inside of the large opening of the trap. The opening of this basket should be the same size as the original basket so that you can fasten the two together. The small end of this cone should point in the same direction as the main cone, and the opening should be about 3 to 4 inches (7.5 to 10 cm) wide. This way fish can be funneled into the cone but will have a difficult time swimming out. Place the trap facing upstream in an area out of the main current, along a shadowed and undercut bank. Fasten rocks to the trap or place them in the trap to keep it in place. Bait is not necessary. Check the trap every few hours.

Hook and Line

If string or line is available, you can fashion a crude pole from a stick. Attach the line to one end of the pole and a hook to the end of the line. If a safety pin is available, you can use it as a hook. You can also make hooks from bone or wood and cordage, as shown in figure 6.7. Hooks can be baited with flies, bugs, worms, or entrails from fish or animals. Drop the hook and line

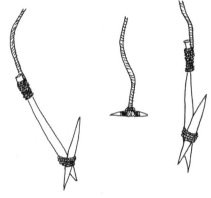

FIGURE 6.7 Various types of fish hooks.

in the water while holding the pole and wait for a tug on the line. When you feel the positive tug of a fish biting, make a quick upward jerk on the pole to set the improvised hook into the fish's mouth and pull the fish to the surface.

Bare Hands

You can catch fish with your bare hands in areas of undercut banks in shallow streams. The best way to begin is to lie on your stomach along the bank and slowly place your hands into the water. You do not need to see the fish to use this method. Allow time for your hands to adjust to the water temperature. Slowly move your hands and fingers along the bank until you touch a fish. Do not make any sudden movements until you are ready to attempt to catch the fish. The objective is to hook your fingers into the gills and quickly throw the fish up onto the bank of the stream. With practice, this can be a viable food-gathering technique.

Spears

Fish spears can be fashioned from a long, straight stick. You can use dead sticks, but for a more durable implement, green wood is best because it can be fire hardened. You can make spears with single, double, or triple prongs; double- and triple-prong spears will hold the fish more securely after it is caught (see figure 6.8). To make a double-prong spear tip, split the end of the stick to create two prongs and force the two sections apart with a small wooden wedge that you can lash into place. Then, sharpen each prong. To make a triple-prong spear, insert a small sharpened stick between the two existing prongs and fasten it into place with cordage. Sharpen the prongs and carve barbs pointing inward into each tip.

Spearing fish requires practice and patience. Practice on a stationary object in the water before you attempt to catch a fish. You will notice immediately that your

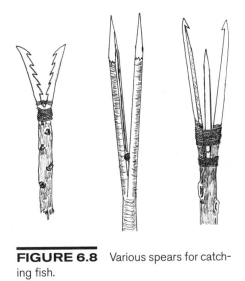

FIGURE 6.8 Various spears for catching fish.

stationary target is not where it appeared to be. Light refracting through the water causes a distortion from your view above the water. To learn how to compensate, place the tip of your spear in the water to see the proper relationship between the spear and the target.

You are then ready to spear a fish. Grasp the spear toward the blunt end of the shaft with your dominant hand. Place your other hand lower down on the shaft for support. Approach the water slowly and smoothly. Just as in stalking or hunting any animal, be quiet and avoid sudden movements. When you find a fish, gently place the tip of the spear in the water. Make a quick jab toward the fish. If necessary, hold the fish against the bottom of the streambed and push the tip through.

Eating Insects

Most insects are edible and are rich in carbohydrate, fat, and protein. They are small but plentiful in almost all environments and can be an important source of food. A variety of species can be found in dark, cool, moist places near lakes, ponds, streams, and marshes. They can often be found under leaves and grasses, beneath the outer layers of the bark of trees and shrubs, and in dead and decaying logs and stumps.

You should observe several precautions when gathering insects for food. Do not use insects that you find dead or feeding on rotting flesh or dung. Most stinging species are edible but not worth the trouble to harvest. Avoid eating furry caterpillars because many of these species are poisonous. The following tips can help you make the best use of some of the common insects that you may find:

- Ants can be gathered into a container from nests and mounds and roasted on a fire. An efficient way to do this is to add hot coals to the container. As the ants cook, the legs and head will shrink, leaving the larger abdomens to be eaten. You can also grind these into powder and add them to other foods.

- You should always cook grasshoppers, cicadas, and crickets to eliminate parasites. Remove the legs, wings, and antennae and then roast the bodies over hot coals.

- Aquatic insects such as dragonflies, water beetles, and mayflies can be collected near ponds, lakes, and streams. Boil them to eliminate any parasites that the insects may carry and to kill parasites and bacteria that may be present in the water.

- Worms and slugs are also edible, although they are best when added to other boiled foods. You can gather them in quantity after a soaking rain.

Using Animal By-Products

During a survival situation, you cannot afford to overlook any resource that could improve your circumstances. Animals provide many important food resources, which you can easily recognize and use. They also offer less obvious materials that you can use to make clothing, shelter, and tools.

Hide

Hides of all animals can be made into usable rawhide, which you can fabricate into bags, footwear, string, and many other useful items. After skinning the animal, stretch and stake the hide onto a flat surface with the flesh side up. Scrape all the flesh and fat from the hide with a knife or stone scraper. You will need to put forth a good deal of effort to complete this process. After you have scraped the hide and washed it thoroughly with water, stake it out tightly stretched until it is completely dry. When the hide is dry, turn it over and restake it. You must then remove the hair from the hide. Do this using the same technique that you used to remove the flesh. Work the hide until you have removed all the hair. Hard labor is required to accomplish this step. The final step is to soften the hide. Place the hide on a soft surface and pound it with a blunt object, such as a blunt stone, until the grain of the hide is broken down and soft. Continue this action until the hide is white and soft. You can then cut and form the rawhide into a variety of useful items.

Bone

Bones can be used for a variety of tools, such as needles, fishhooks, and implement points. You can split bone by hammering or crushing it with a rock and then shaping and sharpening it by abrading it against a coarse stone. Even large bones can be splintered into small pieces for making such items as needles and fishhooks.

Sinew

The tendons from the legs and backs of animals can be stripped into thin strips and used to make extremely strong cordage, which you can use to fasten stone and bone points to wooden shafts for use as a variety of implements. To prepare sinew, remove the tendons from the animal and clean all the flesh from them. Lay them in the sun until they are thoroughly dry. Pound the hard tendons between two rocks until they are soft and feathery. You can then strip the sinew into fine strands. When dampened, the sinew can fasten together many types of items. You simply wrap the sticky sinew around the objects and onto itself. No tying is needed. You can also make extremely strong cordage from sinew. To make cordage, follow these steps:

1. With one hand held comfortably in front of you, hold two strands of sinew parallel and close together between the tip of the thumb and the index finger. Make sure that you have 1 or 2 inches (2.5 to 5 cm) of the material above your hand and the bulk of the material hanging below your hand toward the ground.

2. Begin by twisting the strand on the right in a clockwise direction with the other hand (see figure 6.9).

3. Then fold the strand that you just twisted over the second strand in a counterclockwise direction. This action places the untwisted second strand on the right.

4. Twist the second strand just as you did the first strand.

5. Fold the second strand over the first strand in a counterclockwise direction.

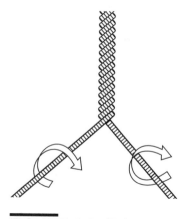

FIGURE 6.9 Technique for making sinew into cordage.

Continue twisting the material together using this technique until you reach the desired length. To splice more material in, begin twisting additional sinew into the strand 1 inch (2.5 cm) or so before the end of the strand. You can use the same technique to fabricate cordage from the fibers of plant materials.

Navigation and Finding Help

IT seems as though you have been walking for a long time—a very long time. A couple of hours have passed since you last recognized any landmarks. The area looks less and less familiar, but you say to yourself, "I'm only tired. If I keep going, I know I'll find my way." In the back of your mind, though, you have a nagging thought that you may not be on the right path. As you travel on, the thought grows increasingly stronger until suddenly you realize that you are standing alone in a strange landscape where nothing is familiar. Although you may be lost, you stand at a well-known crossroad. Many wilderness travelers have been in the same place, and those who have not probably will in the future. The decisions that you make from this point will directly affect the outcome of your experience.

Preventing Disorientation

Getting lost can be frightening, frustrating, and discouraging, especially when traveling in a remote and unfamiliar environment. Anyone can become lost, regardless of outdoor experience, education, or any other personal characteristics. People most frequently become lost when they become separated from a group or when they travel alone and lose their orientation. In both cases, prevention is the best remedy.

When traveling in a group, never lose site of the main party. Use a type of buddy system to keep everyone in close contact. The slowest person should always be kept toward the front of the group. This practice can be a frustration for those who travel at a faster pace, but it prevents problems that arise when people become separated from one another. Radios or whistles are a good investment because they allow a group to communicate if they do become separated.

Whether traveling in a group or by yourself, always be alert to what lies ahead, including weather, terrain, and other hazards. Frequently stop to look behind you and to see what the trail looks like from the other direction so that you will see recognizable landmarks on your return trip. If you are traveling for the first time in an unfamiliar area, carry an appropriate map and compass. Studying the map before you travel is helpful. Take time to make notes of unique landmarks and natural features along the route. This practice will be a great aid on the return trip. If you are traveling in flat featureless terrain or in thick woods, you can mark the trail with rock cairns (small piles of rocks), wooden trail markers made from sticks, or colorful survey tape. Space these markers so that they are visible from one to the next.

Choose a Safety Contact

Always leave the details of your travel plans and itinerary with a responsible person. Let the person know where you plan to go and when you expect to return. You should also let the person know what vehicle you will be traveling in and the license number of the vehicle. Even this minimal information can accelerate the search process and may make the difference between life and death in the event that you do not return on schedule. When you return or if you decide to cancel or change your plans, be sure to update your contact. You want to have people looking for you when you are lost but not when you are sleeping in a warm bed at home.

Reacting Deliberately

When you discover that you are lost or if you suddenly become stranded in an unfamiliar area because of an aircraft emergency landing or crash or some similar event, you should be slow and deliberate in solving the problem. Reacting to the situation impulsively will only make matters worse. The following actions may help you to find your way again or at least prevent your situation from becoming more serious. By using these techniques you will also put yourself in a position where searchers will be more likely to find you.

1. **Orient yourself.** If you have a map, lay it out and try to match it up with the prominent landmarks in the area. This action may solve your problem. Establish the cardinal directions (north, south, east, and west), using whatever means you have (see the section "Finding Your Way" later in the chapter).

2. **Survey the area.** Mark the spot where you are and begin surveying the area, paying special attention to where your marker is. Walk around the area in larger and larger circles. Always keep track of where your marker is. You may be able to follow your own tracks to the spot where you first became lost or divided from the group. Do not become separated from your gear, which will only make survival more difficult.

3. **Make camp.** If you are still lost after using the previous steps, make camp. Start preparing for the night early while light is still available. Build or find shelter, gather firewood and make a fire, and locate a source of water.

4. **Begin signaling.** After completing the previous steps, begin signaling. Of course, if you see or hear people nearby you should begin signaling immediately. The purpose of signaling is to increase your size and visibility. Use signals that contrast with your surroundings. Be creative and use whatever is available. The international distress signal consists of three of anything. See chapter 8 for more information about signaling methods.

Deciding When to Travel

Impatience is a basic human trait, especially when physical or emotional discomfort is involved. People have a strong desire to get back to where they think they should be. This intense drive can be beneficial because it helps people continue pushing forward. But you must balance this determination with the reality of the situation. If you begin traveling with no clear goal about which direction to go, you only worsen your situation. The best option is almost always to stay where you are and continue signaling, especially if you are near a vehicle or downed aircraft. Rescuers will be looking for these large items, which are easier to see than a person is.

But several reasons may require you to leave the actual emergency site:

- After a prolonged time, you have not been rescued. Your resources are exhausted, and you believe that the chance of rescue is nil.

- You are reasonably sure that no rescue effort will be launched. You did not leave word with anyone regarding your travel plans. No one knows where you are and when you intended to return.

- You are sure of your location and know that help is nearby. Even if help is nearby, you must consider many factors before traveling, such as weather, your physical condition, the condition of the group, and the length of travel time. Never expose yourself to additional risks by traveling if waiting would offer more protection and quicker rescue.

Finding Your Way

You can use several methods to determine the cardinal directions. From high-tech equipment such as global positioning systems and electronic compasses to primitive methods that use the sun and stars to show the way, these methods can help you determine where in the world you are and how to get to where you need to go.

Primitive Methods

Primitive techniques are simple to set up and easy to use. They are not as accurate as using a compass or GPS unit, but if followed closely they can keep you on the right track.

The North Star

To find the North Star (or Polaris), locate the Big Dipper and identify the two stars that form the front of the cup part of the dipper. Imagine a line crossing through these pointer stars and extending out beyond the top of the cup. The North Star lies on this line. The distance between the North Star and the top of the cup is about five times the distance between the two pointer stars. True north lies on the earth's horizon beneath the North Star. An effective way to mark this direction is to use sighting sticks. To do this, place a stick about 2 feet (60 cm) long into the ground. Now take a shorter stick and place it in the ground at a position that will allow you to see the North Star when sighting over the tips of both sticks. A line drawn between the two sticks is a true north–south line.

Shadow Stick

The shadow stick uses the sun to create an east–west line on the ground (see figure 7.1). This method is reasonably accurate and probably the easiest method to use. Begin by finding a thin straight stick about 1 foot (30 cm) long. Find a flat, level area and place the stick into the ground so that it is upright and perpendicular to the ground. Then find another thin stick shorter than the first one and place it in the ground at the end of the shadow created by the first stick. As the earth continues to move around the sun, the end of the shadow created by the tall stick will change position. Wait at least 30 minutes and place another short stick at the end of the new position of the shadow. Then draw a line between the two small sticks. This line runs east to west (or vice versa). The more time that you allow to pass from placing the first marker to the placing the second, the more accurate the direction will be. You can also use this method with the moon.

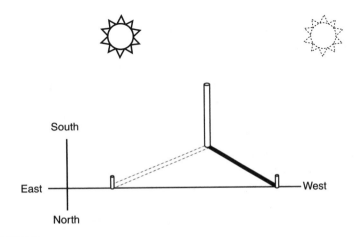

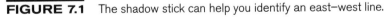

FIGURE 7.1 The shadow stick can help you identify an east–west line.

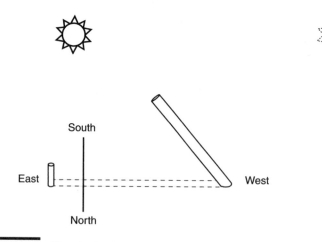

FIGURE 7.2 The shadowless stick provides an indicator for east.

Shadowless Stick

The shadowless stick, illustrated in figure 7.2, uses the same principle as the shadow stick but is more accurate. Again, find a thin stick 1 foot (30 cm) or less in length. On a flat area, push the stick into the ground and point it directly into the sun so that it creates no shadow. Wait until the shadow created by the stick is about 6 inches (15 cm) long. This shadow will be pointing east from the stick. This method also works at night with the moon.

Topographic Maps

Topographic maps represent three-dimensional details on a two-dimensional surface. In other words, they describe the shape of the land by illustrating mountains, valleys, canyons, and flatlands. They also show features like wooded areas, lakes, rivers, streams, and buildings, and they indicate the distance and direction between any two points. When you interpret and apply the language of these two-dimensional maps correctly, you can accurately navigate in the three-dimensional world.

One of the most important features of a topographic map is contour lines, which show how the elevation of the land rises and falls. Contour lines are usually designated by brown (but may be other colors) lines of varying widths that follow the ground surface at a consistent elevation. Each contour line represents a different elevation, so contour lines never cross. Wider lines, known as index contours, are marked with elevations in meters or feet. Narrower lines, known as intermediate contours, help describe the landscape further. The spacing of contour

Direction-Finding Facts and Fiction

A wide array of myths exist about how to find your way in the wilderness. Although some of these suggestions may have some truth in them, others will only lead you to further confusion. Let us examine a few of the common myths:

- *Moss always grows on the north sides of trees.* Hardly. Moss can grow on the north side as well as any other. If you believe this myth, you could be going in circles for days.

- *Observe the direction that geese fly (north in spring and south in the fall).* Movement of geese varies by location. If they have adequate habitat they may not go anywhere or they may fly in various directions. Some birds do head north in spring, but this is not a reliable indication of direction.

- *The sun always rises in the east and sets in the west.* This indicator provides only a general idea of east and west. The further north (or south) you travel and the more the date differs from the spring or fall equinox, the more unreliable this method becomes because of the arc of the sun in relation to the earth.

- *Follow a river or stream downhill to reach civilization.* You should stay where you are, follow the steps presented in the book, and wait to be rescued. This approach will get you home more quickly than any other.

lines reveals whether the topography of an area is steep or gradual. Contour lines that are far apart represent flat or gently sloping terrain, whereas closely spaced lines show steep slopes. The contour interval, the difference in elevation from one contour line to the next, is set by mapmakers to show most effectively whatever landscape is shown on a particular map. For example, the interval could be 10 feet (3.048 m) or 100 feet (30.48 m). The interval is typically printed in the margin at the bottom of the map.

Natural and manmade features are represented by symbols, which are indicated in the map key. Many maps contain a basic map key printed in the bottom margin. Some symbols printed on the map may not be included in the key, so before you go into the field, you should study any maps that you intend to use. Several features are common to most maps. Wooded areas are shown in green; waterways, such as lakes, streams, and rivers, are blue; seasonal watercourses are shown as a blue intermittent line; and buildings usually appear as black squares or outlines. Roads are usually shown in red or black solid or dashed lines and vary by the road size and surface; trails are usually shown as dashed black lines.

Maps are printed to a specific scale, but not all maps have the same scale. Usually, the scale information and a graphic scale bar are printed in the bottom margin of the map. The scale of the map indicates the direct relationship, or ratio, between a unit of measurement on the map and the actual distance that the unit of measurement represents on the ground (in feet, miles, or kilometers). For example, if 1 inch on the map represents 1 mile (or 63,360 in.) on the ground, the scale is 1:63,360. The ratio would be the same in metric terms, and 1 centimeter would represent 636 meters. Maps are printed in a variety of scales, so pay close attention to the scale of the map that you are working with. The graphic scale bar on a map provides an easy way to measure distance. One way to estimate distances on a map is to lay a thin piece of string on the map to create a route. You can then compare the length of string to the scale bar to see how far the distance is.

The most common topographic maps in use for the United States are available from the United States Geological Survey (USGS). The 7.5- and 15-minute series quadrangle maps are the most valuable for backcountry travel. The names come from the fact that the areas shown on these maps are measured in latitude and longitude. Latitude and longitude are measured in degrees, which can be subdivided into minutes and seconds; 1 degree equals 60 minutes and 1 minute equals 60 seconds. One minute of latitude or longitude is about 1.15 miles (1.85 km). The 7.5-minute maps show an area 7.5 minutes in latitude by 7.5 minutes in longitude. Likewise, the 15-minute maps show an area 15 minutes in latitude by 15 minutes in longitude. Maps at this scale show enough detail at a large scale to be extremely usable. Generally, a 7.5-minute map is printed at a scale of 1:24,000. This means that 1 inch on the map represents 2,000 feet on the ground (1 centimeter represents 240 meters). A 15-minute map is generally printed at a scale of 1:62,500, which means that 1 inch represents about 1 mile (1 centimeter represents 625 meters).

Compass

The best type of compass to use with a map has a transparent base plate with a straight edge on both sides (see figure 7.3). The edge of the base pate indicates the direction of travel. Some base plates have

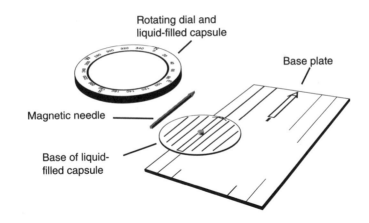

Rotating dial and
liquid-filled capsule

Base plate

Magnetic needle

Base of liquid-
filled capsule

FIGURE 7.3   The parts of a base plate style compass.

printed lines parallel to the edges with arrows indicating the direction of travel. The magnetic needle, usually red on the end indicating north and white or black on the end indicating south, is mounted in a circular liquid-filled housing. The liquid dampens vibration and increases accuracy and legibility. This housing rotates on the base plate and is surrounded by a dial marked with the cardinal directions and the degrees around the circle. An indicator or arrow is on the front of this dial and centered on the base plate. You read or set the bearing at this point. The rotating housing containing the magnetic needle also has a transparent base that is imprinted with the outline (usually in red) of an arrow.

You orient a compass either by rotating the housing on the base plate until the outline of the arrow on the bottom of the housing lines up with the north end of the magnetic needle or by holding the compass

Metal Magnetism

The presence of iron and steel can significantly affect the accuracy of compass readings. Avoid using a compass near items that contain metal, such as watches, jewelry, knives, belt buckles, cameras, GPS units, radios or any electronic devices, electrical power lines, or vehicles. These items contain various amounts of metals, and some of them, especially devices that transmit and receive radio signals or carry electrical current, create electromagnetic fields of their own, attracting the magnetized needle of a compass.

at waist height and level in front of you and rotating your body until the outline in the bottom of the housing is aligned with the north end of the magnetic needle. Although the principles for using any base plate style compass are the same, you should become familiar with the specific compass that you have and read the instructions provided by the manufacturer because models vary. Optional features may include a declination adjustment, a clinometer for measuring the steepness of slopes, or a sighting mirror.

Understanding Magnetic Declination

When you read north on a compass, you are really reading the direction of the magnetic field that points toward the magnetic north pole, which is about 800 miles (1,300 km) away from true geographic north. The powerful geomagnetic field that lies under the earth's surface is generally aligned to north and south but does not run in a straight line from pole to pole. This magnetic field varies in a complex way over the surface of the earth and changes slowly over time. So your compass almost never points to true north.

The difference between true north and magnetic north is called declination. To be accurate in your navigation with a map and compass, you must factor declination into your bearings (see page 135). If you neglect to do this, you could miss your intended target by several miles or kilometers. A diagram at the bottom of maps shows the difference between magnetic north and true north (see figure 7.4). Magnetic north is indicated by MN, and true north is indicated by a star symbol. If the

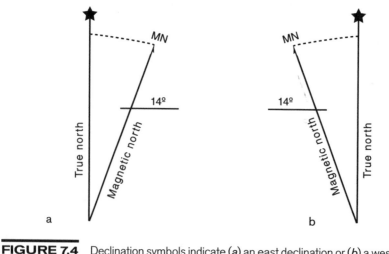

FIGURE 7.4 Declination symbols indicate (*a*) an east declination or (*b*) a west declination.

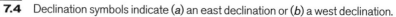

symbol for MN is located to the right of true north on the diagram, an east declination is present. In other words, the magnetic fields of the earth at the particular location that the map describes will cause the magnetized needle on a compass to pull beyond true north toward the east. If the symbol for MN is located to the left of true north on the diagram, a west declination is present. The declination diagram printed on the map is only a representation. Always use the number values rather than the printed directional lines when adjusting for declination.

The magnetic declination that appears on maps is computed when the map is made, so the declination factor provided may not be correct unless it is recent. To obtain current magnetic declination information for any place in the world, go to www.magnetic-declination.com or to the National Geophysical Data Center (NGDC) of the National Oceanic and Atmospheric Administration (NOAA) at www.ngdc.noaa.gov.

Using a Map and Compass

To find the direction or bearing between two unseen points, you need to use a map and compass in combination. Learning to use a map with a compass allows you to plot a course to a particular location without seeing the destination. A compass can also help you locate your position on a map. To do this efficiently and accurately, follow these steps:

1. **Set the declination.** Some compasses have an additional ring or plate on the bottom of the base plate that allows the user to set the declination correction. If your compass has this feature, make sure that you understand how to use it. On this type of compass, you make the declination adjustment by rotating the main housing against the adjustment ring until you reach the desired setting. After setting the adjustment, you can hold it in an offset position (usually by turning an adjustment screw on the back of the compass) until you move to a different setting. You then use the compass normally. It needs no further corrections or calculations as long as you are navigating in the same general area.

   If your compass does not have a declination adjustment feature, or you choose not to use it, you can compensate for declination using the following method. Turn the dial of the compass to 0 degrees. In other words, you should line up the 0 mark on the rotating dial with the bearing indicator located at the front of the dial on the base plate. If the declination grid on the map indicates an east declination, then subtract the indicated number of degrees from 0 and turn the dial to that number. If a west declination is present, add that number to 0 and turn the dial to that number. The following examples provide additional explanation (see figure 7.5):

- You are using a map that indicates 14 degrees of east declination. You first set the compass dial at 0 and then subtract 14 degrees. Set your dial at 346 degrees (figure 7.5*a*).

- You are using a map that indicates 14 degrees of west declination. You first set the compass dial at 0 and then add 14 degrees. Set your dial at 14 degrees (figure 7.5*b*).

- You are using a compass with adjustable declination. After making the adjustment, set the compass dial to 0 degrees.

2. **Orient the map.** Orient the map to true north by first placing it on a flat and level surface. North is always at the top of the map unless otherwise indicated. Now place the compass on the map, and align one side of the base plate with true north on the map (see figure 7.6*a*). If you are using a USGS map, true north will be aligned with the printed edges of the map, not the cut edge of the map. Some maps may not be printed this way, so always check your map and align the edge of the base plate with true north as indicated on the map. Now rotate the map until the north end of the magnetic needle on the compass is directly over the outlined arrow on the housing of the compass (see figure 7.6*b*). The map is now oriented to true north.

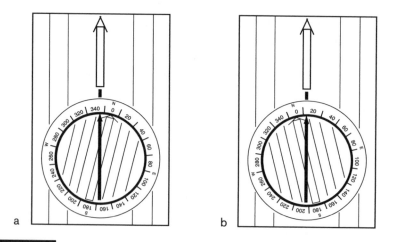

a   b

FIGURE 7.5 To set the declination, subtract the amount of east declination and add the amount of west declination indicated by the magnetic declination symbol on the map.

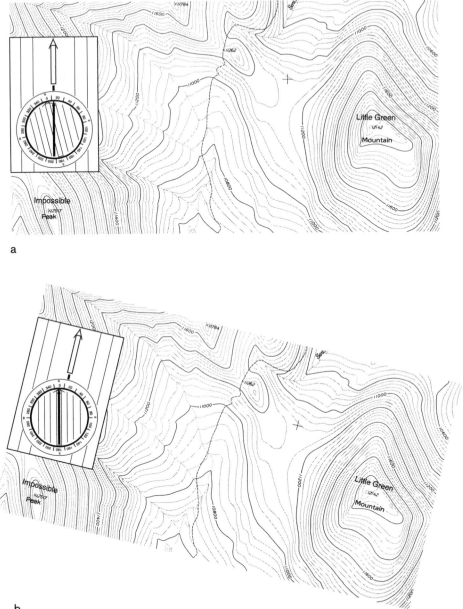

a

b

FIGURE 7.6 To orient the map, (a) align the compass base plate with true north and then (b) rotate the map until the magnetic arrow is on 0 degrees.

3. **Determine the correct bearing.** With the map oriented to true north, place your compass on the map with one edge of the base plate connecting where you are or where you want to begin with your target destination. If the distance between these points is further apart than the length of the edge of your compass's base plate, use a straight edge to draw a line between the two points. You can then align your compass' base plate edge with the line. Leaving the compass aligned with this line, you can set the compass bearing by turning the compass housing until the outlined arrow on the housing is positioned directly under the north end of the magnetic needle (see figure 7.7). The number on the dial that is lined up with the bearing indicator on the base plate is the bearing to your destination.

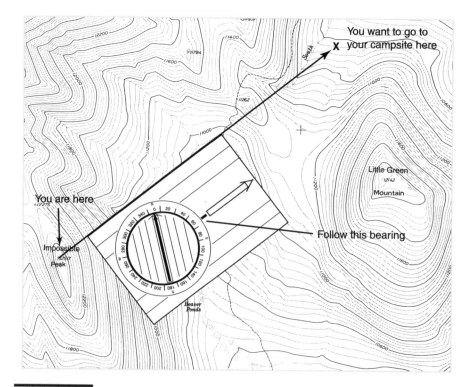

FIGURE 7.7 To find the bearing to your destination, place the compass on a line from your current location to your destination and turn the dial until the arrow on the housing is aligned under the magnetic arrow.

4. **Follow the bearing to your destination.** Remove the compass from the map and hold it at waist height and level in front of you with the direction-of-travel arrow or edge of the base plate pointing straight ahead. Turn your body until the north end of the magnetic needle is directly over the outlined arrow on the housing of the compass. The direction-of-travel arrow now points to your destination. Look up, sight on a landmark and walk to it. Continue to repeat this process until you reach your destination.

Taking a Field Bearing

Taking a field bearing allows you to use a landmark as a reference to follow, even if you lose sight of it. If you are using field bearings without a map, you do not need to correct for declination. To take a field bearing, turn the dial of the compass to 0 degrees and hold the compass level at waist height and point the direction-of-travel arrow at a landmark. Now turn the compass housing until the outlined arrow on the housing is directly under the north end of the magnetic needle (see figure 7.8). The bearing will be indicated by the number on the dial that is lined up with the bearing indicator on the base plate. You can now follow the bearing or transfer the information to the map to find your location.

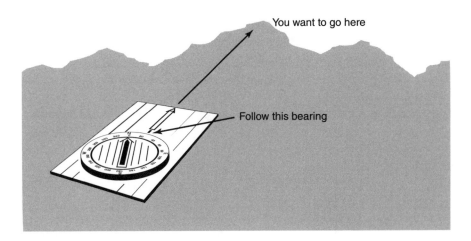

You want to go here

Follow this bearing

FIGURE 7.8 Taking a field bearing to a location in the field.

Finding Your Location on a Map

Taking field bearings from recognizable landmarks enables you to locate your position on a map. To do this, you must first orient the map to true north as described earlier. Using a compass to take a bearing in the field is helpful if you need to verify that you are where you are supposed to be or if you are not sure of your exact location. You then draw these bearings on the map from the specified landmarks, and the intersection of the lines indicates your location on the map (see figure 7.9). The landmarks you choose for reference should be recognizable on the map and more than 30 degrees apart if possible.

Here is how to find or verify your location. Lay your map on a flat area and orient it to true north. Now begin taking field bearings of the landmarks that you have chosen. After taking each field bearing, keep the dial set to the same bearing that you obtained in the field and place the compass on the map with one of the upper corners of the base plate on the corresponding landmark. Now keep the upper corner on

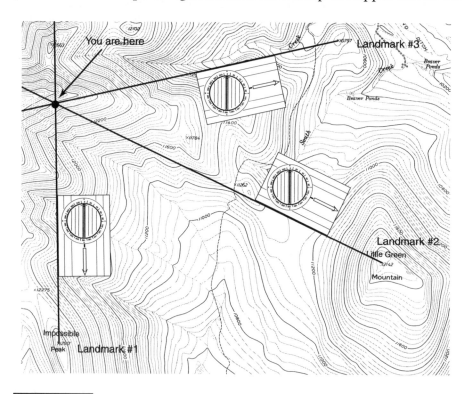

FIGURE 7.9 Find your location on a map by taking the bearing of three landmarks, transferring them to your map, and finding the intersection of lines from each of the landmarks.

the same point of the map and rotate the base plate until the outlined arrow on the housing is directly under the north end of the magnetic needle. Draw a line on the map down the edge of the base plate from the point where the corner of the compass touches the landmark on the map. Use a straight edge to extend the line if necessary. Follow this same process for the other landmarks. Your location is where the drawn lines cross on the map.

Global Positioning System

The global positioning system (GPS) is a satellite-based navigation system made up of a network of 24 satellites about 12,000 miles (19,000 km) above the earth. Each satellite weighs approximately 2,000 pounds (900 kg), measures 17 feet (5.2 m) across with the solar panels extended, and travels at a speed of roughly 7,000 miles (11,000 km) per hour. Placed into orbit by the U.S. Department of Defense, the official name of the system is NAVSTAR. GPS was originally intended for military applications, but in the 1980s the government made the system available for civilian use. GPS works in any weather, anywhere in the world, 24 hours a day.

The GPS satellites circle the earth twice per day in precise orbits and transmit signal information to earth. GPS receivers take this information and use a mathematical principle called trilateration to calculate the user's exact location. Essentially, the GPS receiver compares the time that a signal was transmitted by a satellite with the time that it was received. The time difference tells the GPS receiver how far away the satellite is. With distance measurements from several satellites, the receiver can determine the user's position and display it on the unit's electronic map.

A GPS receiver must be locked onto the signal of at least three satellites to calculate a two-dimensional position (latitude and longitude) and track movement. With four or more satellites in view, the receiver can determine the user's three-dimensional position (latitude, longitude, and altitude). When the user's position has been determined, other information can be calculated, such as speed, bearing, track, trip distance, distance to destination, sunrise and sunset times, and more.

Although the system of trilateration is generally dependable, certain factors can degrade the GPS signal and affect the accuracy of how the receiver calculates its position:

- **Atmospheric delays.** Satellite signals slow as they pass through the atmosphere, which affects the receiver's calculation of its distance from the satellites. The GPS system partially corrects for this type of error by using a built-in model that calculates an average amount of delay.

- **Signal multipath.** The GPS signal may reflect off objects such as tall buildings or large rock surfaces before it reaches the receiver. This effect increases the travel time of the signal, thereby causing errors.

- **Receiver clock errors.** A receiver's built-in clock is not as accurate as the atomic clocks onboard the GPS satellites. Therefore, slight timing errors may occur.

- **Orbital (or ephemeris) errors.** Gravitational fields and solar radiation can cause inaccuracies between the reported location of a satellite and its actual location.

- **Number of satellites visible.** The more satellites that a GPS receiver can receive, the better the accuracy is. Buildings, terrain, electronic interference, or even dense foliage can block signal reception, causing position errors or possibly no signal at all. GPS units typically will not work indoors, underwater, or underground.

- **Satellite geometry and shading.** This term refers to the position of the satellites in relation to each other and to a GPS receiver at any given time. The best satellite geometry exists when the satellites are located at wide angles from one another. Signal interference can result when GPS satellites are in a tight grouping.

- **Intentional degradation of the satellite signal.** Selective availability (SA) is an intentional degradation of the signal that was previously imposed by the U.S. Department of Defense. SA was intended to prevent military adversaries from using the highly accurate GPS signals. The government turned off SA in May 2000, which significantly improved the accuracy of civilian GPS receivers.

Newer GPS units are extremely accurate because they contain 12 parallel channel receivers, meaning that they are able to receive as many as 12 independent satellite signals simultaneously. They are quick to lock onto satellites when first turned on, and they maintain strong locks even in dense foliage or urban settings with tall buildings. Certain atmospheric factors and other sources of error can still affect the accuracy of these GPS receivers, but most are accurate to within about 15 meters.

Differential GPS (DGPS) corrects GPS signals to an average accuracy of 3 to 5 meters. The U.S. Coast Guard operates the most common DGPS correction service, which consists of a network of towers that receive GPS signals and transmit a corrected signal by beacon transmitters. To receive the corrected signal, users must have a differential beacon receiver and beacon antenna in addition to the GPS receiver. Many newer GPS receivers with wide area augmentation system (WAAS) capability can improve accuracy to within an average of 3 meters and do not require additional equipment. WAAS uses 25 ground stations spread across North America to improve the accuracy of GPS satellite signals, so it is currently effective only for GPS receivers operating in North America.

A GPS receiver is an important addition to low-tech navigational techniques, such as map and compass. GPS technology has proved accurate and reliable, and those who venture into the backcountry gain greater navigational capability by carrying a GPS receiver. But relying solely on GPS receivers for navigation is a mistake. As with all high-tech equipment, malfunctions occur. Batteries die, trauma and moisture can damage the unit, and electronic components may simply fail, rendering the devices useless. You should keep your map and compass skills sharp. Never trade these tried-and-true techniques for the false security of electronic circuitry. When all else fails, the skilled use of map and compass will keep you on track.

Signaling

WHEN others believe you to be missing, a search will soon be initiated. If you have communicated your itinerary to someone before you left, this process will begin much more quickly. One of the most profound challenges related to personal survival is making your location known to others, who may or may not be searching for you. Those who have experience with search techniques will attest to the fact that searching for a person in a remote area is like searching for a needle in the proverbial haystack. If you are the needle, you must make yourself stand out from the haystack in a unique and significant way.

Begin your signaling preparation as soon as you realize that you are in trouble. When you realize that you have been found and that rescue is imminent, be thankful. But if the search plane continues to fly by, do not allow despair to creep in. Pick yourself up and prepare again because eventually you will be successful, you will be seen, and you will be rescued.

Principles of Signaling

A few general principles are critical to obtaining successful signaling results with all signaling methods and techniques. The key to success is to appeal to as many human senses as possible when trying to attract attention. We tend to emphasize the sense of sight because searchers are looking for someone. Obviously, sight is the faculty most used in searching, but hearing and smell are also key components, so do not overlook them. The sound of purposeful noise or the smell of campfire smoke has led to the successful conclusion of more than a few search missions. Be creative with your signaling efforts and use whatever is available. Using multiple types of signaling methods will increase your chances of being noticed.

Signal in Open Areas

Search for a high, open space to use as a signaling platform. The larger the area, the more it will stand out to searchers. This principle is a hallmark of successful signaling technique, and those who need rescuing often overlook it. People often stay in the trees or on the fringes of forested areas, believing that searchers can see them. These are appropriate locations for shelters and camps, but you must perform signaling in open areas to be successful. When choosing a location for a survival camp, try to select an area that has the resources you need but also affords easy access to potential signaling areas.

Make Yourself Appear Larger

If your body is the signaling device, you should make as much of yourself as possible visible to your searchers. From overhead, the visible area of an average adult standing still is approximately 225 square inches (1,450 square cm), or 1.5 square feet. The same adult lying flat on his or her back and seen from directly above has a visible surface area of approximately 800 square inches (5,200 square cm), or 5.5 square feet, almost four times greater than when standing still.

You can also increase your visibility by creating large shapes in open spaces by purposefully arranging clothing, equipment, debris from wreckage, tree branches, or other found materials. Use geometric shapes with straight lines and sharp angles. You can also spell out HELP or SOS. Create these patterns with whatever materials are available and make them as large as possible. These designs will draw the attention of searchers because they are uncommon in a natural setting and will stand out as human made.

Use Contrast

One way to use contrast is to wear bright-colored clothing or any clothing you have that contrasts with the surrounding environment. If you are creating signals from shapes, make sure to use materials that contrast with the ground and other surroundings. Use bright-colored clothing and equipment, tree branches, logs, evergreen boughs, or rocks. Make the shapes large enough to be seen by people in passing aircraft.

If nothing else is available, you can use a stick or heel of a boot to scrape shapes or letters into the surface of the ground. In snowy conditions, you can make patterns and shapes simply by walking repeatedly over the snow until you compress it. Impressions created in this manner are more visible from above early and late in the day when the sun is closer to the horizon, creating shadows on the surface of the ground or snow.

Use Motion

Adding motion to a visible signal greatly increases the likelihood that it will be recognized and discriminated from its surroundings. For example, if you lie on the ground to make yourself appear bigger, do not lie still. Instead, move your arms back and forth vigorously. If you happen to be standing, then you should run back and forth or around in circles while waving your arms. Grab a piece of clothing or other fabric in each hand and wave them as you run. You can also construct a flag to create motion (see the section "Flags" on page 150 for more details). This is no time for shyness or quiet behavior; your movements may save your life.

Use Sound

Adding sound to the signaling mix further increases the chances that searchers or others will recognize your efforts. Three of anything is recognized as a distress signal. A sound made three consecutive times followed by a pause and then repeated indicates a distress signal. You can create noises using a variety of techniques. Banging together metal objects such as pots and pans; striking a stick on a log or rock; using gunshots, whistle blasts, vehicle horns; or shouting can be effective in drawing others to your location.

Low-Tech Signaling Methods

You do not need sophisticated or expensive equipment to produce effective signals. Smoke and fire, improvised flags, the chirp of a whistle, or the glint of sunlight from a shiny surface can attract the attention needed to end your survival emergency.

Fire

Signal fires are an effective method for attracting attention at night. Three fires in a row or three fires placed in a triangular pattern are an emergency signal. As with all signaling, build the fires in an open area. When deciding when and how to use fire for signaling, consider all options and take a conservative approach. For example, if you were to torch a remote cabin or an abandoned ranger station, you would create an outstanding signal fire. The original fire or subsequent forest fire would likely draw the intended attention, and if you escape the fire that you created, searchers would probably find you. Such a scenario, however, could endanger you or others, causing injury or loss of life. Your camp and what few resources you have could be destroyed, making your situation even worse.

You should consider the following factors before you light a fire: What is the present fire danger? Are you likely to put yourself and others at risk by building a large fire in this particular place and time? What are your fuel resources? If your signal fires produce no results, will you still have fuel for your survival needs? Are other options available? If you decide that signal fire is your best option, take precautions to prevent the fires from spreading to unwanted areas. Remove any flammable ground material away from the fire area by a distance of 2 to 3 feet (60 to 90 cm) and make sure that no flammable materials are overhead. In high wind, keep your fire small or better yet wait for the wind to die down. After you start the fire, never leave it unattended.

Smoke

Needless to say, the idea of using smoke for signaling has been around for a long while. Smoke is an effective daytime signaling method because it combines the principles of large visible size, contrast, and motion into a single technique that is easy to use. The key to this method is to build a large fire and then add fuel that causes the fire to emit a large quantity of smoke. Smoke-generating fuels include green leafy branches, live wood, evergreen boughs, live grasses, any living plant material, rubber from tires, slow-burning petroleum products like engine oil or grease, plastics, insulating material, synthetic fabrics from vehicle and aircraft interiors, and wiring wrapped with synthetic insulation.

Creating several smoke fires can increase the effect. Multiple fires need not be separated by a specific distance because their purpose is only to generate a greater volume of smoke. As with any signaling attempt, smoke fires should be placed in an open area if possible. As with signaling fires, be sure to follow appropriate precautions. Avoid breathing the smoke from fires when using toxic materials as fuels.

Mirrors

Reflective signals are an extremely effective daytime signaling method that people have used successfully for hundreds of years. Any reflective surface, including polished metal, glass, mirrors, headlight reflectors, flashlight reflectors, and certain types of natural stone, can be used to attract attention. You can improvise a signaling reflector by polishing any metallic object with sand or mud. Potential objects include soda cans, canteens, food cans, mess kits, vehicle and aircraft parts, and belt buckles.

To use reflective material or regular mirrors, follow these steps:

1. Hold the reflector in one hand and reflect sunlight onto your other outstretched hand. This will be your sighting hand.
2. Spread your thumb apart from the fingers on the sighting hand.
3. Aim the reflected light between the thumb and fingers on the sighting hand.
4. Then manipulate the mirror while moving the sighting hand to aid in aiming the reflected light at the target.

Many mirrors made specifically for signaling have a sight built into the center of the mirror. These mirrors are easier to use and more accurate. The translucent sight or grid picks up the image of the reflection created by the sun and allows the user to see exactly where the reflected sun is being projected. The two most common sizes for signal mirrors are 2 by 3 inches (5 by 7.5 cm) and 3 inches by 5 inches (7.5 by 12.5 cm). They can be found at outdoor and camping stores and usually range in price from $10 to $15 depending on size.

Signal mirrors are made from a variety of materials, including glass, metal, and Lexan (polycarbonate resin thermoplastic). Glass is the most reflective of these materials. Signal mirrors made from glass are composed of several layers of thick material. They are more durable than typical window glass but can break if mishandled. Mirrors made with polycarbonates are lightweight and extremely durable. They are slightly less reflective than glass and scratch more easily. Metal mirrors are unbreakable but are the least reflective surface of the three materials. To protect the reflective surface of a signal mirror, store it in a soft pouch or apply masking tape, which can be removed for use.

To use a sighting mirror, follow these steps:

1. Reflect sunlight onto a nearby surface.

2. Keep the reflection from the mirror in the same spot, while slowly raising the mirror up to eye level. Now look through the sight and you will see a bright spot of light on the sighting grid. This spot indicates where the refection of the sun is being directed.

3. Hold the mirror near the eye and manipulate the mirror so that the bright spot in the site is aimed at the intended target.

If you do not have a specific target, such as an aircraft or road, available when signaling, you can slowly sweep the horizon back and forth. On clear days, mirror flashes can be seen many miles away. Even on partially overcast or hazy days mirrors can produce a viable signal.

Canopy Signals

If you are stranded in a heavily wooded area where open areas are scarce, lay contrasting clothing, plastic or other materials in the tops of trees. You must place signals above the forest canopy if they are to be seen from the air. To push improvised signal panels through the canopy, climb as high as possible in a tree and use a long stick to push the material to the top of the trees.

Flags

Flags use motion and contrast to create a noticeable signal. You can create flags from clothing, tree bark or limbs, plastic, or other found materials. A roll of brightly colored plastic survey tape is a useful item to carry. You can make an effective signal flag by tying long streamers of the tape to a stick or pole. Waving this improvised flag back and forth will make you far more visible. You can attach flags to a tree or post and leave them to wave in the wind if you are disabled or are away from the signaling area.

Whistles

Loud whistles can be an effective method of attracting attention. Traditional whistles contain a pea, which is now actually made from a synthetic material. This pea can become damaged, misshapen, or frozen in place during cold conditions, causing the whistle to malfunction. Some modern rescues whistles, such as the Fox 40, use a pealess design and produce a sound of extremely high frequency and high decibel output. A good high-pitched rescue whistle can be heard through other ambient sounds, such as wind and weather noise. Three blasts of a whistle followed by a pause followed by three more blasts is recognized as an emergency signal. Good signal whistles cost less than $10 and can be found at most outdoor and camping stores.

High-Tech Signaling Methods

A variety of high-tech methods exist as aids to signaling. These include pyrotechnic devices such as signal smokes, handheld signal flares, and aerial flares of various types. Other devices employing a variety of technologies are available. These include signal strobes, laser signals, PLBs (personal locator beacons), and personal GPS tracking and notification devices. All these devices offer some advantages over low-tech methods. They can significantly increase your chance of being seen and can hasten an end to a survival experience. But they all have some disadvantages in common. They are much more expensive than low-tech equipment, more difficult to use, and require some degree of maintenance and special handling. Low batteries, severe temperature, moisture, or rough handling can compromise their performance. If you choose to include high-tech devices in your signaling arsenal, you should carry a few low-tech methods as well.

Aerial Flares

You should not use aerial flares until you are sure that someone is in the area looking for you. If you hear a low-flying aircraft in the general area, you would be well justified to fire a flare. If you can see the aircraft, you will have a better chance. Firing a flare to get the attention of a commercial airliner will probably be unsuccessful because these aircraft are usually flying at high altitudes. Be aware that although an aircraft may be searching for you, you may need to use several flares to arouse the spotter's attention, especially during daylight hours.

Several types of aerial flares are available for nonmilitary use. The most common are self-contained manually launched flares, cartridge-type flares that require a pistol-type launcher, and self-launching pen flares. Aerial flares contain a charge that propels a brilliantly colored magnesium meteor. The charge thrusts the meteor, which is immediately ignited, from the end of the flare tube or pistol barrel. The meteor continues to burn as it reaches its highest point, where it begins to arc and fall back to the ground. The average burn time of a self-contained tube flare is about six seconds. Although this is a short time, these devices can be an effective means of attracting attention because of the altitude that they reach and the bright arc that they create. The maximum altitude reached varies with the type of flare and the conditions during launch.

Prices for pyrotechnic signaling devices for land use typically range from $45 to $60 for four hand- or gun-launched aerial flares. Individual handheld flares and smokes cost from $25 to $30 each. Orion Safety Products manufactures some of the most widely available products. Boating and marine supply stores and aircraft pilot supply shops are the best source for these items. Pyrotechnic items are considered hazardous materials, so they cannot be carried during commercial air travel and shipping limitations apply as well.

To use an aerial flare, hold the flare tube or loaded flare pistol above your head, aiming straight up or slightly into the wind. When you pull the trigger or activating mechanism, the flare will launch skyward. Although aerial flares made for land-based operations are designed to burn out before they reach the ground, this may not always occur because of user error, high winds, or a multitude of other factors. These devices are great signaling tools, but they are also great accidental fire starters. Be cautious in handling and using these products. Do not launch aerial flares from a vehicle or where overhead obstructions are present. Never load a launch pistol or flare pen or expose the activation mechanism on a self-contained flare until you are ready to launch the device.

Signal Smokes

After you have drawn the searchers' attention, you can use signal smokes or handheld signal flares. Manufactured signal smokes offer an effective and safe method for daylight signaling. They use the same signaling concept as a smoky signal fire but have the advantages of compact size, lightweight design, and the ability to be deployed instantly without the need to gather fuel or light a fire. They also have the advantage of colored smoke, which offers greater visual contrast than smoke from a typical signal fire. Most signal smokes for land-based use emit orange smoke, although other colors are available. Once activated, the average device will generate smoke for 30 to 120 seconds. You should activate these types of signals only when you are certain that searchers or aircraft are in your immediate area.

Handheld Signal Flares

Handheld signal flares differ from aerial flares in that they are designed to be held in the hand while emitting a brilliant light for a short time, usually about two minutes. Most handheld flares are activated by removing a cap containing a striker, which is used to ignite the tip of the flare. You then hold the device in your hand and wave the flare slowly back and forth. You use handheld signal flares only when you are sure that rescuers are near your location. A caution is in order here: Never hold, light, or launch a flare from inside a vehicle or structure. Stand clear of any flammable materials, either beneath you or overhead. Flares can produce hot molten slag material as part of the burning process that creates the bright light. This slag can cause severe burns and start fires. Road-type emergency flares are not intended for handheld use. They are designed to be placed on a nonflammable surface and left to burn. They produce a bright light, burn longer than signal flares (10 to 15 minutes), and could alert rescuers to your location. They are worth carrying in a vehicle, but for backcountry use, devices made specifically for signaling are a better choice.

Signal Strobes

Small signal strobes are about the size of a medium-sized flashlight and are designed as a short-range visual signaling device (3 to 5 mi., or 7.5 to 12.5 km). They are easily attached to clothing, watercraft, flotation devices, and backpacks. With fresh batteries they will operate continuously for 10 to 30 hours, depending on the design and the temperature at which they are used. Most units are waterproof to a shallow depth, are compact in size, and are easy to carry. They are most effective when used in darkness, but they can be seen to a lesser degree during daylight hours. Signal strobes are available from outdoor and camping stores as well as boating and marine suppliers at prices ranging from $25 to $125.

Signal Lasers

One of the most recent developments in visual signaling technology is the creation of devices that use the piercing visible beam of a laser as a method for emergency signaling. These small handheld units differ from laser pointers in that they have a more powerful laser that projects a widespread beam. These devices are designed to be rotated in a smooth, sweeping back-and-forth motion, perhaps across a specific target. This action produces a bright, pinpoint strobe effect. The manufacturers claim visual distances of 5 to 30 miles (8 to 50 km) from small handheld units depending on time of day and atmospheric conditions. Prices at boating and marine suppliers range from $85 to $200.

Personal Locator Beacons

A personal locator beacon (PLB) is an emergency signaling device of last resort for use when all other means of self-rescue have been exhausted, when the situation is grave, and when loss of life or limb will occur without assistance. You should not activate a PLB because you are going to be a bit late returning from an outing or because you are tired and wet and want to go home. The SPOT satellite tracker (see page 155) is more appropriate for those situations. When you press the activate button on a PLB, many people become involved with your emergency. Because you cannot communicate your specific condition to rescuers through this technology, they automatically assume that your life is at risk. Resources are immediately dispatched to your aid, sometimes putting rescuers' lives at risk.

When activated, PLBs transmit a signal to an international constellation of satellites. When the signal is received, the satellites either triangulate the location of the PLB, which takes about 40 minutes or simply receive the GPS coordinates from a GPS-enabled PLB unit, which takes about 3 minutes. When the location of the PLB is acquired, it is transmitted to a ground-based monitoring station that communicates the coordinates to the appropriate rescue agency. These small, lightweight units have proved accurate and effective as personal emergency signaling devices. Prices range from $550 to $800. Several popular units made by ACR are available from some outdoor and camping stores, boating and marine suppliers, and aircraft pilot shops.

Satellite Tracking and Messaging

One of the newest high-tech signaling tools to be developed is a compact satellite tracking and messaging device called SPOT. These devices acquire GPS coordinates from a GPS receiver built into the unit. The coordinates are then transmitted through a private satellite system to a data center that stores your coordinates. When you turn on the unit, your position is transmitted every 10 minutes and stored. Depending on which annual plan you subscribe to, anyone whom you authorize can access your account and track your location at any time. The information can also be retrieved for later use. The units have the option of sending a request for help to designated friends and family or, by pressing the 911 button on the unit, sending a request for emergency help, which initiates a call to the appropriate rescue agencies. The unit is available from SPOT Satellite Personal Tracker or through outdoor and camping stores, boating and marine suppliers, and aircraft pilot shops. The price ranges from $150 to $169. A yearly subscription fee of $100 to $150 is required to activate the unit. According to the manufacturer, SPOT works around the world, including virtually all of the continental United States, Canada, Mexico, Europe, Australia; portions of South America, northern Africa, and northeastern Asia; and hundreds or thousands of miles offshore of those areas.

Injuries
and Illness

EVALUATING injuries can be overwhelming if you do not know where to begin. Learning how to read and interpret the signals from the body is important for correcting major problems. This chapter describes how to recognize and address major life-threatening injuries involving breathing, bleeding, and heart problems by using an organized problem-solving approach. An organized approach divides the task into a scene survey, a primary survey, and a secondary survey. This chapter also describes how to treat the most common injuries encountered during remote travel. Illness and injuries caused by the environmental effects of heat and cold are discussed as well. Preparation and prevention are the first line of defense against illness and injury, but accidents can occur regardless of your best efforts. You cannot always avoid injuries and illnesses, but you can learn how to recognize and treat them.

Scene Survey

Before you attempt to help another person, you need to survey the scene to protect yourself from injury. You cannot render aid to someone if you become incapacitated in the process. Before rushing into the vicinity of an injured person, you must identify and eliminate any dangers before proceeding with further assessment. When surveying the scene, use all your senses to identify potential dangers, and ask yourself the following questions before entering the scene:

- Is something present that might pose a threat to my life?
- Are environmental hazards present, such as avalanches, floods, falling rock, lightning, and so on?
- Does the area present dangers such as leaking fuel, downed electrical lines, fire, hazardous materials, unstable vehicles, a bridge that is about to collapse, and so on?
- Did dangerous wildlife such as a bear, cougar, or snake cause the person's injuries? Is the animal still present?

After dealing with the possible dangers presented by the scene, try to determine what caused the injuries to the victim. Look for both obvious and subtle signs that indicate what may have happened. Did the person fall? Did environmental factors, such as hot or cold temperatures, contribute to the condition of the injured person? Look for any evidence that could provide helpful information. The cause is called the mechanism of injury, and if you pay attention, it will guide you to the correct conclusions as you assess and treat the person.

Primary Survey

When you are sure that the scene is safe, proceed with the primary survey. The purpose of this survey is to identify life-threatening injuries, which include airway, breathing, and circulation problems, commonly referred to as the ABCs. Life-threatening airway problems occur when something obstructs or constricts these passages, preventing normal breathing function. Breathing problems occur when damage has occurred to the lungs, the respiratory center of the brain, or the parts of the nervous system that connects the lungs to the brain. Circulation problems occur when the heart does not pump normally or damage has occurred to arteries or veins through which the blood flows.

When you enter the scene of an ill or injured person, you must immediately answer four vital questions:

1. Does the person have an adequate airway?
2. Is the person breathing?
3. Does the person have sufficient circulation?
4. Is the person bleeding severely?

If the person is alert and can talk to you, then you know the answer to the first three questions. In this case, you will need to check only for severe bleeding. If bleeding is present, you need to work to stop the bleeding (see "Treating Severe Bleeding" on page 164). After you identify and stop any severe bleeding, the primary survey of an alert and responsive individual is complete. In cases when a person is less than alert or is unresponsive, you must quickly go to work to identify the cause and correct the problem.

Establishing an Airway

A human body can survive for only a few minutes without air. Recognizing and correcting airway problems is the first step in saving a life. The airways consist of the upper airway (mouth, nose, throat and trachea down to the larynx or voice box) and the lower airway (from the larynx to the bronchioles). The most common airway problems are the result of restriction caused by poor airway positioning and alignment; partial or complete obstruction caused by food or other foreign objects; or constriction resulting from the swelling of tissues in the airways caused by infection, ingestion of toxic substances, inhalation of toxic vapors, or allergic reactions. When airways are blocked or otherwise restricted, air cannot properly enter the lungs. To identify airway obstructions in an injured person, use your senses:

- **Look.** Does the chest rise and fall? Do the lips and skin appear blue, gray, or cyanotic? In cold conditions, do you see condensation as the person breathes?
- **Listen.** Do you hear breath sounds? Put your ear to the person's mouth and listen. A person who has a partially obstructed airway may have noisy gurgling breath sounds as air passes around the obstruction. A wheezing sound usually indicates that a person has constricted airways.
- **Feel.** Place your hand on the person's chest. Do you feel it rise and fall? Place your hand or face near the mouth. Can you feel warm breath?

Airway Obstructions and Restrictions

When you determine that an airway problem exists, begin treatment immediately. The basis of treatment is to assure that the airway is unrestricted, which may require repositioning the patient, and to remove any obstructions that may be preventing the free movement of air into the lungs.

1. **Open the airway.** If a victim's airway is restricted because of his or her position, gently reposition the person so that the head and neck are in line with the plane of the body. If possible, place the person on his or her back and use the head-tilt, chin-lift method to open the airway. To do this, place one hand on the forehead to tilt the head back and place the fingers of the other hand under the bony part of chin. Now gently lift upward on the chin until the line from the chin to the jaw is perpendicular to the ground. Be careful not to overextend the neck. Occasionally, this technique will totally correct the problem and the person will begin breathing normally. This result is more likely with unconscious people.

2. **Provide two rescue breaths.** If the victim is not breathing, begin rescue breathing by pinching the person's nose and making a seal over the person's mouth with yours. Use a CPR mask if available. Give the person a breath big enough to make the chest rise. Let the chest fall and then repeat the rescue breath.

3. **Reposition the airway.** If you begin rescue breathing, but cannot get air into the person's lungs, reposition the airway and try again.

4. **Perform abdominal thrusts.** If the breaths still do not go in, perform 6 to 10 abdominal thrusts. To perform the abdominal thrusts, kneel down facing the person in a straddling position with your legs on either side of the person. Position the tops of your knees below the person's waist. Make a tight fist with one hand and place the other hand on top of the fist. Place your hands just below the diaphragm in the middle of the abdomen just above the navel. With quick thrusts, push upward toward the diaphragm.

5. **Open the airway again.** Use the methods described in step 1 and remove a foreign object only if you actually see it.

6. **Attempt two rescue breaths.** If you still cannot get air into the victim, repeat steps 4 through 6. Be persistent and continue this sequence until you are successful.

Constricted Airways

Airway constriction is far different from an obstruction. Constrictions are caused by the swelling of tissues lining the airways, essentially reducing their size and making normal air exchange difficult. Constriction can be brought on by allergies, infections, diseases like asthma, and inhaling substances that irritate the tissues such as smoke or toxins. People will have difficulty breathing, and their breath sounds are usually noisy. Their skin may be cyanotic (bluish) or ashen, and they usually appear extremely anxious. Performing back blows and abdominal thrusts will not be effective.

1. **Identify the cause.** Do what you can to determine the cause of the constriction. Ask the person about a history of allergies to things such as bee stings or foods. Does the person have a history of asthma or other diseases that may affect the airway?

2. **Eliminate the cause.** If possible move the person away from cause of the problem, such as smoke, toxins, or bees.

3. **Help with medication.** Most people who have serious allergies to bee or wasp stings carry an anaphylaxis kit or epi-pen. People with a history of serious asthma usually carry medication inhalers. You can help them administer their medication if they are suffering from a severe reaction.

4. **Adjust the person's position.** A person whose airway is constricted needs more air. Place the person in a position that will make it easier to breathe. This position is usually sitting up and leaning slightly forward. Evacuate to advanced medical care if possible.

5. **Assist the person's breathing.** If a person has stopped breathing, begin rescue breathing.

Choking

Choking takes place when an obstruction suddenly occurs in a breathing person. Unless choking is recognized and quickly corrected, it will lead to cardiac arrest and death. To treat a choking victim, follow these steps:

1. **Observe the person.** Usually a person who is grasping her or his throat is choking. Ask, "Are you choking?" If they cannot cough, speak, or breathe, then they need help.

2. **Call for help.** Tell someone to call 911 if a telephone is available. If you are alone with the person, skip this step until later—fixing the choking is more important.

3. **Give five back blows.** Stand slightly behind the person. Place one arm diagonally across the person's chest for support and lean him or her forward. With the heel of your other hand, strike the person firmly between the shoulder blades.

4. **Give five abdominal thrusts.** Stand behind the person while leaning her or him slightly forward. Make a fist with one hand and place the thumb side of the fists just above the person's belly button. Grab your fist with your free hand. Use quick, upward thrusts to dislodge the object.

5. **Repeat steps 3 and 4.** Repeat back blows and abdominal thrusts until the object is forced out and the person can breathe. If the victim becomes unconscious, follow the procedure for the treatment of obstructed airways on page 160.

Performing CPR

If a person has stopped breathing, the heart will soon stop if it has not already. Cardiopulmonary resuscitation (CPR) is a procedure that can be initiated to provide temporary extension of breathing and a functioning heart.

1. **Check for breathing.** Open the person's airway using the head-tilt, chin-lift method. Put your ear to the person's open mouth and check for three to five seconds to determine whether the person is breathing: *Look* for chest movement. *Listen* for air flowing through the mouth or nose. *Feel* for air on your cheek.

2. **Provide two rescue breaths.** If the person is not breathing, perform two rescue breaths as described earlier.

3. **Provide 30 chest compressions.** Place the heel of your hand in the middle of the person's chest, on the breastbone in the center of the chest between the nipples. Put your other hand on top of the first with your fingers interlaced. Compress the chest about 1 1/2 to 2 inches (3.75 to 5 cm). To provide more volume and better blood flow, allow the chest to recoil completely before the next compression. Perform 30 compressions at a rate of 100 compressions per minute. When performing chest compressions, keep the heel of your hand in contact with the sternum at all times. You may feel pops and snaps when you first begin chest compressions—do not stop! Without CPR the victim has little chance of survival.

4. **Repeat rescue breaths.** Open the airway with head-tilt, chin-lift method again. This time, go directly to rescue breaths without checking for breathing again. Give one breath, making sure that the chest rises and falls, and then give another.

5. **Repeat steps 3 and 4.** Continue for about two minutes, which will be about four or five cycles.

6. **Recheck for breathing.** If the person is not breathing, continue chest compressions and rescue breaths. Recheck breathing every four or five cycles.

7. **Continue CPR.** You should continue performing CPR until the person begins breathing, help arrives, or you are physically unable to continue. CPR is extremely demanding physically. You should not expect to be able to continue CPR for more than about 30 minutes if you are alone. The usefulness of performing CPR for more than 30 minutes on a person with a normal core temperature is questionable at best. For people suffering from hypothermia, continue CPR until they have been rewarmed (see the section "Hypothermia" on page 181). Hypothermia slows the body's metabolism, reducing the requirement for oxygenated blood.

Alternate Types of CPR

CPR is exhausting work. If another person is available, take advantage of the help. The CPR you provide together will probably be more effective.

- **Two-person CPR.** If two or more rescuers are available, follow the guidelines described earlier, but one person should perform the compressions and the other should provide rescue breathing. Trade positions about every two minutes to avoid rescuer fatigue. A convenient way of arranging this is to place rescuers on opposite sides of the injured person. When it is time to change positions, one rescuer moves up to the head and the other moves down to the chest. Make this switch as quickly as possible to limit the interruption to less than five seconds.

- **Hands-only CPR.** Chest compressions are extremely important. If you are unable to give rescue breaths or not comfortable doing so, give the chest compressions without rescue breathing. Try to maintain a rate of 100 compressions a minute.

Treating Severe Bleeding

Significant blood loss causes shock and eventually death. Severe external bleeding must be stopped during the primary survey. Smaller lacerations and wounds can be treated later. Follow this process to stop severe bleeding:

1. **Find the wound.** If you suspect bleeding from an area, remove the clothing from around the wound. You must see exactly where the blood is coming from to stop it.

2. **Apply direct pressure.** Find the specific location where the severe bleeding is coming from and apply pressure directly on that spot. This method is better than using pressure points, and it is better and safer than applying a tourniquet. Use your hand to place sufficient pressure on the wound to stop the bleeding. If the wound continues to bleed, reposition your hand or put more pressure on the wound. If necessary, clamp the two edges of a large wound together between the fingers and the palm of the hand.

3. **Apply a pressure bandage.** After the bleeding is under control, use a pressure bandage to maintain pressure on the wound. To make a pressure bandage create a tight roll of cloth or gauze. Place it directly over the wound. Secure it by wrapping it snugly in place with cloth, gauze, or anything available. Use wide material if possible and wrap only tight enough to prevent the wound from bleeding.

Secondary Survey

When you have corrected all life-threatening problems, you have completed the primary survey and can begin the secondary survey, which consists of three parts, including the head-to-toe exam, the person's history, and vital signs. In some situations, you may never get to this point because of the seriousness of the injuries. The purpose of this survey is to collect information that will help you discover and treat injuries that may not be obvious. These injuries may be rather minor, such as bruises and abrasions, or more serious, such as spine injuries and internal bleeding. During the survey you will collect two kinds of information: what you observe with your senses and what the injured person tells you. You should record the findings of your secondary survey.

Head-to-Toe Exam

The head-to-toe exam is aptly named because you thoroughly examine the person's body from one end to the other to check for injuries that are not as obvious. Do not move the neck, head, or spine if you suspect a spinal injury! Check the following areas during the head-to-toe exam:

- Head—feel for lumps, bumps, and soft spots. Look for blood on your hands, which indicates blood from a head wound.

- Neck—look for swelling or deformity. Run your fingers gently along the cervical spine.

- Eyes—look for general injuries to the eyes. Are the pupils equal and reactive to light? You can briefly shine a beam of light from a flashlight into each eye. The pupils should quickly constrict and then dilate again when you remove the light. You can also shade the person's eyes and watch for the same reaction.

- Ears—look for blood, clear fluids, and any foreign material.

- Nose—is swelling or deformity present? Look for blood, clear fluids, and any foreign material.

- Mouth—ask the person to bite down. Is the jaw in alignment? Look for blood, broken teeth, or foreign material.

- Collarbones and shoulder blades—gently press on the bones. Do you feel grating caused by broken bones?

- Ribs and chest—gently press on the top and sides of the chest, feeling for depressions or irregularities.

- Abdomen—the abdomen should feel soft. If you feel distended or rigid areas or if the person complains of tenderness during the exam, internal bleeding may be occurring, which can cause shock (see page 167).

- Spine—by sliding your hands under the small of the person's back, you should be able to reach the entire spine without moving the person. Do you feel obvious deformities? Does the person complain of pain or tenderness when you touch a certain area?

- Pelvis—place your hands on opposite sides of the pelvis and gently press down. Do you feel grating caused by broken bones?

- Legs—feel for wounds, bruises, and deformities one leg at a time. Ask the person to wiggle the toes. Place your hands against the bottom of the feet and ask the person to push against your hands.

Now place your hands on top of the feet and ask the person to pull against your hands. Does the person's strength seem normal? Is weakness present on one side or the other?

- Arms—feel for wounds, bruises, and deformities one arm at a time. Ask the person to wiggle the fingers. Ask the person to grasp your hands with his or her hands and squeeze. Does the person's strength seem normal? Is weakness noticeable on one side or the other?

Medical History

The person's medical history is an important component of a secondary exam and can reveal vital information that will help in providing appropriate treatment. Collect the following information:

- What happened—listen to what the person tells you. Is the person complaining of pain, dizziness, nausea, a headache, or other issues? Does the person remember what happened? If not, a concussion or head injury may have occurred. Make a note of your observation of tenderness, deformities, blood, bumps, bruises, swelling, discoloration, and so on.
- Last food—when and what did the person last eat? This information may explain why the person is feeling ill. It is also important if the person requires surgery.
- Allergies—ask whether the person has allergies to medications, foods, bites, stings, and so forth.
- Medications—what prescription or nonprescription medications is the person taking? If the victim is transported for further treatment, send the medications with the person.
- Medical history—is the person being treated for any diseases or medical conditions? This information may help you understand what is going on with the person now.

Vital Signs

Take a set of vital signs as soon as possible. This first set will give you a baseline from which to measure any changes that may take place. Then take a set of vital signs every 15 minutes. The trends will give you a good idea of what is happening with the person and how his or her condition is changing. Record the measurement and the time that you take each vital sign. You should check the following:

- Pulse—take either the carotid (neck) or radial (wrist) pulse by counting the beats for 1 minute or counting for 15 seconds and multiplying by four to get a pulse rate for 1 minute. To check the pulse in either location, use the flat part of the ends of your index and middle finger and gentle pressure. The carotid pulse is located just below the jaw along the windpipe and along the throat. The radial artery is located on the thumb side of the inside of either wrist and lies just below the base of the thumb.

- Respirations—look, listen, and feel for breaths and count the number for 1 minute or count for 30 seconds and multiply by two to get a rate for 1 minute.

- Level of consciousness—use the abbreviation AVPU (alert, verbal, pain, unresponsive) to help you assess consciousness. Determine whether the person is alert (knows who and where she or he is, what happened, and so forth), verbal (answers questions but may not say much else), able to respond to pain (does not talk but reacts when pinched), or unresponsive (does not react even when pinched).

- Pupils—use the word PEARL (pupils equal and reactive to light) to help you check the eyes. Are the pupils the same size? Do they become smaller when exposed to light?

- Skin—describe the color (pale, gray, red, blue, and so forth) and temperature (warm, moist, dry, hot, and so forth).

Treatment for Common Injuries

When you complete your surveys of the injured person, you can use that information to begin treating the injuries. Always be alert for changes in the person that may indicate a worsening condition or additional injuries that you may have missed. Think ahead and try to anticipate problems before they happen.

Shock

Shock occurs when the body cannot provide adequate oxygenated blood to the vital organs. True shock is not the same as "acute stress response," which can be triggered by psychological stimuli like fear and panic and can cause people to faint or feel ill. This condition generally resolves within a few minutes. True shock is life threatening and will continue to progress, eventually causing death, if left untreated.

Expect shock to develop in all people with serious injuries. Severe internal or external bleeding, breathing and respiratory problems, heart problems, severe burns, spinal cord damage, severe infections, severe vomiting, diarrhea, severe dehydration, and reactions to stings, medications, or food can cause shock. Early treatment can help prevent shock from developing or worsening. People suffering from shock need specialized treatment, and many need surgery to repair internal injuries. Timely transport to a medical facility is a priority for people who are suffering from shock.

Early signs of shock include increased pulse rate, increased respirations, anxiousness, pale skin, and decreased urine output. Later signs of shock include a rapid weak pulse, rapid respiration, altered levels of consciousness that lead to confusion and unconsciousness, cool pale skin, and decreased urine output. Symptoms may include thirst, nausea, and feeling weak, faint, or dizzy. Internal bleeding quickly leads to shock. Symptoms for internal bleeding include significant trauma to the chest or abdomen, a bruised or rigid abdomen, blood in the urine or stools, or vomiting blood that resembles coffee grounds.

To treat shock, stop all external bleeding. Place the person in the shock position by laying the person on his or her back and elevating the legs 12 inches (30 cm). If this elevation causes pain or breathing becomes labored, lower the legs. Keep the person warm and protect the airway. People suffering from shock often become nauseated. If vomiting occurs, turn the person on her or his side and clear the airway. Reassure the person. If you suspect shock, evacuate the person as soon as possible to a medical facility. If you are in the backcountry where help is hours away, do not hesitate or waste time trying to decide what to do. If you think that the person is bleeding internally or that shock is present or may develop, go for help immediately.

Fractures

Assessment of fractures and dislocations is a straightforward process that involves evaluating the mechanism of injury along with signs and symptoms. If the forces involved in the mechanism of injury were sufficient to cause a fracture and if during the exam you find positive signs and symptoms indicating a fracture, then you treat the injury as a fracture. If the injured person is complaining of pain to a limb or joint but no mechanism of injury for a fracture is present, you should continue to look for other causes. The signs and symptoms of fractures include the inability to bear weight on or use the body part; significant pain, tenderness, and swelling; an observable deformity or angulation; or a bone protruding through the skin or visible in the wound. Additionally, people may describe hearing a crack.

Treat all suspected skeletal injuries, including fractures (broken bones), strains (stretched or torn muscles), sprains (stretched or torn ligaments), and dislocations (joints that are or were out of place), as if they are fractures until proved otherwise. The correct treatment for fractures is splinting. A properly applied splint stabilizes the bone in its normal anatomical position. The splint prevents the movement of the fractured bone ends, which left unsplinted can cause further damage to bone, blood vessels, muscle, and nerve. Considerable pain and additional bleeding and swelling will result.

Traditional methods of first aid teach that fractures should be splinted in the position found. In a backcountry situation that is hours or even days from a medical facility, this method is neither practical nor advisable. Bones and their underlying structures of muscles, connective tissue, nerves, and vessels will function better and be less painful when placed in their anatomically correct position. Gentle manipulation of the fracture is required, as described here.

- **Use traction in position.** This task is accomplished by gently grasping the proximal (closest to the center of the body) part of a limb above the fracture site and holding it in the position found. Apply steady traction to the distal (farthest from the point of attachment) part of the fracture by using your free hand to grasp the limb firmly below the fracture site and gently apply downward pressure on the limb. While maintaining this downward pressure, slowly and gently bring the limb into its normal anatomical position. Traction in position (TIP) is safe and usually relieves pain when done properly. Discontinue TIP if it causes considerable pain or if the movement of the distal part of the fracture is met by resistance. In this case splint the fracture in the position found.
- **Make the injury hands stable.** Hold the fracture in a stable position until you can apply the splint.
- **Make the injury splint stable.** Apply the splint to provide stability to the fractured bone.

Before applying a splint, check the CSM (circulation, sensation, and movement) below the fracture site. Can you feel pulses below the fracture site? Is the skin color normal below the fracture? Does the person have normal sensation below the fracture, or does it feel numb? Is the person able to wiggle fingers or toes? If the person does not have normal CSM, attempt to ascertain why. Adjust or remove tight or constrictive clothing, or reposition the injured limb.

If you are working alone, gather all the splinting materials needed and have them nearby before you begin the process. If the person is conscious, willing, and able, the person can use his or her hands as an extra aid under your direction. You can improvise splints from almost any material strong enough to serve the purpose. Some materials to consider are skis, poles, backpacks and frames, aluminum stays from frameless backpacks, snowshoes, paddles, life jackets, insulated sleeping pads, belts, boot laces, climbing rope, sticks and boughs, duct tape, compressed clothing, webbing, cargo and accessory straps, parachute cord, tent poles, cardboard, fence posts, scrap metal and wood, and bicycle pumps. The basic principles of splinting for several types of injuries follow:

Fractures of Long Bones

- Splint in the anatomically correct (or inline) position.
- Immobilize the joint above and the joint below the fracture. For example, to splint a forearm fracture, immobilize the wrist and elbow.

Fractures of Joints

- Splint in the position found or in the midrange position.
- Immobilize the bone above and the bone or bones below the fracture. For example, to splint a knee, include the femur (thighbone) and the tibia and fibula (bones in the lower leg) in the splint.
- Fractured joints are generally already in a position to be splinted. Exceptions to this include extremely deformed joint fractures or a loss of sensation or circulation below the joint. In these cases, use gentle traction to move the joint into normal anatomical midrange position.

Open Fractures

- Fractures with protruding bone ends should be gently cleansed but left uncovered before applying traction or splinting.
- Use traction in position as with other long-bone fractures. The exposed bone ends may pull below the skin surface when traction is applied. This occurrence is normal.

Splints should be snug but not so tight that they restrict circulation or cause pain. The best splints are multidimensional—splint material is applied to two or more sides of the fractured part. Use enough padding to prevent discomfort where the splint comes in contact with the fractured part. Compact or compressed padding works best. Loose fluffy padding will cause a splint to be sloppy and ineffective. Swelling near the fracture site may increase for the first 24 hours. Increased swelling can cause decreased circulation to extremities below the fracture site because the swelling causes the splint to become too tight. Check the splint often to ensure that it does not become too tight or loose. Check the CSM below the fracture frequently. If the person complains of pain, adjust the splint.

Spine Injuries

Forces great enough to cause injuries to the head, such as a fall or being hit by a falling object, can cause injuries to the spine. The neck (cervical spine) is the most vulnerable to injury. Any force causing major trauma to a person should be considered a positive mechanism for spine injury. If a mechanism for spine injury exists, be sure that your secondary survey includes a thorough exam of the complete spine, paying particular attention to tender areas, obvious deformities, and altered sensation, movement, or strength in the extremities. The general signs and symptoms of spine injury include the following: the person complains of spine pain, the spine is tender to the touch, and tingling, numbness, or weakness occurs in the extremities.

Treatment of spinal injuries in the field requires great thought and care. You must make every effort to protect the spinal cord from injury, especially if you must move the injured person during treatment. In a setting where access to advanced medical treatment is nearby, people who have a positive mechanism for spine injury should be treated for a spine injury, whether or not they have positive signs and symptoms.

In remote situations, where access may be difficult and transporting a person to a medical facility will be difficult, a more thorough assessment is required before making the decision to immobilize the person. If a person has a mechanism for spine injury in a remote setting, but no signs and symptoms indicate a spine injury, the person need not be treated for a spine injury. This judgment applies only if you consider the person reliable.

When assessing a person for a spine injury, you should have confidence that she or he is giving you candid and accurate information so that your treatment will result in the best outcome. In other words, is the person reliable? If the person is fully conscious and alert; is not under the influence of alcohol, drugs, or other substances; and is not suffering from a head injury, shock, or medical conditions that would alter consciousness, then he or she can be considered reliable. If, on the other hand, the person has a decreased level of consciousness for any of the reasons listed or you just do not feel comfortable with your own exam, then consider the person unreliable.

For example, if a woman falls 20 feet (6 m) from a cliff and lands on rocks below, you would automatically suspect, because of the mechanism of injury, that she might have a spine injury. When you examine the woman you find that she has a gash on her head, which you bandage, and some abrasions on her legs. She does not complain of pain in her neck or back, and you find no deformities or tenderness there either. She does not remember falling and keeps asking you what day it is. She says that she is OK and just wants to go home. This woman is not reliable because the fall caused a decreased level of consciousness. Because a positive mechanism of injury is present and she is not reliable, you should treat her for a spine injury, even though a problem with her spine is not obvious and she is not complaining about pain or discomfort.

The following summaries can help you assess spine injuries in a remote setting.

Reliable Person

- Positive mechanism of injury + positive signs and symptoms = spine fracture
- Positive mechanism of injury + negative signs and symptoms = no spine fracture

Unreliable Person

- Positive mechanism of injury = spine fracture

If you have determined that a person has an injured spine, send for help. If you are alone with the person, stabilize him or her first and then go for help. Spinal injuries require the same treatment as long-bone fractures do. Immobilize the joint above and below the injury to stabilize the spine and prevent further injury. For the spine, almost the entire length of the body must be immobilized—the head, neck, shoulders, and hips. As with fractures, you should stabilize a spine injury by using traction in position and making the injury hands stable and splint stable.

Because of the mechanics involved in accidents, a person can be tossed and turned and end up in an extremely twisted position. To stabilize and treat the person, you must place the person on his or her back in a normal, anatomically correct position. During this process you must make every effort to protect the spine from further injury. If you are alone and need to roll a person who is facedown onto his or her back, follow these steps:

1. Rotate the person's arms until they are lying on the ground fully extended above the head. The arms in this position will serve to stabilize the head and neck while you roll the body.

2. Kneel down beside the person's torso and use one hand and arm to hold the person's arms securely together near the head.

3. With your other hand and knees pushing toward the person, begin rolling the person over onto her or his back while continuing to stabilize the head and neck.

4. Continue this rolling motion until the person is completely on her or his back.

If you have help, perform the following steps to place a person on her or his back. The scenario is described with four people, but you can adjust it for more or fewer. The process is the same no matter what position the person is in. The person in this scenario is lying facedown in a twisted position.

1. One person takes a position behind the head of the injured person. This person automatically becomes the leader and directs the others through the process. Two people take places on either side of person's torso, and one person is at the feet. Their job at this point is to stabilize the person in the position in which you found him or her, paying particular attention to the shoulders, hips, and legs.

2. The leader places her or his hands on either side of the base of the person's head and pulls gentle traction on the head and neck area while at the same time rotating the head and neck and bringing it into alignment with the shoulders and torso.

3. The leader then directs the person at the feet to straighten the victim's legs and move them in line with the shoulders and hips. The others hold their positions and stabilize the person.

4. The injured person's hips, shoulders, head, and legs are now aligned, but the person remains facedown. On the leader's order, the group now slowly rolls the person onto his or her side in

unison (often called a log roll)The leader sets the pace by how fast she or he turns the head. The others watch and listen to the leader, taking special care to keep the shoulders and hips aligned with the head and neck. The leader calls, "Stop" when the person is on his or her side.

5. Use the same procedure to roll the person onto his or her back.

To make a spine injury hands stable, you need to maintain the proper inline position during any lifting, moving, or carrying. Continue applying gentle traction to the head and neck. To make the injury splint stable, secure the head, neck, shoulders, and hips in place, usually to a litter or full-length backboard. When these items are not available use the flat ground itself as a splint. Natural materials and items of gear and clothing can also be used to maintain a correct position. Place padding between the ground and the person, such as a thin closed-cell foam pad. Place tightly rolled clothing along the person's sides, head, and neck for stability. Keep the person warm and as comfortable as possible while waiting for help to arrive.

Wounds

Wounds occur when an object breaks or penetrates the skin, causing disruption to tissues, vessels, and nerves. Deep wounds can also cause injury to organs, bones, connective tissue, and major blood vessels. The following are the signs and symptoms of major types of wounds:

- **Shallow wounds.** These wounds are scrapes and abrasions that disturb the skin but do not reach into the soft tissue and are usually not associated with significant blood loss.

- **Lacerations.** These wounds are caused by the tearing of skin and tissue. Lacerations are usually jagged or irregular and may result in a flap of skin and flesh, or avulsion, that remains attached. They may be shallow or penetrate deep into soft tissues and other underlying structures. Lacerations can cause severe blood loss.

- **Puncture wounds.** These wounds are caused by sharp pointed objects. The entry wounds from punctures are small but may extend deep into the soft tissues. Infection is common because bacteria and other material carried by the penetrating object remain in the closed wound.

- **Amputations.** These wounds involve the loss of a body part such as a finger, leg, or foot. Amputations may cause significant blood loss.

The treatment of wounds starts by applying direct pressure to control bleeding. Apply a pressure bandage if needed. With amputations when you cannot control bleeding by direct pressure, you can use a tourniquet. Apply the tourniquet as close to the end of the stump as possible and tighten it only as much as needed to control bleeding. (If you can locate the amputated part, take it to the hospital with the victim. Surgical reattachment is sometimes possible.) When you have controlled the bleeding and the wound begins to clot, wash the wound area with soap and drinkable water, and then irrigate with plenty of water. Remove any pieces of debris, including dead skin or pieces of flesh, dirt, or any foreign material. Do not attempt to cleanse the wound until you have completely controlled bleeding.

Apply a clean dry dressing over the wound. Hold the dressing in place with a snug (but not tight) bandage. Check wounds daily and apply clean dressings. Minor swelling, redness, and drainage are normal during wound healing. Watch for signs of infection, including significant swelling, drainage of pus from the wound, increasing redness that is spreading from the wound, increasing pain, and fever. If these signs develop and persist, seek advanced medical care.

Impaled Objects

Impalement is caused by any object that penetrates the skin and remains lodged into underlying tissues or structures. Never remove an impaled object! Impaled objects may be holding pressure against damaged tissues, organs, and vessels, and their removal can cause severe bleeding and related problems. To treat impaled objects, make every attempt to stabilize the object in place for transport. In a backcountry environment, where evacuation may be slow and difficult, stabilizing the object may cause more damage or may be logistically impossible. Consider removal of the object if it prevents a safe and timely evacuation and if it is easy to remove. If you can substantially stabilize the object, you can trim it to facilitate transport of the victim. For example, if a tree branch has impaled a person, you could trim the branch with a saw to make the person easier to transport. You must take great care to prevent movement of the object from causing additional damage.

Burns

Burns to external skin and tissues as well as the body's internal system can result from contact with open flames, hot objects, gases, or certain chemicals. The depth of a burn determines it seriousness. The various types of burns and the signs and symptoms for identifying them are as follows:

- **First-degree burn.** The skin is still intact and no blisters are present. The burn appears red and painful. An example is common sunburn.
- **Second-degree burn.** The outer layer of the skin surface is damaged. Blisters are present along with redness and pain.
- **Third-degree burn.** The full depth of the skin is damaged, including blood vessels and nerves. The burn appears charred black, or ash in color, and no blisters are present. The burn may not seem painful because of nerve damage.
- **High-risk burns.** This category includes burns affecting the airway and respiratory system, burns covering more than 30 percent of the body no matter what their degree, third-degree burns covering more than 10 percent of the body, and electrical and chemical burns.

To treat burns, stop the burning by removing the heat and immediately begin cooling the area by immersing it in cool water. You can use ice or snow, but you should apply it initially for only a few minutes to avoid cold injury to the wound area. If the burn is not serious, clean, dress, and treat it just as you would a shallow wound. You should immediately evacuate people with high-risk burns to advanced medical care.

Head Injuries

Head injury refers to brain trauma caused by a significant blow to the head that disrupts the normal function of the central nervous system. The hard shell of the skull protects the brain, and it is surrounded by fluid, which serves as a liquid shock absorber. A blow to the head of sufficient force can force the brain against the inside of the skull, causing injury to the brain itself. Serious head injuries cause swelling to the brain tissues, resulting in increased intracranial pressure (ICP). Increased ICP causes loss of circulation to brain tissues and further loss of function.

The signs and symptoms of minor and severe head injuries follow. A minor head injury, or concussion, results in temporary loss of normal neurological function. Symptoms usually improve over time. To recognize severe head injuries, you need to be aware of the signs of increasing ICP.

Signs and Symptoms of Minor Head Injury (Concussion)

- A concussion causes a temporary loss of consciousness or momentary lapse of memory. A person suffering from a concussion may have no memory of the actual event.
- The injured person may feel nauseated.
- Symptoms of concussion improve over time.

Signs and Symptoms of Severe Head Injury

- The person has an altered level of consciousness that progresses downward toward U on the AVPU scale. The person may be restless and combative.
- Persistent vomiting occurs.
- The person complains of severe head pain.
- The person's pupils are unequal. This is a late sign of increasing ICP and should not be relied on exclusively without the presence of other indicators.
- Irregular breathing and seizures are other late signs.

The treatment for a minor head injury or concussion includes monitoring the person for signs of increasing ICP. If you are in a remote setting, begin making plans to evacuate the person to advanced medical care. To treat a severe head injury, provide basic life support (ABCs) and evacuate rapidly to advanced medical care.

Chest Pain and Heart Attack

A heart attack is caused by inadequate circulation to the heart muscle, usually because of blockage or constriction in a blood vessel that supplies the heart. The signs and symptoms of heart attacks follow:

- The classic symptom is crushing pain in the center of the chest, sometimes radiating to the jaw and left arm.
- A person having a heart attack may also complain of pain in the back, neck, or stomach.
- The person may have shortness of breath, sweating, nausea, or lightheadedness.
- Irregular heartbeat may or may not be present.
- The person will usually have a history of similar medical problems.

- Many people do not present with all these symptoms. Be thorough in your exam and obtain a good medical history from the person.

Chest pain can also be caused by muscle or rib pain, respiratory infections, and indigestion. After quickly evaluating and ruling out other causes, treat the person for symptoms of heart attack by providing basic life support (ABCs). Reassure the person, help the person take his or her heart medication, and evacuate rapidly to advanced medical care.

Chest Trauma

Trauma to the chest and ribs can result in a variety of injuries to the lungs, including bruising, swelling, and punctures, all of which can quickly develop into life-threatening problems. Look for the following signs and symptoms of chest trauma:

- External bruising to the chest area
- Impaled objects or visible penetrating injuries to the chest
- Labored or difficult breathing
- Blood or pulmonary edema (pink froth) produced in the lungs and visible around the mouth
- Cyanotic or bluish tint to the lips and skin
- Gurgling or noisy breath sounds caused by fluid in the lungs
- Decreased level of consciousness caused by lack of sufficient oxygen

People with serious respiratory problems cannot be treated in the field and require rapid evacuation to advanced medical care. Until you reach professional help, position the person in way that will make breathing easier, usually sitting up. Reassure the person and have the person breathe with you, taking in long, slow breaths and exhaling fully.

People with traumatic injuries to the chest should lie on the injured side to stabilize the injury and reduce pain. For open chest wounds, make an airtight seal from plastic or similar material. This temporary fix will prevent air from entering the chest cavity when the person breathes and should improve respirations. If the person's condition quickly worsens after applying the seal, remove it. If the person stops breathing, begin ventilating immediately with rescue breaths.

Environmental Illnesses and Injuries

Prolonged exposure to difficult conditions can overwhelm compensating mechanisms, causing deadly cold- and heat-related illnesses to develop. Prevention is the best treatment for environmental illnesses and injuries. One of the most important weapons in your preventative arsenal is proper clothing and the knowledge of how to use it.

Dressing With Layers

The layering system is a simple method of using individual layers of clothing to maintain an optimum level of comfort and protection from the surrounding environment. The system is extremely flexible and allows wide adjustment in response to increasing or decreasing work levels and changing weather. During cold conditions the ideal balance is to be comfortably warm without sweating. If you become too cool, add a layer. If you begin to perspire, remove a layer. All materials in the layering system should be water tolerant (i.e., should insulate even when wet). Effective natural fabrics include wool and silk. Synthetic polyester fabrics perform extremely well and are widely available in jackets vests, hats, gloves, and pants. The characteristic that these fabrics share is that they absorb only a very small percentage (less than 1 percent) of their weight in moisture and dry quickly.

The layering system consists of the three main layers:

- **Base layer.** This thin layer placed next to the skin is probably the most important layer in the system. The primary purpose of the base layer is to manage moisture by wicking or carrying perspiration away from the skin, moving it to the outer surface where it can evaporate without cooling the body. Base layer materials should be thin and lightweight and have a close but nonrestrictive fit.

- **Middle layer.** This layer provides the bulk of the insulation by trapping warmed air close to the body. Vests and jackets made of the appropriate materials are excellent for this purpose. The insulation layer can actually be made up of more than one layer depending on the temperature and activity level.

- **Shell layer.** The outer layer, or shell layer, should stop wind, rain, and snow. A proper shell garment will prevent wind and water droplets from penetrating but allow water vapor to escape. Waterproof nonbreathable fabrics are not ideal because water vapor cannot escape, but the condensation problem can be reduced by properly ventilating the garment by loosening zippers and sleeves. Waterproof breathable shells consist of a membrane or coating that is applied or laminated to a durable outer fabric. Gore-Tex is one example.

When the head and neck are left exposed, large amounts of heat are lost. An uncovered head and neck act as a chimney that funnels heat upward away from the body. Closing collars, adding an insulated cap, and covering that with a shell can dramatically reduce heat loss.

You should also use the layering system with gloves and footwear. Wearing a thin polyester glove inside an insulated glove or mitten and then placing them in a glove or mitten shell is a great combination. This setup allows you to remove your hand from the insulating layer to accomplish fine motor movements. Insulated pak-style boots include a removable water-tolerant liner inside a durable weather-resistant shell. Socks should have wicking capabilities as well. Wearing a thin polyester sock next to the skin with an insulating sock on top of that is a good combination. Tight-fitting boots or thick socks that cause constriction reduce blood flow and are the leading cause of cold injuries to the feet.

In hot and dry environments, light-colored, loose-fitting clothing helps reflect solar heat away from the body and allows sweat evaporation and air movement close to the body. A wide-brim hat or loose covering to provide shade for the head, face, and neck is also important. In humid conditions, reducing layers and the thickness of clothing will promote evaporation of perspiration. Polyester and cotton blends, polyester and wool blends, or merino wool garments offer moisture wicking capabilities with an extended evaporation time to prolong the cooling effect.

What About Cotton and Goose Down?

Cotton fabric should never be used in a cold-weather layering system. Instead of wicking moisture away, cotton absorbs it like a sponge. During cold, wet conditions, cotton kills. Goose down is extremely lightweight, compressible, and has an excellent weight-to-warmth ratio. Unfortunately, down must be kept dry to maintain its positive qualities, which makes it a poor choice in some situations.

Hypothermia

Hypothermia usually does not occur suddenly. Instead, cold wind and dampness slowly take their toll on the unsuspecting and unprepared. When hypothermia begins to take control of the body, it drives the body's temperature lower and numbs the mind while forcing critical systems to malfunction and shut down. Without intervention, hypothermia leads to a cold and silent death. Avoiding hypothermia requires a basic understanding of how external factors influence the body's internal mechanisms and how our efforts can help keep these things in balance. In a cold environment, the following factors work in combination to determine thermal balance:

- **Heat loss.** The loss of body heat to the surrounding environment occurs in several ways. The prevention of hypothermia depends in a large part how well you control this loss.

  - Radiation is the method for most heat loss. As metabolic processes of the body produce heat, it radiates from the surface of the skin.

  - Convection occurs when the movement of air carries heat away from the body. Wind chill factor is a way of describing heat loss by convection (see figure 9.1). Immersion in cold water causes convection to occur at a much greater rate.

Calm	Temperature (°F)																	
Wind (mph)	40	35	30	25	20	15	10	5	0	-5	-10	-15	-20	-25	-30	-35	-40	-45
5	36	31	25	19	13	7	1	-5	-11	-16	-22	-28	-34	-40	-46	-52	-57	-63
10	34	27	21	15	9	3	-4	-10	-16	-22	-28	-35	-41	-47	-53	-59	-66	-72
15	32	25	19	13	6	0	-7	-13	-19	-26	-32	-39	-45	-51	-58	-64	-71	-77
20	30	24	17	11	4	-2	-9	-15	-22	-29	-35	-42	-48	-55	-61	-68	-74	-81
25	29	23	16	9	3	-4	-11	-17	-24	-31	-37	-44	-51	-58	-64	-71	-78	-84
30	28	22	15	8	1	-5	-12	-19	-26	-33	-39	-46	-53	-60	-67	-73	-80	-87
35	28	21	14	7	0	-7	-14	-21	-27	-34	-41	-48	-55	-62	-69	-76	-82	-89
40	27	20	13	6	-1	-8	-15	-22	-29	-36	-43	-50	-57	-64	-71	-78	-84	-91
45	26	19	12	5	-2	-9	-16	-23	-30	-37	-44	-51	-58	-65	-72	-79	-86	-93
50	26	19	12	4	-3	-10	-17	-24	-31	-38	-45	-52	-60	-67	-74	-81	-88	-95
55	25	18	11	4	-3	-11	-18	-25	-32	-39	-46	-54	-61	-68	-75	-82	-89	-97
60	25	17	10	3	-4	-11	-19	-26	-33	-40	-48	-55	-62	-69	-76	-84	-91	-98
Frostbite times in minutes					30			10					5					

FIGURE 9.1 Wind chill index.

Adapted from National Weather Service, 2001, NWS windchill chart. [Online]. Available: http://www.weather.gov/om/windchill/index.shtml [April 29, 2009].

- Conduction is the direct transfer of heat from one object to another. When the body comes in contact with a material that has a lower temperature, heat is lost through conduction. Sitting or lying on uninsulated ground can cause significant heat loss. Immersion in cold water causes extremely rapid heat loss.

- Evaporation is the process through which liquid changes to a gas. The evaporation of perspiration and moisture from the skin is an efficient way of keeping the core temperature normal during periods of heat stress, but evaporation of perspiration can be dangerous during cold conditions.

- **Heat production.** Exercise produces heat through the burning of calories. Factors that affect this process are the amount of calories already stored in muscles and organs, the kind and amount of calories eaten as fuel is expended, how well the body is hydrated, and the level of exercise being performed. Not all calories are the same. Simple sugars are like tinder and kindling. They are quick to start burning, but they burn for only a short time. Complex carbohydrates are like sticks that are slower to burn than simple sugars but last longer. Fat and protein are like logs that provide steady energy over several hours.

- **Heat retention.** Body size and shape and individual metabolism affect heat retention. Body fat has no actual insulation value, but it contains less blood supply than muscle and, therefore, loses less heat to the environment than muscle does. Beyond these natural factors, the only way to increase the retention of body heat is to add layers of clothing.

- **Cold challenge.** When the cold challenge overcomes the body's ability to produce and retain heat, the body is no longer thermally balanced and its core temperature begins to fall. Factors that affect the extent of the cold challenge include temperature, wind, humidity, and precipitation.

- **Cold response.** When the body is exposed to cold, blood is shunted by vasoconstriction (blood vessels becoming smaller in diameter) from the shell to the core. This mechanism, called the shell core response, keeps the blood deeper in the core to protect the vital organs and causes decreased function in the extremities. More fluid in the core results in an increase in urine production. This loss of fluid is important to consider when treating hypothermia, because it must be replaced to rewarm the body.

Hypothermia can be classified as mild or severe. You must be able to differentiate between the two levels because the treatment is different for each.

Mild Hypothermia

The clinical definition of mild hypothermia is a core temperature between 90 and 95 degrees Fahrenheit (between 32.2 and 35 degrees Celsius), but accurate measurement is not practical in the field. Therefore, look for the following signs and symptoms to determine whether someone has mild hypothermia:

- Shivering increasing to uncontrollable shivering as core temperature falls
- Increased urine production
- Abnormal level of consciousness
- Apathy
- Impaired judgment
- Slowed reflexes and loss of coordination and slurred speech
- Moody and irritable disposition

If you observe any of these signs, begin immediate treatment for mild hypothermia. Quick and aggressive field rewarming is the key to successful treatment of mild hypothermia. First, you need to reduce the cold challenge. Find or build shelter to block wind and precipitation, and remove wet clothing and replace it with dry clothing. You can increase the victim's heat production by encouraging the person to eat simple sugars. Then add complex carbohydrates and work up to fats and proteins. The body cannot effectively use calories from food in a dehydrated condition so give the person fluids. Use warm liquids if they are available, but if not, drinking cold water will not cause additional harm to a hypothermic person. Do not allow the person to eat snow and do not use heavily sweetened, caffeinated, or sports drinks. The concentration of electrolytes in sports drinks makes them difficult to absorb. . Exercise can be used to increase heat production.

You also need to add external heat to the victim. Huddle as a group around a person in the early stages of hypothermia to provide shelter and transfer heat by radiation and conduction. Two people can cuddle together to conserve and share body heat. Skin-to-skin contact is an efficient method of heat transfer. To do this, place the hypothermic person and a nonhypothermic rescuer in a sleeping bag. Both the victim and rescuer remove all clothes and cuddle together. The rescuer must be careful not to become hypothermic while attempting to rewarm the victim. If more than one rescuer is available, take turns warming the victim. Use radiant heat from a fire, candles, or chemical heat packets. Place heat packs on areas with concentrated blood flow near the surface of the skin, such as the neck, under the arms, and the groin. Cover heat packs in a dry sock or cloth before placing them on the skin.

Severe Hypothermia

When the core temperature falls below 90 degrees Fahrenheit (32.2 degrees Celsius), especially to 86 degrees Fahrenheit (30 degrees Celsius) or lower, the heart muscle becomes more irritable. Sudden movements or rough handling can cause an abnormal heart rhythm to occur, which can quickly lead to the loss of all cardiac activity. Shivering also stops at a core temperature below 90 degrees Fahrenheit (32.2 degrees Celsius). The following signs and symptoms indicate severe hypothermia:

- No shivering—the presence of this symptom with other symptoms is a definitive sign of severe hypothermia
- Muscular rigidity
- Pale or bluish skin
- Weak, slow, irregular, or undetectable pulse
- Undetectable respirations
- Profound confusion, memory loss, or unconsciousness

When the body has reached a level of severe hypothermia, it no longer has the ability to warm itself. Without intervention, death will occur. The victim needs a controlled rewarming procedure that can be effectively accomplished only at a medical facility. Therefore, the primary field treatment for severe hypothermia is preventing further heat loss during evacuation. In this case, do not add external heat. Rewarming should be attempted in the field only if the victim cannot be evacuated to a medical facility within a few hours. Package the victim in a weather-tight wrap during evacuation to reduce the cold challenge and prevent further heat loss. Do reduce the cold challenge by finding or building shelter and removing all wet clothing and replacing it with dry layers.

Whether you are able to evacuate a victim or must attempt field treatment, gentle handling of a victim of severe hypothermia is critical. Any exercise or sudden rewarming can have lethal consequences. Be

Hypothermia and CPR

The standard technique of chest compression has uncertain value with a cold heart and may cause ventricular fibrillation in a cold but functioning heart. Several general guidelines can help you decide what to do when assessing cardiac or respiratory activity in a hypothermic person. Check for a carotid pulse, spending plenty of time (up to two minutes). If you detect a pulse, do not initiate CPR. If you do not detect a pulse, consider all the circumstances, including your own physical condition, and use your best judgment as to whether to begin CPR. Respirations may be extremely slow and shallow. Holding an item made from glass, such as a mirror, a shiny cup, a pair of eyeglasses, or goggles near the mouth or nose will reveal condensation if a person is breathing. You should assist breathing whenever respirations are not present or appear to be inadequate, especially when dealing with a severely hypothermic person, even without a detectable pulse.

careful to avoid dropping, jostling, or in any way handling the victim in a rough manner. Do not attempt to exercise the person. Do not allow the person to walk and do not rub the extremities to promote circulation. Keep the victim lying flat during evacuation or during rewarming in the field (if evacuation is not possible).

If rapid evacuation is not possible, you must carefully initiate field treatment. This slow process may take as long as 24 hours. Add external heat using methods such as skin-to-skin conduction, heat packs, and radiant heat from fire. Apply these methods conservatively and slowly. If the person is conscious and can swallow, give food and liquid in small amounts. As the level of consciousness improves, you can give more food and liquid. Never attempt to give food or liquids to an unconscious person. Hypothermia victims are not considered dead until they are warm and dead. So never give up on a seemingly hopeless hypothermia person.

Cold Injuries

When the temperature falls below 32 degrees Fahrenheit (0 degrees Celsius), exposed tissues are at risk of freezing. Areas of the body with less circulation, such as fingers, toes, ears, nose, and face, become particularly vulnerable. Factors like the cold response, tight-fitting boots, and smoking can increase the likelihood of injury because they can all reduce circulation to the extremities. To prevent cold injuries, use an effective layering system, especially on the head, face, and extremities. Keep well hydrated and continue adding appropriate fuels to the body. Do not delay rewarming an extremity when early warning signs appear.

Frostnip

Frostnip describes early stages of ice crystal formation in tissues. Frostnip can be easily rewarmed in the field, and if it is done without delay no loss of tissue or function will occur. The early recognition of frostnip is crucial so that it can be treated before it progresses to frostbite. Frostnip is soft. It will feel stiffer than normal tissue but will still be pliable, and the skin will move over joints and tendons.

Numbness is the earliest indication of cold injury. As numbness increases, the pain and cold sensation disappear. The total loss of sensation is an indicator of early frostbite. Frostnipped areas of flesh appear white and waxy. This condition is difficult to assess on yourself, especially in areas around the cheeks, ears, and nose. During cold, windy conditions frequently place a bare hand on these areas to assess sensation. If you are in a group, buddy up and do regular visual checks for white or discolored areas.

Reduce the cold challenge by finding or building shelter and begin rewarming. Conduction is the best method to use for rewarming. Skin-to-skin heat transfer is especially effective. Be cautious with the use of radiant heat sources for rewarming. Cold skin is highly sensitive to heat and can be easily burned. Applying the correct amount of heat to an extremity that has no sensation is especially difficult. Heat packs can be used, but do not place them directly on the skin.

Rewarm your hands by placing them under your arms or in your groin area. Feet can be warmed by placing them on the bare abdomen of a rescuer and closing layers of clothing around them. Cheeks, ears, and nose can be warmed by covering these areas with a warm gloved hand.

Rewarming from any cold injury is painful. The duration and level of the pain is directly related to the severity of the injury.

Frostbite

Frostbite, indicated by solid ice crystal formation in the tissues, can cause significant loss and damage to tissues as well as considerable loss of function. Frostbite injury is classified in degrees, first through fourth. The degree of injury is difficult to determine until rewarming is complete. Frostbite is a devastating injury with long-term consequences, and you should take every precaution to prevent it. As with frostnip, the early signs of frostbite are numbness. Act quickly when you feel the first signs of numbness. Complete loss of sensation in the affected area is a sign of frostbite. The frostbitten part may feel like a wooden club. Frostbite appears solid and discolored, and ice crystals may be visible in the tissue.

The correct treatment for frostbite is controlled rewarming at a medical facility. Rewarming in the field is difficult and should be avoided if possible. Treat frostbite by reducing the cold challenge and taking precautions to prevent further freezing to the area. Frostbitten tissue may rewarm spontaneously through normal metabolic processes, but you should make no active attempt to rewarm the frostbitten area during evacuation. If frostbitten tissue does thaw, protect it from any trauma and refreezing. This means that that it can no longer be used. Do not rub the frostbitten tissue in an attempt to rewarm it. Rubbing frozen tissue with snow is especially harmful. Evacuate as quickly as possible. If you are alone, you should walk out on a frozen foot to a place where you can receive appropriate treatment.

Hyperthermia and Heat Illness

Hyperthermia develops when a combination of heat being produced within the body by exercise and external heat from the environment overwhelms the body's heat response mechanism, resulting in a core temperature above normal. The factors that influence hyperthermia include the following:

- **Heat challenge.** Factors that affect the heat challenge are temperature and humidity. Together, these are often referred to as the heat index, which represents the efficiency of evaporation. Another factor is heat produced by the metabolic processes within the body.

- **Heat response.** Heat response involves the same mechanisms that occur in cold response but in reverse. Through vasodilation (blood vessels becoming larger in diameter), blood moves from the core to the shell. This mechanism, called the core shell response, is the body's attempt to maintain normal core temperature by increasing heat loss through radiation to the outside air. In addition, the body sends moisture in the form of perspiration to the surface of the skin to improve the efficiency of the cooling process through evaporation.

In addition, dehydration plays an important role in heat illness and should be avoided at all costs. When traveling or working in hot conditions, slow down, take regular breaks in the shade, drink plenty of water, and wear a full-brim hat.

Heat Exhaustion

Heat exhaustion is caused primarily by dehydration and typically does not indicate a significant change in core temperature. Those suffering from heat exhaustion are usually weak, thirsty, and nauseated. This combination of symptoms is common and is a strong indicator of heat exhaustion. The person's respirations and heart rate increase, and vomiting may be present. Skin appearance may vary from pale to flushed and clammy to sweaty. Urine output is reduced and concentrated, and the person will have a normal level of consciousness.

Treatment is aimed at preventing further fluid losses and replenishing fluid volume to normal levels. Stop sweating by reducing exercise levels and moving into a shaded area. Remove excess clothing to allow natural cooling. Restore fluid volume with small sips of plain drinking water every few minutes. Avoid giving large amounts of water too quickly because doing so can cause vomiting. Even if vomiting is present, continue to slowly replenish fluids, which will help stop the vomiting. Do not give sweetened drinks. Sugars reduce the absorption of fluids and can cause nausea and vomiting. Electrolyte drinks are not necessary if food intake is normal. If a person has not eaten food regularly, a pinch of salt can be added to a liter of water. Avoid salt tablets because their extreme concentration of salt may irritate the stomach.

Heatstroke

Heatstroke occurs when the heat challenge overwhelms the body's heat response mechanism, causing the core to overheat to a critical level (above 105 degrees Fahrenheit, or 40.6 degrees Celsius). Heatstroke can occur without volume depletion if the heat challenge is extreme enough. Heatstroke is a true emergency that requires immediate and radical efforts to cool the body's core.

Changes in mental status and consciousness are the most reliable signs of heatstroke. Early signs include bizarre, agitated, or aggressive behavior. The victim may be disoriented and confused, and may experience hallucinations. The skin may appear flushed or pale, and hot to the touch, and sweating may or may not be present. As the condition progresses the person may exhibit lack of muscle coordination, muscle twitching, seizures, and unconsciousness.

The best chance of survival from heatstroke comes from immediate and radical cooling in the field. Use the concepts of radiation, conduction, evaporation, and convection to cool the victim quickly. Immersion in cold water is probably the most effective treatment. This method combines the principles of conduction and convection to remove heat quickly. If only limited water is available, use convection by creating artificial wind and water. Strip the person and splash or spray small amounts of water on the skin while vigorously fanning the person with items of clothing and gear. If water is not available, urine will suffice. Watch for signs of cooling and be careful not to cool the person to the point of hypothermia. When the person is able to drink, begin replenishing fluid volume with water. After field treatment has begun, evacuate the person to a medical facility as soon as possible.

Dangerous Animals and Environments

ALTHOUGH traveling through remote wilderness terrain is for the most part a safe experience, some very real dangers may be lurking. Your situation can change from tranquility to tragedy in a moment if you do not recognize and heed warning signs. You can avoid accidents and injuries from natural hazards if you know how to recognize them and then take measures to avoid them. Do not wait until you are running from a bear or up to your neck in roiling snow before you realize the importance of learning how to deal with dangerous animals and environments. Take time to read this chapter and learn before you venture into the backcountry. Digesting this information will not take long, and doing so can ensure that you will be around to enjoy many outdoor adventures.

Dangerous Animals

Animals found in their natural habitat are not inherently vicious or dangerous. Humans and animals can adequately coexist if the humans take the time to learn something about animal behavior and habitat and take the precautions necessary to avoid situations that could develop into dangerous encounters.

Bears

Two commonly known species of bear inhabit North America: the black bear and the grizzly bear. The most widespread is the black bear, which is found in most of Canada and Alaska; on the west coast of the United States from the Canadian border through California to Mexico; in the Rocky Mountain states; in northern Minnesota, Wisconsin, and Michigan; in the New England states; in New York and Pennsylvania; in the Appalachian Mountains; and in Florida and southern Louisiana. The grizzly, or brown bear, ranges from Alaska and the Yukon and Northwest Territories through most of British Columbia, western Alberta, and into the northwestern United States, including the states of Montana, Idaho, and Wyoming. The species have many physical and behavioral characteristics in common, but they also display some distinct differences that affect how they respond to people. You should be able to distinguish the species and know how to adjust your behavior to avoid a dangerous encounter.

Do not use color as a means of identification. Black bears can be black, many shades of brown, or cinnamon, and a few are even white. Grizzlies can be black, brown, blond, or anywhere in between. One of the major differences between black and grizzly bears is the grizzly's pronounced muscular shoulder hump, which a black bear lacks. A grizzly's foreclaws are also much longer and lighter in color than those of a black bear. The facial profile of a grizzly is generally concave in appearance, whereas black bears have a flatter nose profile and larger, more pointed ears. Grizzly bears are usually larger than black bears.

Evidence of bear activity includes overturned logs and rocks, rotten stumps torn apart, excavated anthills and rodent burrows, berry bushes that have been broken or torn apart, decaying pieces of prey, and trees marked with tooth and claw marks. Bear scat is usually dark brown and cylindrical and is similar to a dog's in appearance but may contain animal hair, seeds, and grasses. Bears also have a rather unpleasant odor.

Bears have an extremely keen sense of smell and hearing. They see in color, and their sight is similar to that of a human. Their acute sense of smell guides them to food sources and warns of intruders and other dangers. Bears can move extremely quickly for their size, reaching speeds of over 30 miles (48 km) per hour both uphill and downhill. They can easily outrun a human. Black bears are good tree climbers, but grizzlies generally lack this skill.

Bears are intelligent and curious. They are not malicious by nature, but they will fiercely defend their interests, like food and family. When bears identify a threat they can become defensive immediately. Their behavior is rather predictable, except when injured or sick. They generally go to great lengths to avoid humans, but when they have become habituated or accustomed to the presence of humans their behavior is less predictable and sometimes even predatory. Grizzlies are generally known to be more aggressive than black bears.

Avoiding an Encounter

Most of the unpleasant encounters between humans and bears happen for two reasons. The first occurs when a human enters a bear's space by surprise. The second occurs when bears are attracted to a camp because of food or other odors. You can avoid the first situation by making your presence known to bears from a distance, giving them time to move away from you. When moving through bear country, travel in groups and make sufficient noise such as talking or singing to alert bears to your presence. The use of bear bells or similar items can be helpful.

You can avoid the second situation by carefully using and storing food items and by preventing the presence of other smells in your camp. Never store any type of food item in your tent or sleeping bag. Store, prepare, and eat food away from camp. Seal all food items in resealable plastic bags, place them in a container, and hang it from a tree at least 10 feet (3 m) from the ground and 10 feet (3 m) from the nearest tree trunk. If trees are not available, then hang or place the food in a location inaccessible to bears. Wash your hands, face, and eating utensils thoroughly when finished with meals, store the utensils away from camp, and discard the wash water away from camp. Do not bury any trash or food but instead place it in a bear-resistant container. Do not sleep in the same clothes that you wore when preparing food.

Keeping your food out of the mouths of bears has a greater implication than you may think. A bear that becomes habituated to humans and their food is a dangerous bear because it will frequently seek out an easy meal. At the end of the story the bear is usually destroyed, and humans may experience tragic results as well. So take care to protect your food from bears. You will be safer, and so will the bears.

Besides limiting food odors, you should control other smells in your camp. Take care not to spill petroleum fuels near camp; the odor that they give off is known to attract bears. Use only unscented personal hygiene products. Store these items and any other items with an odor (such as toothpaste) away from camp. Do not urinate or defecate within 100 yards (30 m) of camp. These smells can also attract bears.

Although no evidence exists that bears are attracted to menstrual odors more than any other odor, a few precautions are recommended for menstruating women to reduce the potential risks of attack: Use premoistened, unscented cleansing cloths, use tampons instead of pads, use only unscented or lightly scented products, and do not bury tampons or pads. Double bag all used feminine products in resealable bags and store them in the same manner as food.

These additional guidelines can help you avoid bear encounters:

- Learn about the area before you go. Will you be traveling in bear country? What species are you likely to encounter?

- Wear and use neutral-colored clothing and gear because bright, flamboyant colors may attract bears, who see in color.

- Carry an approved bear spray and know how and when to use it. Bear spray is different from mace or sprays made to ward off a human attacker, so make certain that the spray you carry is made specifically as a bear deterrent. Bear spray should be accessible and available for use on a moment's notice. Do not pack it away in a backpack.

- Look, listen, and smell for signs of recent bear activity.

- Adjust your routes so that you do not travel through thick bear habitat like berry bushes or near streams where bears usually fish.

- Keep your deterrent and a flashlight near you at night.

Escaping an Encounter

If despite your efforts to avoid a bear encounter you find yourself in the presence of a bear, remain calm and assess the situation. Try to identify the bear. Is it a black or a grizzly? Are cubs or an animal kill nearby? If the bear is in the distance, retreat and find another way around the area. Never try to approach a bear, for any reason. If you have a close encounter with a bear follow these guidelines:

- Get your deterrent ready for action. If you do not have deterrent, improvise something such as sticks and rocks.

- If you are with other people, keep the group together.

- Talk to the bear in a calm voice.

- Slowly back away in the direction from which you came. Never turn your back on a bear and do not run. At this point the bear may leave.

- When a bear is in a defensive mode it may swat the ground while snorting or make a bluff charge toward you to persuade you to leave. Remain calm and nonthreatening while backing away. Continue to talk softly to the bear. Do not make any sudden or aggressive movements toward the bear.

If the bear is following you or continues to act aggressively toward you even as you are attempting to back away, take these additional steps:

- Stop and face the bear. Stand tall, appearing as large as you can. Take a step or two toward the bear. This movement may persuade it to leave.
- If the bear persists in following, act aggressively toward the bear. Shout and stamp your feet. Show the bear that you will fight back if attacked.
- Use your deterrent.

If a bear should happen to attack, the way that you react depends on whether the bear is in a defensive mode or predatory mode. Bears will fiercely defend their cubs, a fresh kill, or a food cache. Try to determine which mode the bear is in so that you know how to respond. If a bear attacks in a defensive mode, such as a mother bear that is defending her cubs, do not act aggressively but deploy your deterrent. If the bear continues the attack, drop to the ground, lie face down, and play dead. Your legs should remain slightly apart, and your hands with fingers locked should cover the back of your neck for protection. This position shows the bear that you are not a threat. Try to remain in this position, even if you become injured. If the bear rolls you over, try to continue rolling until you are face down again. When the attack is over, remain in this position until you are sure that the bear is no longer in the area.

When a bear attacks after following and stalking, it is acting in a nondefensive, or predatory, manner. If the bear makes physical contact after you have deployed deterrent, fight with everything that you have in you. Use whatever weapon you can lay your hands on—a knife, rock, or stick. Kick, punch, or hit, concentrating on the nose, eyes, and face. When a bear begins to eat you, the attack is no longer defensive. You must fight for your life.

Mountain Lions

Mountain lions, also known as cougars, pumas, panthers, and cata-mounts, are the largest species of cat that still roams parts of North

America. Although they were once found in all of the continental United States and Canada, their range has been significantly reduced as their habitat has disappeared. They now inhabit western British Columbia and southern Alberta south through California and the western states of the United States. A very small, endangered subspecies also resides on the Florida peninsula. As human development continues to encroach on their natural habitat, encounters between mountain lions and humans are on the rise and will continue to increase.

Mature mountain lions are generally uniform in color but may vary from yellowish brown to dark brown, cinnamon, or gray. The chest and belly are light gray or white, and black appears on the tip of the tail and ears. Their size and weight varies with habitat and season. Full-grown males can reach a length of 9 feet (2.7 m) including the tail, and they weigh 160 pounds (73 kg) or more. Females can measure up to 7 feet (2.1 m) in length and weigh 100 to 125 pounds (45 to 57 kg).

Mountain lions are solitary creatures and seek to avoid contact with humans and other predators. Mountain lions prefer rugged, remote terrain that is rich in game, and they travel great distances to hunt. They have keenly developed senses of smell, sight, and hearing, which help them detect intruders and prey from a great distance. They are adept climbers and are extremely stealthy when approaching prey. They have been known to jump vertical distances of 20 feet (6 m) and horizontal distances of 40 feet (12 m) in a single leap. They are extremely fast and can reach speeds of 35 miles (56 km) per hour in short bursts. The mountain lion makes varied sounds, including hisses, growls, and screams. Their mating call is especially memorable because it sounds similar to a woman screaming.

Signs of mountain lions include food caches in which a partially eaten kill has been covered with loose sticks and leaves and scratches on trees used as scratching posts. Mountain lion tracks are large, rounded, and 3 to 4 inches (7.5 to 10 cm) long. Tracks show four toes and no claw marks. Their scat may vary from masses to large segmented cylindrical droppings and pellets, usually containing hair and pieces of bone.

Avoiding an Encounter

Prepare yourself with knowledge about the area and appropriate deterrents before you go. Have sightings or encounters occurred recently in the area? A few general guidelines will help keep you safe:

- Avoid traveling alone in mountain lion country.
- Keep small children close to an adult. Alone, they appear as easy prey to a mountain lion.

- Avoid taking pets into mountain lion country. If you must take them, keep them leashed.
- Minimize activity at dawn and dusk because mountain lions are most active then.
- Carry a deterrent and keep it within reach at all times. Possible deterrents include firearms, knives, rocks, sticks, and whatever else you can find. Anecdotal evidence suggests capsaicin-based sprays (like bear sprays) may be effective.
- Look, listen, and smell signs of mountain lions.

Escaping an Encounter

Understanding the basics of mountain lion behavior will help you know how to respond to an encounter. When a mountain lion is at a distance of 50 yards or greater and appears interested in you or your group, it may only be curious. An interested mountain lion may watch you closely, change positions, and follow you. This behavior represents a low risk for adults, but it presents an increased risk for children so they should kept close to adults. When you encounter a mountain lion at a distance, follow these guidelines:

- Begin moving away from the mountain lion while keeping it in your peripheral vision.
- Do not turn your back on the animal and do not run. This action could trigger a predatory response and precipitate an attack.
- Ready your deterrent or improvise a weapon such as rocks or sticks in the event that the situation changes.
- Find another route or come back later.

When you encounter a mountain lion at a distance of less than 50 yards and the lion is hiding and intensely staring at you, it may be preparing to attack. If this behavior continues and the animal is crouching and creeping, an attack may be eminent. When you find yourself in this situation, follow these guidelines.

1. Remain calm and fight panic.
2. When you have a close encounter, slowly back away, maintaining eye contact. Eye contact shows the lion that you are aware of it.
3. Do not turn your back and do not run.
4. Talk loudly or yell at the animal.
5. Make yourself appear larger. Raise your arms over your head and make waving motions.

6. Do not bend over, which makes you look smaller and like easier prey.

7. If you are with children, pick them up without bending over. Keep eye contact with the animal while doing this.

8. Be prepared to deploy any means of deterrent that you have available.

9. If attacked, remain standing and fight for your life. Do not play dead. Use a knife, stick, rock, camera, or any weapon or object that you can find to defend yourself. Mountain lions typically attack their prey by biting the back of the neck. Take special care to protect this area of your body.

Venomous Snakes

North America is home to four types of venomous snakes—coral snakes, rattlesnakes, copperheads, and cottonmouths—and 20 sub-species. Coral snakes belong to the elapid family and are relatives of the cobra. Rattlesnakes, copperheads, and cottonmouths belong to the pit viper family. Characteristics unique to pit vipers include elliptical catlike pupils, a blunt snout, and a wide triangular-shaped head. Their most notable feature is the small heat-sensitive pits located between their eyes and nostrils that help detect warm-blooded prey.

Venomous snakebites are a serious medical emergency and require rapid evacuation to a medical facility where the proper antivenin can be administered. One of the greatest risks from a venomous snakebite is the massive tissue damage that can occur. The extent of damage is related to the type and amount of toxin injected, the location of the bite, and the length of time before receiving treatment. This last factor has the greatest effect on the long-term outcome for the victim. Not all bites from venomous snakes result in the injection of venom. Experts say that about 25 percent of bites result in a "dry bite."

Venomous snakes use their venom sparingly, primarily to acquire food. They also bite if they feel threatened but only after other attempts to fend off an intruder fail. Pit vipers defend themselves by placing their bodies in a close coil with their heads raised. From this position, they make a quick strike toward their intended target. They use their retractable and hollow daggerlike fangs to inject venom into their victims. During the strike, they open their mouths, extend their fangs, and sink them into the flesh of the target, instantly injecting venom into the tissues. The snake then recoils and readies itself for another strike. This strike sequence happens in a flash, leaving the surprised victim with a painful and dangerous bite. People occasionally receive bites from pit vipers without even seeing the snake.

Pit viper bite wounds appear as one puncture mark or two puncture marks placed close together. Pit viper envenomation causes severe pain and swelling at the bite site almost immediately. The systemic effects take much longer to appear. If a pit viper bites you and no severe pain or swelling occurs, you may not have been envenomated. In the field, accurate determination of whether venom has been injected is not possible; therefore, immediate medical treatment should be sought. Nonvenomous snakebites also need to be treated as soon as possible because of the risk of bacterial infection of the bite wound.

Coral Snakes

Three species are found in the United States. The eastern coral snake ranges from Florida north to southeastern North Carolina and west to eastern Texas and northeastern Mexico. The Texas coral snake can be found in many locations in Texas, and the Arizona coral snake ranges from central Arizona to southwest New Mexico into Sinaloa, Mexico.

Coral snakes are blunt-nosed and glossy. North American varieties can be identified by their alternating wide red, wide black, and narrow yellow or white rings, which encircle the body. On a North American coral snake, red always touches yellow or white, and the tip of the head is black to the angle of the jaw. Some nonvenomous snakes, such as some varieties of the king snake, are similar in appearance, but their rings follow a different pattern. The rhyme "Red and yellow, kill a fellow; red and black, friendly jack" (alternate versions end with "venom lack") accurately describes how to identify a North American coral snake. The average length of a coral snake is 18 to 30 inches (45 to 75 cm).

In the east, coral snakes live in wooded, sandy, and marshy areas and spend most of their lives burrowed underground. In the west, they prefer rocky areas, arroyos, and river bottoms. They are reclusive and avoid human contact, but they will bite if handled or stepped on. Unlike pit vipers, coral snakes have two tiny fixed fangs and do not strike. Instead, coral snakes need to hold on to their victims to get a good bite and inject their venom. They produce a dangerous and potent neurotoxin, which can shut down human respiratory and cardiovascular systems. The effect of their venom may not happen until as long as 12 hours after the bite occurs.

Rattlesnakes

The rattlesnake is widespread throughout the continent and is the most common snake encountered. Many species of rattlesnake are distributed throughout the United States, Mexico, and southern Canada. They can be found in almost any climate zone or terrain type across the lower 48 states of the United States, living at altitudes from sea level to as high as 11,000 feet (3,400 m).

Their color and pattern varies by species and may be dark olive, gray, blue gray, or tan. Patterns appearing on the back can be speckled, hexagonal, or diamond shaped and may contain cross-bands. All rattlesnakes have a small, segmented rattle at the end of the tail, which produces a buzzing or rattling sound when the snake is threatened. Mature rattlesnakes reach an average length of about 30 inches (75 cm), but some species such as the eastern diamondback rattlesnake may be as long as 5 feet (150 cm).

Bites from any variety of rattler are dangerous and sometimes fatal. The type and potency of venom produced by rattlesnakes vary between species. Most produce hemotoxic venom that destroys blood and tissue cells. This type of venom can cause serious, long-term tissue damage near the bite site. The Mojave rattler of the western United States and timber rattler of the Southeast are particularly dangerous because they produce a neurotoxic venom that attacks the central nervous system, causing paralysis, respiratory, and cardiac failure.

Copperheads

The copperhead snake is named for the coppery red coloration of its head. Generally, the snake is chestnut colored and has darker cross-bands that become narrower at the midline of the back. Young copperheads can be recognized by the yellow tip on their tails. Copperheads are found in northern Florida and all other states in the southeastern United States. They extend as far north as Virginia, Maryland, Washington, D.C., Pennsylvania, West Virginia, southern Indiana, and southern Illinois, and as far west as Missouri, Oklahoma, and Texas.

Mature copperheads are 24 to 50 inches (600 to 127 cm) in length and live in wooded areas, along hillsides, near rock outcroppings, and near streams, ponds, and swamps. They can be found basking in the sun during spring and fall but become nocturnal as the days grow warmer. The copperhead does not have a rattle at the end of its tail, but when cornered it will sometimes vibrate its tail, producing an audible warning as the tail makes contact with surrounding materials such as leaves and brush.

Copperheads are generally more aggressive toward intruders than rattlesnakes and cottonmouths are. They populate areas close to cities and towns and are easily provoked; consequently, they account for most venomous snakebites in the United States. Fortunately, their hemotoxic venom is less potent than that of other venomous snakes in North America. Even so, their bites are painful and can cause serious tissue damage and in some cases death.

Cottonmouth

The cottonmouth, also known as the water moccasin, is the only semi-aquatic pit viper in the world. Cottonmouths are found in the eastern United States from Virginia south through the Florida peninsula and west to Arkansas and southeastern Kansas. Growing to lengths of 3 to 4 feet (90 to 120 cm), cottonmouths are usually found in or near water, and they prefer shallow, slow-moving lakes and streams. They are proficient swimmers and have successfully colonized islands off the Atlantic and Gulf coasts. Cottonmouths have blunt snouts with broad heads that are distinct from the neck. Their bodies have a heavy build, narrowing to a slender tail. Young cottonmouths are brilliantly colored by bands with dark borders and pale centers. This pattern fades as they grow older.

Not usually aggressive, the cottonmouth is named for its unique defensive behavior. When threatened, this snake often stands its ground by coiling itself, tilting its head back, and gaping at the threat, exposing the white lining of its mouth. The venom of the cottonmouth is hemotoxic, and bites are painful. As with other snakes that produce this type of venom, bites can cause severe tissue damage at the bite area. Deaths are rare but do occur.

Avoiding an Encounter

Although snakes are predators and possess superior hunting and stalking skills, they avoid contact with humans and other large predators. Most venomous snakebites occur when people accidentally make contact with a snake or purposely attempt to handle them. By applying basic knowledge of snake behavior and using common sense, you can avoid both of these situations. The following guidelines will help you avoid problems with venomous snakes:

- Learn about the snakes that might inhabit the area in which you will be traveling.
- Be alert for signs of snakes. Listen for the audible warnings, such as the rattling or buzzing of rattlesnakes.

- Do not provoke venomous snakes. If you do not attack them, they will not attack you. They will, however, defend themselves if they feel threatened. Many snakebites occur when people handle snakes, so when you see them, leave them alone.

- Take special care around loose rocks, thick brush, caves, leaf piles, and downed logs when hiking or camping in a known snake habitat. During the summer in the heat of the day, snakes seek cool, shaded areas. Never place your hands or feet where snakes might be hiding before investigating first. If you are working or walking in an area known to have a large number of venomous snakes, consider wearing snake-proof boots, leg protectors, or snake-proof chaps.

- Be aware that snakes are nocturnal hunters and are active at night. They are especially active during spring when they emerge from hibernation in search of food.

- Know the proper treatment for snakebites and be prepared by carrying the proper medical gear.

- Stay out of striking distance. When pit vipers strike, they can extend themselves well beyond their coil. If you have inadvertently cornered a coiled pit viper, back away and stay well beyond its strike range.

Escaping an Encounter

If a venomous snake bites you or a companion, follow these steps:

1. Get to a medical treatment facility as quickly as possible. Do not wait for help to arrive. If you have a means to communicate, call for outside medical and rescue help and alert hospital staff so that they can be prepared with the appropriate equipment and medications.

2. Identify the species of snake that inflicted the bite if possible, but do not spend a lot of time trying to identify the snake. Do not put yourself in danger by trying to kill the snake.

3. Remove any rings or jewelry that might restrict blood flow when swelling occurs.

4. Wash the bite with soap and water.

5. Use a suction device within the first few minutes. A suction device designed for snakebites may provide some benefit when placed over the bite to help draw venom out of the wound.

6. Immobilize the bitten area and keep it lower than the heart. If you apply a splint, monitor swelling and make sure that the splint does not restrict blood flow in the extremity. Always check for adequate pulse and sensation above and below the splint. In general, a person should avoid using an extremity that has been bitten, but this directive should be balanced with the need for rapid transport.

7. Apply a compression bandage if you cannot reach medical care within 30 minutes. A compression bandage wrapped 2 to 4 inches (5 to 10 cm) above the bite can help slow the venom. The purpose of the bandage is to provide light compression only; it should not stop the blood flow from arteries or veins. The bandage should be loose enough that you can slip a finger under it. Check it frequently to make sure that it does not constrict blood flow.

8. Transport the victim as rapidly as possible. If you cannot quickly accomplish the treatments explained in the previous steps, abandon them and concentrate on getting to the hospital. Effective life-saving treatment cannot be accomplished in the field.

9. Sustain basic life support functions: airway, breathing, and circulation.

Several improper methods of treatment are mistakenly thought to be proper when someone has been bitten by a snake. The following instructions can prevent you from causing further injury or wasting time on treatment methods that will not help:

- Do not cut and suck. Cutting into the bite site can damage underlying organs, increase the risk of infection, and does not result in venom removal.

- Do not apply ice. Ice does not deactivate the venom and can cause frostbite.

- Do not use electric shocks. The shocks are not effective and could cause burns or electrical problems to the heart.

- Do not offer alcohol. Alcohol may deaden the pain, but it also dilates the local blood vessels, which can increase venom absorption.

- Do not use tourniquets or constriction bands. These have not proved effective, may cause increased tissue damage, and could damage the extremity.

Lightning

Although lightning can strike low open areas of land and water, the most susceptible areas are mountain tops and sharp ridge lines, tall trees in open areas, structures such as towers, poles and buildings, and boats on the water. Lightning is not drawn to metallic objects to a greater or lesser degree than it is to other materials. But metal is an excellent electrical conductor, and once struck, it will carry the current with little resistance. Long metallic objects like railings, power lines, bridges, phone lines, metal fences, metal pipe, and rail tracks act as power conduits, transferring dangerous levels of current over considerable distances. Other wet materials such as an extended rope will also act as a conduction path for lightning.

Lightning occurs when the bottom of a storm cloud becomes negatively charged while the surface of the earth takes on a positive charge. The intense electric field between the two begins to ionize the air, and eventually a conductive path forms between the two. Several paths of ionized air, called stepped leaders, begin stemming from a cloud, seeking a path to the earth. When a negatively charged stepped leader gets close to the earth, objects on the surface begin responding to the strong electrical field by sending up positively charged streamers. Any object on the earth's surface can produce these streamers, including the human body. When a stepped leader meets a positive streamer, the conductive path is complete and massive amounts of electrical current flow between the earth and the cloud. The flash of a lightning strike is a result of the intense heat produced by the electrical discharge. The heat causes the air around the strike to expand so rapidly that it explodes. Thunder is the sound of the explosion.

Lightning can cause a variety of strikes and other dangers that can be harmful or deadly:

- **Ground strikes** usually occur directly below the cumulonimbus clouds of a thunderstorm, but many injuries and fatalities from lightning strikes occur before the main storm complex is overhead. Lightning can move great distances horizontally from a cloud, striking miles (km) from a storm, well beyond the rain area and visible thundercloud. Lightning can also strike from diminishing clouds several minutes after the main thunderstorm has dissipated.

- **Direct strikes** happen to people when a stepped leader coming from a cloud connects with a streamer coming from the body, causing the return stroke to pass through or over the surface of the body. The massive return stroke has a typical current of 30,000 amps, which is 2,000 times greater than household current. Obviously, this amount of current can cause major damage to all major systems of the body.

- **Side flashes** occur when lightning strikes an object near a person and the lightning splashes or arcs from the object to the person.

- **Ground current** results when lightning strikes the earth and currents flow in concentrated channels on the surface or in the soil. Ground current can injure people nearby. How far the current flows varies widely, depending on the strike current and ground conductance. The ground current is stronger close to the strike.

- **Streamer currents** are strong electrical currents discharged from the tops of elevated objects and people near the descending stepped leaders near the strike point. These currents are much smaller than the powerful return stroke current but intense enough to cause injury or death.

- **Contact voltage** is the lightning current that is carried through things such as telephone cable, power lines, and other metallic objects. People can be seriously injured or killed if they are in physical contact with these materials during a strike, even when it occurs some distance away.

Lightning can cause several problems for the human body, including electrical damage, trauma, and burns. Electrical impulses are especially critical to the heart and respiratory system. High currents of electricity suddenly applied to the body can cause cardiac or respiratory arrest. Electrical damage to the central and peripheral nervous systems can cause memory and function disorders as well as numbness and paralysis. Lightning can cause various types of trauma. The volatile force of a lightning strike and explosive release of energy can cause blunt force trauma to a person who is near the strike. The massive current can also create powerful muscle spasms, which can throw a person or cause the person to fall.

Lightning strikes produce massive currents that can result in significant burns. Surface and flashover burns are created as current flows over the body. Metallic objects like pack frames, climbing gear, tools, jewelry, and belt buckles that are attached to or near the body can also cause burns. Burning fabric from clothing and equipment can contribute to secondary burns. Flashover burns can be serious and may be associated with internal burns. Lightning current can enter the body, causing major damage to organs, tissue, and bone as it literally burns a path through the body. Internal burns are characterized by large entry and exit burn wounds, which may be close together or separated. Entry and exit wounds that are close together do not necessarily indicate a short internal burn path. Current can move randomly through the body before finally exiting.

Avoiding a Lightning Injury

Plan your work or recreational pursuits around potential thunderstorm activity. Nature is not concerned with your schedule, so be flexible, adjust your plans, or reschedule if needed. If you know that storms usually begin forming at 11:00 a.m., make sure that you are out of potential danger zones by then. Set turnaround times and be rigid about enforcing them. Do not wait until you are standing on a peak above timberline with lightning strikes flashing nearby to think about retreating.

When you see or hear the first evidence of an electrical storm, begin retreating to a safer place. Thunder produced by a lightning strike travels 1 mile (1.6 km) every five seconds. You can estimate your distance in miles from a strike by counting the number of seconds between the flash of the strike and the sound of the thunder and dividing by five (the distance in kilometers is the interval in seconds divided by 3). This rule provides general information, but do not use it as a reason to delay your retreat from the storm.

If you are near civilization, the safest place to be is inside a building. Stay away from exterior doors and windows, pipes, wires, electrical appliances, lighting fixtures, electrical outlets, and corded telephones. If you cannot reach a substantial building, an enclosed vehicle with a solid metal roof and sides is the next best choice. When you are inside, close the windows, lean away from the door, put your hands in your lap, and do not touch the steering wheel, ignition, gearshift, or radio. Open framed vehicles and equipment and those made with plastic or fiberglass are not appropriate for lightning protection.

If you are in the backcountry or otherwise outside with no chance of reaching a building or vehicle and lightning is striking nearby, move to a lower elevation immediately. Do not stop in open areas or take shelter under tall trees, especially those located in or near open areas. Do not take shelter in open-sided buildings. Stay away from sharp ridges and peaks. When descending from a ridge or peak, move toward the least intense part of the storm if possible. By far the most important action you can take is to descend quickly.

Sometimes lightning will provide a few seconds of warning when a strike is imminent. If you feel the hair on your head, legs, or arms standing on end; if your skin tingles; or if light metal objects begin to vibrate or hum, you are in immediate and severe danger. Immediately remove metal items like tools, gear, and pack. If you are in a group, spread out so that people are several body lengths from one another. Then get into the lightning position to make your body as low as possible and your footprint as small as possible: Put your feet together, squat down, tuck your head, and cover your ears with your hands. Do not lie on the ground, do not stand or squat with your feet separated, and do not touch the ground with any part of your body other than your feet. You must minimize the area of body contact with the ground to lessen the chances of contacting currents traveling across the ground caused by a strike. Placing a nonconductive material, such as a foam pad, between your feet and the ground may help prevent contact with ground currents. When the immediate threat of lightning has passed, continue moving to a safer place.

Responding to a Lightning Injury

The normal concepts of triage cannot be applied to lightning injuries. Deaths from lightning strikes result from cardiac or respiratory arrest. Therefore, you should direct all available resources to those with no pulse or respirations by providing CPR and respiratory support. Injuries caused by trauma and burns during a lightning strike are also common and must not be overlooked. Some injuries from a strike take time to manifest themselves, so anyone injured, no matter how slightly, should be evaluated at a medical facility as soon as possible.

Avalanches

Avalanches are one of the most powerful and misunderstood phenomenon of nature. In fact, they have been seriously studied only within the past 50 years. The number of avalanches that occur each year worldwide is unknown because many happen in isolated areas, but many parts of the world possess terrain and weather that combine to create a fertile breeding ground for dangerous avalanches.

About 100 people are caught in avalanches each year in North America, but this number may be inaccurate because many incidents that do not involve fatalities or significant injuries are never reported (www.avalanche.org). The fatality rate is generally increasing as more people take to the winter backcountry to enjoy a variety of activities. As gear and equipment, such as snowmobiles, have become more sophisticated and powerful, more people are able access avalanche terrain than ever before. Unfortunately, without avalanche training and skills, many people place themselves at serious risk without knowing it. From 2000 through the 2007 to 2008 winter season, 336 people died in avalanches in North America. Table 10.1 shows the breakdown of the activities that those people were involved in.

Although avalanches vary greatly in size and type, most fatalities in the backcountry are caused by slides that are 2 to 3 feet (60 to 90 cm) deep at the fracture line, about 150 feet (45 m) wide, fall about 400 feet (120 m) in elevation, and reach a speed of about 50 miles (80 km) per hour. The average duration of slides is less than 30 seconds. But avalanches can be much larger, involving the release of entire mountainsides of deep snow and reaching speeds of over 100 miles (160 km) per hour. Their massive force is enough to destroy buildings and structures made of concrete and steel. But do not make the mistake of thinking that large slides are the only ones that kill. Many avalanche fatalities occur in slides that fall less than 100 feet (30 m), and some deaths occur in slides that fall less than 40 feet (12 m).

Avalanches are of two types: loose-snow avalanches and slab avalanches. A loose-snow avalanche is a cohesionless mass of snow, such as new snow that has not bonded or snow that has become wet during a

Table 10.1   Avalanche Fatalities by Activity, 2000 through 2007–2008 Season

Victims by sport or activity	Number of deaths	Percentage of total number of deaths
Snowmobilers	125	37%
Skiers	118	35%
Climbers	39	12%
Snowboarders	37	11%
Other	17	5%
Total	336	

Adapted from American Avalanche Association, 2009, Avalanche accidents database. [Online]. Available: http://www.avalanche.org/accidents.php [April 29, 2009].

thaw cycle. It starts at a single point and spreads out as it moves down slope, forming a triangle. This type of avalanche usually involves a small amount of snow near the surface and is not considered as deadly as a slab avalanche. But do not underestimate loose-snow avalanches because they can sweep you into a narrow terrain trap, such as a gulley, which can result in a deep burial.

A slab avalanche consists of one or more snow layers on a slope, which bond into a large cohesive slab. Gravity places stress on the slab, constantly pulling it downhill until the force overcomes the

FIGURE 10.1 A slab avalanche is a cohesive unit of snow that breaks loose and slides down the slope.

strength of the snow. Finally the slab breaks loose from its anchors at the top, bottom, and sides, and it begins sliding down slope (figure 10.1). Slab avalanches may contain blocks or chunks of snow, some larger than a refrigerator. Slabs can range in thickness from 1 foot (30 cm) or less to as deep as the entire snowcover down to the ground, which can be several feet (a meter or more). Unstable slabs develop with the added weight of new or wind-deposited snow or the weight of a person. Human triggers are a common cause of slab avalanche release.

For a slab avalanche to occur, four components must be present: a steep slope, a cohesive slab, a weak layer in the snowpack, and a trigger. Snow falling to the ground becomes part of the snowpack, which develops in layers. Each new storm adds snow to the existing snowpack, and redistribution of snow by wind may add more snow. As falling or windblown snow reaches the snowpack, the flakes immediately begin to change, binding their crystals together to form a cohesive slab. Factors such as temperature and moisture determine how well the slab forms and how well the new and old layers of snow bond together. When a snow layer achieves sufficient cohesive strength, the first component of a slab avalanche has been established.

Weather has a profound effect on how layers bond within the snowpack. Extremely cold temperatures delay the development of cohesive layers in the snow and lead to weak layers and instability. A prolonged period of sunny days and cold nights can produce surface hoar, which is a type of frost characterized by loose broad crystals. This coating becomes a weak layer when new snow is deposited onto the snowpack. When a strong layer develops on top of a weak layer on a sufficiently steep slope, almost all the components are in place for an avalanche.

The final component is the trigger, which may occur naturally by the weight of additional snow, the constant force of gravity, or the concentrated impact of snow falling from a slope or cornice above. The weight of a person, snowmobile, or snowcat, or the intentional detonation of explosives can also be a trigger. The trigger causes the weak layer to collapse, and the strong layer above fractures and separates from the snowpack, sliding down the slope. In most cases, people trigger the avalanche in which they are buried.

Avoiding an Avalanche

Attempting to predict exactly when and where avalanches will occur is difficult at best. Rules of thumb do not work well with avalanches. A studied, well-reasoned approach is needed here. Try to put emotion aside and make decisions based on measurable evidence that you can acquire through your senses. The three main variables to consider are weather, terrain, and snowpack. By understanding these variables, you will have a better chance of predicting and avoiding avalanche danger.

Weather observations include the amount and intensity of precipitation, wind speed and direction, and temperature. Gathering information before entering avalanche terrain is vital. Call the local avalanche information center or check current avalanche conditions online. These important resources will give you a base of information from which to start. Pay attention to these specific aspects of the weather:

- **Storms.** The risk of avalanches is greatest during major storms. About 75 to 80 percent of avalanches occur during or shortly after major storm cycles. The additional weight of new snow on steep slopes stresses an already burdened snowpack. This is no time to add the weight of a human trigger to the mix.

- **New snow.** Pay close attention to how much new snow has fallen and the rate of accumulation. Snowfall rates of 1 inch (2.5 cm) or more per hour increase avalanche danger. If more than 12 inches (30 cm) of new snow accumulates during a single storm, the avalanche danger is considered extreme.

- **Wind.** Winds in excess of 15 miles (24 km) per hour increase the avalanche hazard significantly. Such winds can transport substantial quantities of snow from windward slopes onto leeward slopes (those facing away from the wind). Even on a sunny day windblown snow can have the same effect on leeward slopes as a major snowstorm and can create dangerous cornices on the leeward edge of exposed ridges. Evidence of high winds can be seen as snow plumes stretching from high peaks and ridges.

- **Temperature.** Warmer temperatures in the range of 20 to 32 degrees Fahrenheit (–7 to 0 degrees Celsius) help the snowpack stabilize rapidly. Snow remains unstable in colder temperatures because of the temperature difference between the snow and ground surfaces. Problems also arise when temperatures rise well above freezing because meltwater percolates through the snowpack. This infiltration weakens the bond in the snowpack and causes significant instability.

Learning to identify avalanche terrain is critical in recognizing and evaluating avalanche hazard. With experience you will learn to get a feel for the angle of a slope. An extremely helpful tool to carry is slope meter or clinometer. Many compasses have built-in clinometer as an option. The following aspects of terrain influence the likelihood of an avalanche:

- **Slope angle.** Slope angle is the most prominent factor leading to avalanches. As the slope steepness increases, so do the natural forces that place stress on the snowpack. About 90 percent of all avalanches release on slopes of 30 to 45 degrees. Steeper slopes tend not to hold a significant amount of snow because of gravity. During unstable conditions avalanches can be triggered from shallow slopes below steeper ones. Fractures starting at the bottom of the slope can shoot upslope, causing the slab to release.

- **Slope orientation.** The orientation of a slope is also an important factor. Leeward slopes are more dangerous because of the addition of wind-deposited snow. North-facing and shaded slopes tend to be more dangerous during midwinter because of colder surface temperatures. South-facing slopes tend to be more dangerous during spring because of solar heating and meltwater in the snowpack.

- **Slope profile.** Slope profile concerns the shape of the slope—flat or curved, convex or concave. As shown in figure 10.2, convex slopes are likely to fracture at the bulge. Concave slopes provide a degree of support at the base but are still capable of avalanching.

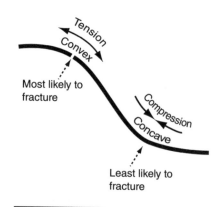

FIGURE 10.2 Convex slopes are more likely to fracture because gravity creates tension at convex locations.

- **Vegetation.** Vegetation such as large trees and thick brush, as well as rocks and other terrain features, can help anchor the snow. These anchors become less effective as snow covers them fully. Do not depend on natural anchors to protect a slope from sliding. Even thickly wooded slopes provide little protection from slides that start from open slopes above.

- **Past avalanche activity.** Signs of past avalanche activity include avalanche debris from earlier slides, open paths between forested or brushy areas, bent or broken trees, and groups of young trees growing in swaths among more mature timber.

The snowpack provides its own clues about stability. Through close observation and by employing all the senses, you can reach strong and accurate conclusions about the stability of a specific area of the snowpack.

- **Recent avalanche activity.** Hearing or seeing avalanches or debris from recent slides in the area is an obvious signal that additional avalanches may occur on similar slopes. Do not ignore this warning; take heed and stay on moderate terrain.

- **Recent wind loading.** Recent wind loading is another indicator of avalanche danger. Look for scoured or wave patterns on hard snow surfaces. Cornices and snow plumes from ridges and peaks are indicators of wind-transported snow, which can develop dangerous wind slabs because the crystals collide many times while the snow is blown.

- **Hollow sounds.** Hollow or "whoompf" sounds that occur under your feet indicate unstable slab conditions. Feeling the snow drop or settle is also an indicator of unstable layers in the snowpack.

- **Shooting cracks.** Avoid any slope where you see cracks in the snow around you, especially if they shoot out from your tracks as you move across the snowpack. Stay off slopes with a similar profile and orientation.

Your route selection is another key way to help you avoid avalanches. When traveling through valleys, stay well away from the base of potential avalanches and run-out zones, the areas where debris from avalanches comes to rest. Travel on the windward side of ridgelines, slightly away from the ridge top. In most cases this line of travel will keep you in areas of shallower snowpack and away from dangerous cornices. Avoid narrow gullies that could act as terrain traps. Although these features seem benign, a small slide can quickly fill them up with deep snow. If you must cross a dangerous slope, follow these guidelines:

- Before crossing, prepare yourself for the worst. Add layers to your clothes, including hat and gloves. Pad and insulate yourself in the event that you are caught in a slide.

- Loosen or remove ski pole straps from your wrists. Unbuckle the waist belt of your backpack and carry it over one shoulder. If you are caught in a slide, discard all your equipment immediately. Equipment such as skis, snowshoes, and backpacks will tend to drag you deeper into a slide.

- Only one person should cross at a time. This method places the risk on just one person at a time and reduces stress on the snowpack. All other party members should watch from a position of safety. If the person crossing is caught in a slide, all eyes should be riveted to that person, paying specific attention to the point at which the victim went out of sight.

- Everyone should cross in the same track. This method is quicker and puts less stress on the snowpack.

- If you must ascend or descend a potential avalanche slope, go straight up or straight down. Traversing the slope could cause the snowpack to fail. Travel as close to the sides of the slope as possible, always looking for an escape route if a slide occurs.

- Never assume that a slope is safe because someone crossed it just before you.

- Do not consider a slope safe just because you crossed it earlier the same day. Significant changes can take place over short periods, creating serious weaknesses in the snowpack.

- Use areas of dense timber, ridges, or rock outcrops as islands of safety. Arrange your route to go from island to island. This technique reduces the time that you are exposed to the hazard.

- Always carry and be proficient in the use of avalanche rescue gear. Required items are an avalanche rescue beacon, collapsible probe pole or probe ski poles, and an avalanche shovel (see page 23 for more information).

Responding to an Avalanche

If you are buried in a slide, digging yourself out can be nearly impossible. Concentrate your efforts on avoiding an avalanche, but if you are caught in one, follow these guidelines:

1. Shout out! You want to alert other party members of your predicament. Discard any equipment that will drag you down. If you are on skis or a snowmobile, try to remain upright and maneuver to the side of the slide. If you are pulled down in the slide, release your ski poles or snowmobile.

2. After you are down and caught in the avalanche, concentrate on swimming with the slide. Use any kind of swimming motion, always working yourself toward the side of the slide. Fight being pulled under by thrusting your body upward with your swimming motions. The closer you are to the surface, the greater your chances for survival.

3. As the slide is coming to a stop, curl your body into a fetal position and put your hands in front of your face with your elbows against your chest. Try to make an air pocket in the snow by moving your head and hands back and forth. Take a deep, slow breath and hold it until the snow settles around you. As you come to a stop, try to thrust a hand to the surface.

4. If you see light, you may be able to dig yourself out. If you cannot see light you are probably buried too deep for self-extrication. Conserve your energy.

5. Do not panic! Make your breathing slow and deliberate. Remain calm and wait for rescue.

If other members of your party are caught in an avalanche, you must act quickly to rescue them. The most important factor in a successful avalanche rescue is time. When the slide stops, the clock starts ticking. Only 50 percent of victims survive after being buried for 30 minutes. About 33 percent survive after an hour, and only 10 percent survive after three hours. The choices that you make as a rescuer in the moments after a slide will have a profound effect on the ultimate outcome of the search. Burial depth is closely tied to survival rates as well. About 90 percent of victims buried to a depth of 1 foot (30 cm) or less survive. Usually these people are easy to locate or are able to dig themselves out. People buried between 1 and 2 feet (between 30 and 60 cm) deep have a 53 percent survival rate, and only 39 percent of those buried to a depth of 4 feet (120 cm) survive.

If someone in your group is caught in a slide, do not go for help unless that help can be at the slide location in less than five minutes. The clock is ticking, and you must do all that you can before the time runs out. Use every available person during the search. Usually help is miles or hours away, and when it finally arrives, precious time and resources have been lost. Of course, if communications are available, call for help immediately and then begin or continue the search.

If you are with others, someone, usually the most experienced person, must take charge and direct the rescue effort. The leader must organize the group, make assignments, and explain specifically to the rescuers what they are to do. Before moving into the slide area, look for further avalanche danger and establish an escape route in the event of a second slide. If your team is large enough, assign a member to act as a lookout from the side of the slope. The lookout's job is to alert the rescuers if a second slide releases. If your group is too small to have a lookout, each rescuer should constantly be watching and listening. Rescuers should not expose themselves to unreasonable risks during a rescue effort. Do not let yourself or a member of the group become another statistic.

After making your way into the slide area, mark the spot where the victim was last seen. Search downhill from this spot. Perform an avalanche beacon search if you have beacons. Avalanche beacons are small short-range radio location devices that can be manually switched from transmit mode to receive mode. When entering an area of potential avalanche danger, each person turns his or her beacon to the transmit mode and straps the unit securely to the chest. If someone is caught in an avalanche, those who have not been caught can begin a beacon search by switching their beacons to the receive mode. (All units must be switched to prevent the transmission of false signals.) The signal strength of the buried beacon is directly related to the proximity of the transmitting unit. With a little training and practice, a buried beacon can be quickly located. If multiple people are buried, be sure to turn off each victim's beacon when he or she is found so that the signal does not interfere with the remaining buried beacons.

If you do not have beacons, start with a scuff search. Kick the snow surface looking for clues just under the surface. If you find something, such as an article of clothing or a ski pole, uncover it, and then leave it in place for future reference. Probe the area beneath the clue to determine whether the victim is attached to or beneath the clue. You can use collapsible probe poles, inverted ski poles, tent poles, or even long, thin tree branches stripped bare with a small blunt end as probes. Begin probing by inserting the probe into the debris and pushing it through until you reach an object or the ground. Be quick but gentle so that your probe will not cause injury to a buried person. You are probing for a dense but pliable object, which will feel different from a rock, log, or the ground. If you think that you have struck a buried person, begin to dig until you reach the object.

If you do not locate the victim during the scuff search, begin probing for the victim around trees and rocks, in depressions in the snow, and in places where slide debris has accumulated (see figure 10.3). In addition, search the lower end of the debris field. Many victims end up there. After thoroughly probing all likely burial spots, establish a probe line working from the bottom of the debris field uphill to the last seen point. In organizing a probe line, all rescuers form a line across the area to be searched. They stand elbow to elbow and place their probes between their feet. When the leader gives the command to probe, all rescuers should then probe. At the next command, all rescuers pull their probes out of the snow and advance uphill together, approximately 1 foot (30 cm), and repeat the probing process.

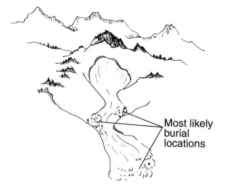

FIGURE 10.3 Search at bends and at the bottom of a slide path.

For the probe line to be efficient, the team must work as a unit and never deviate from the pattern. If someone encounters a strike (something that feels as if it could be the victim), that person drops out of line and begins shoveling. The probe line continues probing. If the group is large enough, people not part of the probe line can be assigned to shovel so that no one has to drop out of the line when a strike is encountered. An organized probe search for an avalanche victim is time consuming and requires many people and resources to be effective. Usually, when you reach the point of considering an organized probe search, you have done all that you can do as an individual or small group, and it is time to go for help.

Choosing to go for help is an agonizing decision for which there is no firm guideline. Ultimately, this decision is a personal one. You can end the search and go for help when you believe that you have done all that can be done or you are physically unable to continue the search because of exhaustion or injury. Other reasons may include severe weather, threat of hypothermia or frostbite, or threat of another avalanche.

When an avalanche victim is initially uncovered, immediately check the person's airway. Do not wait until the digging is complete. Move quickly toward the head and clear the airway of snow. If the victim is not breathing, begin ventilations immediately. Continue ventilations while the digging operations are completed. Start CPR if needed and always treat for hypothermia. Because of the forces involved in an avalanche, look for signs of trauma and be especially careful with the neck and spine while handling and moving a slide victim.

Flash Floods

Flash floods occur suddenly and typically arrive without much warning. Flash floods are powerful enough to roll boulders, tear out trees, destroy buildings and bridges, and scour out new channels. Rains that produce flash floods can also trigger catastrophic mudslides. The crashing roar of water and debris rolling through what was just a few minutes earlier a dry wash is a sobering event to witness. Rapidly rising water can reach heights of more than 30 feet (10 m). In fact, most flood deaths result from flash floods.

Two key elements contribute to flash flooding: rainfall intensity and duration. Topography, soil conditions, and ground cover also play important roles. Flash flooding is usually caused by slow-moving thunderstorms, repeated thunderstorms moving over the same area, or heavy sustained rains. Occasionally, debris dislodged during a storm can become jammed, creating a natural dam that restricts the flow of water. Flash flooding can occur downstream if the obstruction should suddenly release.

Streams and dry washes in sandstone formations are especially susceptible to flash flooding because the soil is able to absorb only a small fraction of the rain. The steep slopes and narrow canyons funnel the storm runoff into small creeks and dry washes, transforming them into raging torrents. In this terrain, where deep canyons are cut like narrow slots into stone, flash floods can travel from a storm many miles away, bringing tragedy to unwary explorers. All areas with elevated slopes and soil types are subject to flash flooding. When soils become saturated and rains continue, the water has no choice but to gather and begin flowing to the lowest point.

The following guidelines can help you avoid flash floods:

- Plan ahead by gathering information about current conditions and weather forecasts for the area where you will be.

- Be flexible and willing to change or reschedule your plans according to the conditions. Your schedule should never take priority over safety.

- Stay away from streambeds and other drainage channels during and after rainstorms or when heavy rain is possible. If you are near a stream and water begins rising rapidly, treat the situation as a flash flood. Mountain streams can rise several feet (a meter) or more in just a few minutes.

- Do not camp along streams and washes. A flash flood can catch you while you are sleeping. Locate your camp on ground that is significantly higher than the stream or canyon floor.

- Pay attention to thunder, lightning, and other signs of distant rainfall. Rain upstream, even many miles away, can roar down a canyon and catch you completely by surprise.

- Climb to higher ground and safety if you see or hear a flash flood coming at you during a hike or in camp.

- Do not cross flowing water or flooded trails where water is above your knees.

- Never attempt to cross flooding or rising waters in a vehicle. Only 24 inches (60 cm) of water is needed to float most vehicles. If you cannot move a vehicle to a safe place away from possible floodwaters, leave it and move to higher ground immediately.

Survival Kits

EVERY year many people are killed or injured in weather-related accidents. Typical emergency survival incidents happen in cold or hot weather when mechanical problems or severe weather disables vehicles, equipment, or aircraft. Incidents also develop in the backcountry when travelers become lost or when inclement weather develops. Trauma resulting from crashes and emergency landings causes some deaths and injuries, but many of the deaths and injuries occur from the effects of hypothermia, hyperthermia, dehydration, carbon monoxide poisoning, or other environmental factors. Basic survival knowledge and a few items of vital emergency gear could prevent many of these deaths and injuries.

Survival Kit Basics

Survival kits can contain a variety of tools and materials. Modern technology has provided a plethora of gadgets and products that are effective aids to survival. Choosing among all the useful items that are available can be a challenging task. A useful survival kit should be small, lightweight, and compact. The components of a survival kit should fulfill essential needs for survival, including shelter, fire (or heat), water, food, and signaling methods. The kit should also include light sources, tools, and medical supplies. Ideally, an emergency survival kit should help sustain life for a minimum of 72 hours. Sustaining life does not mean living in comfort with no hunger or thirst; it means living in a survival mode with minimal food, water, and shelter until rescue takes place, roads reopen, weather changes, or the situation otherwise changes for the better.

Kits can be assembled for a variety of applications, including use in automobiles, snowcats, snowmobiles, and aircraft and for purposes such as family preparedness and backcountry use. A kit for a vehicle of any sort should accommodate two to four people. Configurations for families and other special uses should include appropriate quantities for the planned use. Packaging and components should be high quality and durable. Choose items that can withstand exposure to heat and cold. Nutrient content, caloric density, and shelf life are the key features to consider in selecting food items.

You can package components in a variety of cases and bags. Hard cases offer superior protection for components and equipment, but do not offer much flexibility if you need to add additional items. Waterproof soft cases are flexible and easily stored under or behind seats in a vehicle or aircraft or in a pocket in your pack. You can package a personal backcountry kit in a small soft case that you can carry when traveling or hiking. A pocket-sized kit that you can easily carry on a quick trip away from home or keep in a vehicle is also useful. The following sections provide recommended components for kits for various survival situations and outlines their possible uses.

Shelter

Protection from the elements is basic to survival, and you can take many approaches to meeting this need, as discussed in chapter 2. Survival kits should contain items that you can use to fabricate at least minimal shelter protection. For small, lightweight kits, use just a few essential lightweight items. If you have more space available, include additional items. Refer to the techniques in chapter 2 for specific instructions regarding shelter construction. Depending on your needs, you may want to carry all or some of the following items:

- **Emergency blankets.** Lightweight, compact, and useful, emergency blankets are available from outdoor and camping stores for $2 to $3. The metalized Mylar material provides a sealed barrier, which prevents wind and moisture from passing through and slows heat loss from the body. Outdoors, you can use blankets to construct a shelter, or you can simply wrap up in one to reduce heat loss. Inside a vehicle, you can use them to construct a small shelter. By covering the windows and draping the blankets down from the ceiling, you reduce the space that you need to heat. Use tape or safety pins to construct the enclosure. Cold-weather electrical tape works well. Always crack a window for ventilation and never make the shelter airtight, especially when using candles to heat the enclosed space. Always use a carbon monoxide detector. The disadvantage of emergency blankets is that they are easily torn. After being torn they soon self-destruct, so use care to keep them intact.

Enviro-Tech International manufactures a product called the SafeShelter that is designed to enclose a smaller space inside a vehicle. You can then heat that smaller space with a candle. Suspended from the ceiling, the SafeShelter drapes down to form a shelter inside a vehicle large enough to accommodate three or four people. The SafeShelter is adjustable and can be used in vehicles varying in size from small cars to snowcats and large trucks. The cost of the SafeShelter is $80.

- **Emergency bags.** These bags are made of the same material as emergency blankets but are fabricated into an enclosed bag with an opening at the top. They are more effective at preventing heat loss than emergency blankets because the sides are sealed. The price range for Mylar emergency bags, available from outdoor and camping stores, is $6 to $8. An effective and inexpensive substitute is a thick 55-gallon (200 L) trash bag, which you can find at grocery and hardware stores.

- **Poncho or tarp.** This is a useful item to carry if you have the space. A poncho or tarp with grommets installed in the corners and a few evenly spaced along the edges is a versatile item for creating a shelter (refer to chapter 2 for information on building a poncho shelter.) An excellent alternative to a tarp made of plastic or coated fabric is to make your own from Tyvek. This material, produced by Dupont, is made from flashspun high-density polyethylene fibers. The material is extremely strong, lightweight, waterproof, and breathable. Tyvek can be purchased in two forms: hard structure and soft structure. Hard-structure Tyvek, which has a hard and brittle feel, can be found at building supply stores and is sold in rolls as home wrap. You can soften it by machine washing. A 9-foot-by-150-foot roll costs about $150. Soft-structure Tyvek, which feels like soft fabric, is used to make clothing and covers for vehicles and boats. You can buy it in rolls or cut sheets from Material Concepts (materialconcepts.com) at a cost of about $40 for an 8-foot-by-10-foot (2.4 by 3 m) sheet.

- **Carbon monoxide detector.** As noted in chapter 2, carbon monoxide poisoning deaths can occur when people shelter in a vehicle during winter conditions. Snow can quickly block the exhaust outlet of a vehicle, forcing carbon monoxide into the cab. When sheltering in your vehicle, always use a carbon monoxide detector. Simple, inexpensive card-type detectors cost less than $10 and can be ordered from aircraft pilot supply shops.

- **Cordage.** Cord has many uses. If you need to go outside the vehicle or shelter for any reason during whiteout conditions, you can use cord as a lifeline by tying one end around yourself and the other to some stationary object. People have lost their lives just a short distance from their vehicle, home, or barn after becoming disoriented in a whiteout. Cordage is also indispensable for shelter construction, fabricating tools, and general utility. A length of at least 50 feet (15 m) is recommended. Cordage is available from hardware stores and outdoor and camping stores for less than $10. Many types of cordage are available. One very versatile and useful type is paracord, a lightweight nylon kernmantle rope originally used in the suspension lines of military parachutes. It consists of several strands of nylon covered by a strong braided sheath.

- **Sleeping bag.** Carrying a bag for each person is ideal if space is available. Sleeping bags can be purchased from outdoor and camping stores at a cost of $50 to $200.

Fire and Heat

Fire is particularly critical for survival because it provides heat, light, security, and signaling capability. As discussed in chapter 3, always carry at least three methods of starting a fire. These should be reliable methods that you are familiar with and may include any of the following items:

- Matches, including strike on the box, strike anywhere, waterproof, or wind and waterproof.

- Metal match or any device that uses ferrocerium to create a spark.
- Butane lighters
- Fire-starting aids including petroleum-based products, candles, and steel wool.

Besides serving as a fire-starting aid, candles can provide heat and light for a long stay in a vehicle, primitive shelter, or snow shelter. Candles intended to produce long-term heat should be larger than the small candles and candle stubs used as fire-starting aids. Long-burning candles are usually made from paraffin, which is a petroleum by-product, or beeswax. Candles that are self-contained in a can are convenient and easy to use. Many larger candles include multiple wicks that can provide more heat for a particular application like cooking. When burning a candle always ensure that you have sufficient ventilation. Candles use oxygen and produce small amounts of gases that can be dangerous if not vented.

Many types of candles available for emergency use have rated burn times from 4 to 120 hours or more. Candles can be found at outdoor and camping stores at prices ranging from $3 to $20. Some of the brands to look for are Coghlans, NuWick, Sterno, and MPI Outdoors. You can make your own candles by melting wax and pouring it into an empty can or mint tin. You can use paraffin, beeswax, or other candles. Paraffin and candlewick material can be purchased from craft supply stores. You can also find paraffin in the canning section of grocery stores. Follow these steps:

1. Use a clean, dry metal container. Secure a wick or wicks to the bottom of the container with hot glue or tape. The wicks should extend 1/4 inch (.6 cm) above the top edge of the container.

2. Melt the wax. Use caution so that the wax does not overheat and ignite. Use a double boiler setup. An easy way to do this is to place a metal container or can containing the wax to be melted inside a pot that contains water. Simmering the water in the pot will generate enough heat to melt the wax. Do not place the can containing the wax directly on the heat source.

3. When the wax melts sufficiently, slowly pour the liquid wax into the candle container, taking care to keep the wick or wicks upright. When the candle cools completely it is ready for use

You can make a longer-burning version of this candle by mixing fine sawdust into the wax. To make this type of candle, follow these steps:

1. Use a metal container as described earlier but do not install the wicks yet. In a separate mixing container made of metal (this will be the container in which you will mix the wax and the sawdust) place a sufficient quantity of fine sawdust.

2. Prepare the wax using the method described earlier.

3. After the wax melts, begin pouring it into the container with the sawdust. As you pour, mix the wax into the sawdust with a stick. When the wax cools enough, you can use your hands to mix the material together thoroughly.

4. While the material is still soft, place enough of it into the candle container to fill it to within 1/4 inch (.6 cm) or so of the top. Press and smooth the mixture until it evenly fills the container. Use a length of wire or a nail to create the hole for the wick or wicks. The hole or holes should reach the bottom of the container. Then place the wicks into the holes.

5. After inserting the wicks, pour melted wax into the wick holes and seal the candle by filling the container with the melted wax to the top of the container. Allow it to cool thoroughly before use.

Chemical heat packs, which produce heat without fire, are a viable option that you may want to consider for use in a survival kit as an addition to fire sources of heat. Products such as Hot Hands offer temporary relief from the cold and are especially helpful as an aid in preventing a localized cold injury such as frostnip and frostbite. These products create heat by a chemical reaction caused when several dry ingredients are combined and exposed to air. They are manufactured in several sizes and generate heat of 100 to 180 degrees Fahrenheit (38 to 82 degrees Celsius) for a duration of 5 to 16 hours depending on the model. Prices range from $1 to $7, and they can be found at outdoor and camping stores.

Light

Besides illuminating the dark, a light can provide a feeling of safety and security as well a means for signaling. Modern portable light technology offers many reliable, durable, and weather-resistant products. Choose from among the following light sources based on the type of application and the space available in your kit:

- **Flashlight.** Carry a reliable light with extra batteries and an extra bulb. LED (light-emitting diode) lights provide a soft but bright light source and use far less current than standard lights, which means extended battery life. Many LED lights contain several LEDs and have a variable position switch, which allows the user to control the number of LEDs that are turned on, conserving battery life even further. Combination lights have both LEDs and incandescent bulbs, used when a brighter beam is needed. Headlamps allow hands-free operation. Portable lights are available through outdoor and camping stores and range in price from $5 to about $100.

- **Light sticks.** These items produce light from a chemical reaction for up to several hours. They are lightweight, compact, and require no batteries or power source. The amount of light that they produce is directly related to the ambient air temperature. In cold conditions they emit dim light. They cost less than $3 each at outdoor and camping stores.

Water

Water is essential to survival, but packing enough water for all your needs into a survival kit is impractical. But you can carry a limited supply as well as other items that will help you collect and purify more. In vehicles, carry at least 2 gallons (7.6 L) of water in sturdy containers. Remember not to fill the containers full during winter because of the breakage that may occur. When you are not traveling in a vehicle, you have a variety of options for carrying and obtaining water:

- **Water packets.** These small foil packets are filled and sealed by the manufacturer. They usually contain about 4 ounces (120 ml) of water and have a shelf life of up to five years. The packets are available from some outdoor and camping stores for about $.50 per packet. Quantities can be ordered from the following companies: Emergency Preparedness Service (www.emprep.com), Meyers Custom Supply (www. meyerscustomsupply.com), and Nitro-Pak Preparedness Center (www.nitro-pak.com).

- **Collapsible container with a resealable cap.** This item does not use a lot of space and is useful for collecting and storing water. Containers are available from outdoor and camping stores. A 2.5-gallon (9.5 L) container costs about $9.

- **Water purification tablets or filters.** See chapter 4 for more information about chemically treating water and where to obtain tablets and filters.

Food

Carry a reliable food source that stores well in both heat and cold. Make sure that those who have access to the survival kit understand that this food is for use only in an emergency. It is an extremely discouraging experience to reach for the survival kit in a genuine emergency and find the food and other items missing. The best food choices are products with a long shelf life that require little or no preparation. Larger survival kits can include a few packets of tea and dried instant soup along with a metal cup. Include small energy bars in addition to more substantial items such as MREs (meals ready to eat) and survival rations.

MREs, originally designed for military use, contain complete meals that can be eaten without preparation. Some versions have self-heating mechanisms that can heat the meals within a few minutes. MREs have a shelf life of about three years. A meal with a heater costs $6 to $8. You can find MREs at some outdoor and camping stores or order them from the following companies: the Epicenter (www.theepicenter.com), MRE Foods (www.mrefoods.com), Meyers Custom Supply (www. meyerscustomsupply.com), and MRE Depot (www.mredepot.com).

Dry survival rations are a baked food ration formulated to provide a balanced minimum daily diet with limited water resources. They come packaged in a 1,200-, 2,400- or 3,600-calorie compact bar or brick and have a shelf life of five years. The price for a 3,600-calorie food ration is $5 to $7. Survival rations can sometimes be found at outdoor and camping stores or can be ordered from the following companies: Emergency Preparedness Service (www.emprep.com), Meyers Custom Supply (www. meyerscustomsupply.com), and Nitro-Pak Preparedness Center (www.nitro-pak.com).

In situations in which you need to catch your own food, you will want to have a few of the following supplies available. See chapter 6 for more information about trapping and snaring animals and catching fish.

- **Snare wire.** Wire used to make snares should be thin, strong, and flexible. Stranded wire has the benefit of strength and durability. Copper, brass, and stainless steel are common materials that work well. Carry at least 20 feet (6 m) of wire because it can serve many useful purposes during a survival situation. Thin picture-hanging wire or used guitar strings also work for making snares. Local sources for wire include hardware and building supply stores and craft stores.

- **Fishing kit.** A useful kit contains five or six hooks of various sizes, two or three small lures, a wire wound leader, a few split-shot sinkers of varying sizes, a small bobber or float, some salmon eggs for bait, and 50 feet (15 m) of 12-pound (5 kg) fishing line. These inexpensive items are available at outdoor and camping stores.

Signaling Methods

As with fire-starting options, you should include multiple signaling methods in a survival kit. Remember, as emphasized in chapter 8, you want to make yourself louder, larger, noisier, and brighter. Choose items that are reliable, easy to use, and familiar to you. Include both high-and low-tech devices from among the following:

- Signal mirror
- Bright-colored survey or flagging tape
- Aerial flares
- Handheld signal flares
- Signal smokes
- Laser signal
- Signal strobe

Tools

Including a few essential tools in a survival kit will enhance your ability to accomplish basic tasks such as building a shelter, making a fire, collecting firewood, and gathering and trapping food. Each of the following items can be essential in a survival situation:

- **Knife or multitool.** A necessary component to any survival kit, a knife is useful for cutting, scraping, and creating other tools and implements for survival. Buy the best that you can afford. Knives range in price from $40 to about $150 and can be found at outdoor and camping stores.
- **Wire saw.** A wire saw is a coil of braided wire about 3 feet (1 m) in length with a handle loop on each end. Wire saws work effectively on a variety of materials. By stretching the wire between a bowed stick, you can create a small bow saw. You can also make a snare loop for catching animals by passing one handle of the saw through the other to create a self-tightening

loop. Wire saws range in price from $6 to $10 and can be found at outdoor and camping stores.

- **Shovel.** Shovels are useful for clearing snow away from the exhaust system of a vehicle, digging out, digging snow shelters, and many other tasks. If space will not permit carrying a full-sized shovel, then carry a smaller collapsible avalanche shovel or entrenching tool.

Medical Supplies

Always carry a first aid kit tailored to your specific needs. Many commercially made kits are available that may serve your needs, or you can make your own. Quantities of components will change based on group size and intended use. Be sure to include a supply of any medications that you use regularly as well as a splint, an irrigation syringe, and some moleskin. The SAM Splint is a strong yet flexible ready-made splint that can be cut and bent to provide support to any injured limb. A 60-milliliter irrigation syringe can be used to thoroughly cleanse wounds. Moleskin, a thick synthetic felt-like material with adhesive applied to one side, can be used to prevent foot blisters. Table 11.1 lists items that could be included in a basic first aid kit.

Table 11.1 Basic First Aid Kit Supplies

Bandages	Medication	Tools
Adhesive tape	Pill vials for medications	Safety pins
Adhesive bandages of assorted sizes	Antiseptic wipes	Ziplock bags
Knuckle bandages	Triple-antibiotic ointment	Needles
Fingertip bandages	Sunscreen	Scissors
Butterfly bandages	Cortisone cream	Scalpel blade, sterile
Adhesive pads (nonstick)	Antacid tablets	Irrigation syringe
Sterile gauze pads, 4 by 4 in. (10 by 10 cm)	Ibuprofen, aspirin, or acetaminophen tablets	Cotton-tipped applicators
Conforming gauze roller Bandages, 3 in. (7.5 cm)	Antidiarrheal tablets	Tweezers
Moleskin, 3 by 4 in. (7.5 by 10 cm)	Povidone iodine prep pads	Small notebook and pencil
Triangular bandage		
Elastic bandage, 3 in. (7.5 cm)		
SAM splint		

Keeping Your Survival Kit Current

Whether you buy a premade kit or build your own, you must inspect and replace outdated components regularly. If you are storing the kit for an extended time, check batteries and food items at least every six months and replace them if necessary. Certain pyrotechnic signaling devices have expiration dates on them, and you should replace them on or before that date. Test water bags and containers for leaks, make sure that matches are not damp or damaged, and be sure that metallic items are not rusted or inoperable. Keep an inventory card with a checklist in the kit to indicate when items were last inspected and replaced. Inventory the kit and replenish items after each use. Do not wait for an emergency to discover that components are missing or unusable.

Personalizing Your Survival Kit

Building a survival kit is an individual effort. The examples presented on pages 230 through 232 have been created from years of experience and trial and error. They describe a basic selection of items in each category that are useful for various uses and situations. You can modify the exact items and quantities of each item according to your needs and individual preferences. Even if you use a commercial kit, you should modify it and add other items to suit your specific needs. Manufactured survival systems and kits for different applications can be ordered from my company, Enviro-Tech International, or other suppliers. Make sure that the equipment that you carry will work for you. Study it, become familiar with it, play with it, and learn how to use each component. Your life may depend on it.

Vehicle Kit

The items in this kit are appropriate to include for use in cars, trucks, snow-cats, aircraft, and other vehicles. Group individual items into categories and store them together in ziplock bags for easy organization and identification. The main package could be a duffle bag, backpack, flexible dry bag, or hard-shell case.

Shelter	Fire and heat
100 feet (30 m) of parachute cord 2 emergency bags 4 emergency blankets 1 roll cold-weather electrical tape	4 emergency candles (long burning) 1 box of wind- and waterproof matches 1 match safe with waterproof matches 1 magnesium fire-starter kit with metal match 1 fire-starting pack with steel wool and various fire-starting aids 4 chemical heat packs

Light	Water
1 LED flashlight 3 cyalume light sticks	8 emergency water packets 1 bottle of water purification tablets 1 collapsible water container (1 gal, or 4 L)

Food	Signaling methods
2 survival food rations (3,600 calories) 1 assortment of tea and soup 1 metal cup	3 aerial flares 2 handheld signal flares 2 signal smokes 1 signal whistle 1 signal mirror

Tools	Medical supplies
1 multitool with pliers 1 emergency wire saw 1 carbon monoxide detector	1 basic first aid kit

Personal Backcountry Kit

This type of kit should be small enough to be thrown inside or strapped onto a backpack. Typically, a small zippered soft case with dividers, elastic loops, and foldout mesh pockets makes an excellent container for this kit.

Shelter	Fire and heat
50 feet (15 m) of parachute cord 1 emergency bag 1 emergency blanket	4 stick or tub candles 1 match safe with wind- and waterproof matches 1 magnesium fire-starting kit with metal match 1 fire-starting helper pack (includes steel wool and petroleum impregnated cubes)

Light	Water
1 LED flashlight 1 cyalume light stick	1 bottle of water purification tablets 1 collapsible water container (1 L)

Food	Signaling methods
2 high-calorie food bars 1 assortment of tea and soup 1 metal cup	2 aerial flares 2 signal smokes 1 signal whistle 1 signal mirror

Tools	Medical supplies
1 multitool with pliers 1 emergency wire saw	1 personal first aid kit

Pocket Kit

The items in this kind of kit can be assembled in a small waterproof tin or durable plastic container. A small tin can double as a cooking pot over a fire.

Shelter	Fire and heat
50 feet (15 m) of parachute cord 1 emergency blanket or bag	2 tub candles 1 match safe with wind- and waterproof matches 1 metal match 1 fire-starting helper pack (includes steel wool and petroleum impregnated cubes)

Water	Light
1 bottle of water purification tablets 1 collapsible water container (1 L)	1 mini LED flashlight

Food	Signaling
small quantity of hard candy	1 signal whistle 1 signal mirror

Tools	Medical supplies
1 mini multitool with pliers 1 emergency wire saw 1 snare wire, 4 ft (120 cm) long 1 fishing kit containing small fishhooks, lures, float, and line	Small assortment of adhesive bandages Small quantity of adhesive tape Needles Scalpel blade Small vial containing aspirin, ibuprofen, acetaminophen, and other personal medication

ABOUT THE AUTHOR >>

Since 1978, **Randy Gerke** has been teaching survival techniques to the general public and groups from corporations and government agencies. He is a former captain and a member of the Ouray Mountain Rescue Team in Ouray, Colorado, and a graduate of Brigham Young University. He has been a technical advisor to the television programs *Rescue 911* and *Worst-Case Scenario*. He has been personally involved in many search-and-rescue operations in a variety of terrains and weather conditions during every season of the year.

Gerke is the founder and owner of Enviro-Tech International at www.etisurvival.com, a company devoted to teaching wilderness survival and rescue, wilderness medicine, and aircraft crew survival. Gerke has taught survival and rescue courses from Maine to Washington state. His clients have included the U.S. Department of Energy, U.S. Air Force, U.S. Navy, Verizon Wireless, U.S. Department of Homeland Security, and the Federal Aviation Administration.

Gerke lives in Montrose, Colorado.

BOCA RATON PUBLIC LIBRARY, FLORIDA

3 3656 0540750 7

613.69 Ger
Gerke, Randy, 1954-
Outdoor survival guide

JUN   2011

You'll find other outstanding outdoor sports resources at

http://outdoorsports.humankinetics.com

In the U.S. call 1-800-747-4457

Australia 08 8372 0999 • Canada 1-800-465-7301
Europe +44 (0) 113 255 5665 • New Zealand 0064 9 448 1207

HUMAN KINETICS
The Premier Publisher for Sports & Fitness
P.O. Box 5076 • Champaign, IL 61825-5076 USA